FROM KEYNESIANISM TO MONETARISM

Long-term mass unemployment, which Keynesianism seemed to have banished, is again at the top of the political agenda. This brings a new significance to understanding how Keynesianism in Britain gave way to Monetarism, two decades ago.

From Keynesianism to Monetarism: The evolution of UK macro-econometric models explains this dramatic change in economic policy through the study of the evolution of macroeconometric models of the whole economy from the mid-1960s to the early 1980s. These computer-based models have long been of interest because of their use in economic forecasting – particularly when these forecasts prove wrong. However, the models were the creation of some of the leading academic economists who sought to influence – and often radically alter – the conduct of economic policy in Britain from the late 1960s onwards. As such, they and the extensive documentation surrounding them, form a rich source of information, which provides insight into the arguments behind the policies of the time. The book, divided into three parts, examines macroeconometric models in a non-technical way. Part I discusses the importance of macroeconometric modelling; Part II examines the rise and fall of Keynesian income–expenditure models; and Part III evaluates the evidence and presents a critique of how we can learn from these models now and in the future.

Peter Kenway is lecturer in economics and econometrics at Reading University. He has extensive experience of designing and using computer models for policy analysis in public transport planning in Britain and the United States. He has written previously on Keynesian and Marxian economics and on social transformation in Eastern Europe.

FROM KEYNESIANISM TO MONETARISM

The evolution of UK macroeconometric models

Peter Kenway

London and New York

First published 1994
by Routledge
11 New Fetter Lane, London EC4P 4EE

Simultaneously published in the USA and Canada
by Routledge
29 West 35th Street, New York, NY 10001

© 1994 Peter Kenway

Typeset in 10/12pt Garamond by
Ponting–Green Publishing Services,
Chesham, Buckinghamshire
Printed in Great Britain by
Biddles Ltd, Guildford and King's Lynn

British Library Cataloguing in Publication Data
A catalogue record for this book is available from
the British Library

Library of Congress Cataloging in Publication Data
has been applied for

ISBN 0–415–09398–8

CONTENTS

CONTENTS

FIGURES

TABLES

ACKNOWLEDGEMENTS

Among the many people who gave me help during the course of my research into the development of macroeconometric modelling, I would particularly like to thank Ron Smith for his contribution over a number of years. I would also like to thank Peter Hart, Andrew Godley and Maxine Frerk for their reading of draft versions of this book and their trenchant criticisms of it. I also wish to record my appreciation of the Centre for Economic Forecasting at the London Business School for allowing me access to their archives.

Part I

UK MACRO-ECONOMETRIC MODELS

1

WHY STUDY MACROECONOMETRIC MODELS?

This book is a study of the evolution of the computer-based models, of the United Kingdom economy between the middle 1960s and the early 1980s. The significance of this period is that it spans the decline and fall of Keynesianism and its replacement by Monetarism. The significance of these models – macroeconometric models, to give them their proper title – is that they chart this progression from one economic regime to the other.

One way of putting it would be to say that the book treats the models as archaeological artefacts. As solid objects, which have been preserved almost intact, they, and the often considerable amounts of documentary information about them, form a precise and detailed record of the economic beliefs of the economists who created and used them. These were not ordinary economists, but rather the select few who had (or sought) both the ear of government and access to media through which to promulgate their views on government economic policy.

Many of these economists are still in positions of influence today, promoting many of the same views. One question of interest, therefore, which this book examines, is how those views were reached. For me, however, the most interesting thing about the macroeconometric models is the light that they shed on the relationship between Keynesianism and Monetarism. It is normal, I think, to see them as opposites, and in many crucial respects this is true. But what the models show is that the elements of continuity, including the mutations within Keynesianism that prefigured Monetarism, are at least as important as the evident contrasts. This gives rise to the idea that the progression from Keynesianism to Monetarism was a process of *evolution*. This idea is the book's central theme.

Macroeconometric modelling is now a specialist area of economics,

3

employing advanced analytical methods and an array of technical terms. This book, however, has been written for a wider audience. It is intended as a history of one part of modern economic thought. Mathematics and econometrics have been kept to a minimum and the many detailed points, with which these disciplines deal, have a secondary status here. Likewise, although the models are a window on economic policy, the book avoids the plethora of detail that comes from studies written by those who have been close to the policy-making process and the policy makers themselves. These omissions are deliberate and the reason for them is that what this book is trying to do is to pick out the fundamental features of the pattern behind the shift in thinking and policy that began what are now some thirty years ago.

STRUCTURAL ECONOMETRIC MODELS AND FORECASTING

A macroeconometric model is a *structural* model in empirical form. A structural model purports to represent the way in which the economy works. It is composed chiefly of *estimated* relationships which are held to represent aggregate behaviour: for example, aggregate consumption as a function of income, or expenditure on imports as a share of total expenditure. The primary function of macro-econometric models is to help with the formulation of *policy advice* to government, principally in the area of what could be called the 'management of the economy'. The appendix to this chapter provides a basic introduction to the main characteristics of such a model.

The macroeconometric models therefore occupy a niche shaped by the interaction of three sets of factors: firstly, economic theory, which supply ways of representing the workings of the economy; secondly, the historical data, which supply the material from which the estimates are obtained; and thirdly, the policy problems of the day, which largely determine the issues that the models must address. It is the combination of the three factors that makes macro-econometric models interesting and valuable to this study.

The thing for which the models are best known, though, is not so much policy advice as *forecasting*. Although the published forecasts that are produced nowadays with the aid of macroeconometric models tend to look beyond just the next two years, it is their assessments of these short-term prospects that attract the most attention. This type of forecasting is a routine activity, with forecasts published typically two, three or four times a year. Rather like weather forecasts, the ones that get remembered are those that turned out to be badly wrong. The most memorable mistakes in weather forecasting are probably linked to freak events like hurricanes. But the economy does not behave in that way. Changes in behaviour take time to build up, with the result that the most spectacular errors of those forecasting the economy occur when they fail to foresee either the magnitude of some event, or its duration, rather than the event itself.

Economic forecasting has been dogged by this type of problem since the middle of the 1970s, and the problems since the middle of the last decade have been worse than before. Firstly, economists failed to predict the extent of the economic boom in the late 1980s; then they failed to predict both the depth and length of the subsequent recession, which began in 1990. Naturally, the forecasting record of the British government's Treasury has excited the greatest attention, but, in its failure to forecast both the boom and the recession, this government department has been not the exception among forecasters but the norm, as studies by both the Treasury and independent academics have shown.[1] Those who are most closely associated with the models devote a considerable amount of attention to the analysis of the forecasting performance in order to diagnose which parts of the model are at fault.[2]

One of the particular problems for macroeconometric models is that it often seems (and is sometimes true) that better forecasts can be obtained using methods that are cheaper and simpler. These range from different types of computer-based model through to informal procedures that do not rely on a formal model at all. For example, one of the few economic forecasters to have conveyed at least some sense of the depth of the recession that began in 1990 gave up using computer models a few years ago on the grounds that they were giving the wrong results.[3]

A poor forecasting record may be evidence that a model is unreliable for policy analysis; but the converse does not apply. This is because, to formulate economic policy, one needs a knowledge of how the economy works, whereas such knowledge is not necessarily needed for forecasting. There is an analogy here with horse racing. I may, by studying the form, be able to make a fortune betting at the races, but you would be ill-advised, on that basis alone, to entrust me with the training of your horse. My success depends on knowing a successful horse when I see one; your success, if you are to have any, depends on finding someone who understands how a successful horse is produced in the first place.

The proper response to the inferior forecasting performance of a structural model is to attempt to improve its ability in that area by borrowing from the other, more successful methods.[4] This was one of the primary motivations behind the synthesis of structural econometrics and time-series methods that took place in the United Kingdom in the 1970s, and this tradition has since then had considerable influence on the development of macroeconometric modelling in Britain.[5] A poor forecasting record is a spur to improvement but it is in no way an argument against structural modelling itself.

THE USE OF MODELS FOR POLICY ANALYSIS

The case for employing a macroeconometric model to help with the task of policy analysis rests on arguments for abstraction, which apply to models in general, and for using an empirical form, which apply to econometric models in particular.

A macroeconometric model is, necessarily, a highly simplified representation of how the economy works. This simplification applies not only in relation to the economy itself but also in relation to the rich diversity of economic thinking that lies behind, and informs, the construction of a model. This thinking typically has its gaps, ambiguities and contradictions. It is surrounded by all sorts of qualifying conditions that are intended to limit its applicability. An approach that expresses the economy by means of just a handful of empirical equations cannot possibly capture more than a few fragments of the background economic thinking.

The particular role of the model is to separate out what is thought to be capable of systematic representation. It is a distillation of a view of how the economy works which shows the most important elements, and their inter-relationships, in a precise and quantified manner. It is a view of the economy stripped down to its bare essentials. Clearly, it would be wrong to treat such models without regard to the theoretical background; but the builders of macroeconometric models do not usually commit this error.

The use of a macroeconometric model for policy analysis has a number of advantages. The first is the clarity that is afforded by the inherent precision of any mathematical form. The benefits to be had from this precision probably accrue principally to the people who actually build the model: the very act of trying to translate what are rich, incomplete and perhaps even, at times, incoherent thoughts into this form is an invaluable discipline. Secondly, the model provides a framework that allows many different policy alternatives to be explored in a *consistent* fashion. Thirdly, the model is a (relatively) transparent way of representing economic thinking.

The fourth advantage stems from the inherently empirical nature of a macroeconometric model, which means that all of the effects that can be represented by it have to be fully quantified. This is particularly important as far as practical policy-making is concerned, where what is decisive is the magnitude, or scale, of the effects of some policy rather than just the effects themselves. An example that illustrates this point perfectly is the use of the exchange-rate as an instrument of policy. The question of whether Britain should depart from a fixed parity for the pound was the subject of debate as long ago as the early 1960s. In a later reflection on that debate, Brian Tew observed that none of the people involved thought it necessary or even possible to quantify the effects:

> Yet without quantification the debate was almost bound to be inconclusive, since the possible adverse side effects of a departure from the $2.80 peg (retaliation by other countries; speculation against the pound; deterioration in our terms of trade; a rise in the cost of living; leading possibly to a wage–price spiral; breaking faith with overseas holders of sterling; damage to the city's prestige) all depended very much on the percentage by which the pound's external value would have to fall.
>
> (Tew 1979: 310–11)

The importance of quantification is a point that will recur through the book, as will the effect of altering the exchange rate. Indeed, the question of the proper use, if any, of the exchange-rate is one that has been central to the debate on macroeconomic policy in Britain since the 1960s. A measure of its importance in this study is that a change in the answer to this question is the thing that, above all else, distinguishes each phase in the transition from Keynesianism to Monetarism.

KEYNESIANISM AND MONETARISM

'Keynesianism' and 'Monetarism' are words that carry many meanings. Of the two, Monetarism is the more conservative, admitting perhaps no more than one principal variety to the basic strain.

Keynesianism, in contrast, comes in at least half a dozen different flavours and many of these (for example, 'new', 'neo', 'post', 'international', 'left', 'IS–LM', 'income expenditure') are themselves subject to further fissuring. Nevertheless, it is possible to distinguish the one group from the other by their assessment of the ability of a free market to produce the beneficial results promised by neoclassical economic theory. Put simply, Monetarists affirm that the free market is so capable while Keynesians deny it.

This, though, is an unsatisfactory distinction in as much as it defines Keynesianism in a negative way, by what it is not, rather than by what it is. Since the Keynesianism with which this book will deal is the one that guided the conduct of economic policy making in Britain for three decades from the early 1940s, it is appropriate to look for a positive definition. The one I shall use focuses on the objectives that are set for the conduct of the government's *macroeconomic* policy:

> in a market economy the total amount of goods and services produced is not (or not normally) determined by the amount of scarce resources at its disposal, and the efficiency with which they are utilised, but on certain features of the process of income generation which will tend to establish an equilibrium level of effective demand which will limit the amount produced, irrespective of potential supply. Keynes' theory has shown how the economy can be managed so as to secure the full utilisation of resources, in particular the full employment of labour, mainly by government action in the fiscal and monetary field, without any radical change in the framework of institutions of a market economy.
>
> (Kaldor 1971: 2)

On this view, Keynesianism is, therefore, the use of fiscal and monetary means to achieve full employment. This, of course, was not the only objective to be attained by these means; others included the control of wage inflation, the achievement of a certain rate of economic growth and the maintenance of a satisfactory balance of payments with the rest of the world.[6] Monetarism, in contrast, sees the principal role of government fiscal[7] and monetary policy as the control of inflation.

It is important to emphasise here that the difference lies not in the objectives themselves – Keynesianism recognised the problem of inflation just as Monetarism recognised the importance of the 'real' economy – but in the means for achieving them and, in particular, whether those means should be macroeconomic or microeconomic. The point of this distinction is that microeconomic means are not really within the control of the government: the government can influence them indirectly by creating a more or less conducive environment, but it cannot affect them directly. Thus the question is this: is the government *directly* responsible for the macroeconomic variables, such as employment and the balance of payments, or is it only *indirectly* responsible? Kaldor suggested that, under Keynesian-ism, governments of both political parties believed these variables to be their direct responsibility and the fact that they published targets bore testimony to that interpretation. Monetarism, though, adhered (and adheres) to what these Keynesians saw as the old, orthodox view about the proper role of government in relation to the economy:

> up to recently – up to the Second World War in fact – the tasks of economic policy were mainly thought of as the creation of a framework of laws and institutions which provided the best environment for the operation of market forces, and not the direct manipulation of those forces.
>
> (Kaldor 1971: 1)

In employing the late Nicholas Kaldor as the spokesman for Keynesianism, I am choosing someone whom many economists would see as an extremist. Certainly, there are many modern Keynes-ians who would have little difficulty in subscribing to what Kaldor saw as the old orthodoxy (and which is of course the current orthodoxy), that the proper role of the central authorities, beyond the control of inflation, is to *enable* the economy to work better so as to achieve its goals, rather than to act themselves to achieve them.

The reason for choosing Kaldor is the close affinity between the ideas articulated by him and the policies that were promoted by the leading developers of macroeconometric models, particularly in the early 1970s. This applies not only to the 'New Keynesians', of the Cambridge Economic Policy Group, who were directly linked to Kaldor, but also to the London Business School economists, who were, for a time, the most vigorous proponents of Kaldor's 'radical alternative' of devaluation to secure export-led growth. The affinity, though, extends beyond specific policies to the very conception of how applied economics should be practised. There are moments when Kaldor spoke of it as problem solving, which, when conducted on this grand scale, is much more the province of operations research than it is of economics. There is no doubt that the macroeconometric models of the late 1960s and 1970s would be acceptable as models within operations research, even if economists and econometricians questioned their pedigree.

The progression from Keynesianism to Monetarism was, in the first place, a shift in what were held to be the proper objectives of macroeconomic policy. But serious economists do not change their minds on a matter as significant as this without good reason. Of course the circumstances and problems of the time play their part in shaping what economists believe to be important, but ultimately this alone is not enough. Such a drastic change of opinion regarding the appropriateness of policy, or the appropriateness of using some instrument of policy to achieve those objectives, requires nothing less than a change of view about how the economy works. The old Keynesianism lost its hold within economics, not because economists ceased to believe in the importance of unemployment, or growth, but rather because they ceased to believe the Keynesian account of how those variables were determined and, in particular, the means by which the government could influence them. The transformation from Keynesianism to Monetarism required, therefore, a transformation of views about how the economy worked. And it is precisely this – the way in which the economy is believed to work – that a macroeconometric model, as a structural model, represents. To study the models is therefore to concentrate on the way in which the understanding of the economy's structure evolved and altered.

THE PRINCIPAL CHARACTERS

Whose understanding? To answer this question involves introducing the principal macroeconometric modelling groups accompanied by an indication of their importance to the story to be told here. The institutions at the centre of British economic policy – Her Majesty's Treasury and the Bank of England – have long possessed macro-econometric models of their own. So too has the National Institute of Economic and Social Research, which is independent of government but which nevertheless enjoyed close links with the Treasury, secured principally through exchange of personnel. The models are publicly available and, indeed, groups of economists quite independent of the Treasury can, and do, use its model to prepare projections of the future course of the economy. But none of these official or semi-official models was responsible for any significant advance in modelling within the time-frame of this study. I will deal with the spread of modelling to these institutions (chapters 2 and especially 4), but attention here will be focused principally on the groups who were responsible for major innovations within UK macroeconometric modelling, first and foremost among which is the London Business School.

The first macroeconometric models of the British economy were built in the 1930s, and a variety of types began to appear from the late 1950s onwards (chapter 2). It was, though, the model that was built by James Ball and Terence Burns at the London Business School, in 1966, that rapidly came to define 'the' UK macroeconometric model. As well as 'inventing' the model in the first place (its roots and the reasons for its successful proliferation are dealt with in chapter 3), Ball and Burns and their colleagues developed the model type and helped spread it to other institutions (chapter 4). They were responsible for introducing the exchange-rate as an instrument of policy in the models in the early 1970s (chapter 5). As the decade proceeded, they first altered their minds – and their model – about the effect of exchange-rate changes and then later shifted from their previously Keynesian position to one that was consistent with International Monetarism (chapter 7). The question of how they managed this progression from Keynesianism to Monetarism is obviously one of the central problems for this book to address (dealt with at length in chapter 8).

The second group of model innovators was the economists of the Cambridge Economic Policy Group. These economists, led by Wynne Godley, were best known for their consistent advocacy, from the middle 1970s onwards, of a policy of quantitative import controls in order to alleviate the balance of payments constraint on the rate of growth of the UK economy. This policy, coupled with their oft-expressed scepticism towards formal econometric methods, left them with very little support among fellow academics. Yet these economists, both individually and as a group, made a far deeper impression on the course of macroeconometric modelling than their position as 'extremists' might suggest. Godley was responsible for a number of the crucial developments in the pre-model period of the early 1960s (chapter 3) while the Group was the first of the UK model builders to shift attention away from the traditional short-term (or cyclical) fluctuations, to the underlying (or 'trend') path of the economy (chapter 6). This shift of focus, and the accompanying change in what were held to be the principal determinants of the course of the economy, pre-figured a number of later moves by other economists who were promoting quite different strategies from those of the Policy Group.

This is nowhere more true than with the third group of model innovators: the economists based at Liverpool University and led by Patrick Minford. In the chronology of this book, these economists are 'post-Monetarists' in that their chief contribution came after the shift from Keynesianism to Monetarism had been made. Yet, in their role as 'supply-side' innovators, Minford and his colleagues were following in the footsteps of the Policy Group: not (of course) in the remedies that they espoused, but in the problem, of the underlying path of the economy, that they addressed. The contrast between these two groups' different approaches to what was the same question is another important issue dealt with later in the book (chapter 9).

THE HISTORICAL SETTING

However, what gives this account of macroeconometric model development its spice is the historical setting in which that development took place. In particular, the Business School's model came into being within months of the event that, with the benefit of hindsight, seems to mark the beginning of the end of Keynesianism. During the long post-war boom, the United Kingdom had enjoyed something close to full employment, with unemployment fluctuating between only 1 and 2 per cent of the workforce. But by the middle of the 1960s, it was proving increasingly difficult to reconcile, on the one hand, a rate of economic growth sufficiently high to sustain full employment with, on the other, the need to restrict the import of goods and services into the UK to a level that was consistent with a satisfactory position on the balance of payments. The Labour government that came to power in 1964 was beset with this problem of the balance of payments. In July 1966, that government, which had three months before been re-elected with a parliamentary majority of ninety-seven, took action to try to deal with this problem. It did so, firstly by deflating the economy, thereby causing unemployment to rise, and, secondly, by introducing a freeze on pay, voluntary in the first instance but made statutory a short while later.

The history of the models charts firstly the increasingly desperate attempts to revitalise Keynesianism – to find other means by which to maintain full employment consistent with the need to balance payments with the rest of the world – and in due course to replace it with Monetarism.

This leads on to the last of the book's major themes concerning the relationship between Keynesianism and Monetarism and, in particular, the reason for the demise of the one and the triumph of the other. Was Keynesianism defeated by Monetarism in the late 1970s because the latter accorded an overwhelming priority to the defeat of inflation at a time when the annual rate of inflation had topped 25 per cent? Or did Keynesianism collapse owing to its failure to cope with increasingly hostile circumstances? The significance of this now is that, with more than 3 million unemployed and little hope of this figure being reduced, the circumstances might be thought once again to favour a doctrine that gives priority to employment over inflation. Yet if Keynesianism collapsed without the help of Monetarism, then the appearance of conditions reminiscent of the 1930s may be of no help. The question whether or not we can now return to Keynesianism is discussed in chapter 10.

APPENDIX: MACROECONOMETRIC MODELS

A macroeconometric model represents a national economy in the form of a set of empirical equations. Although the very smallest model that was intended to be serious had six equations, we will use just four equations to demonstrate the essential features of such a model.

This model contains two behavioural equations and two identities. The first equation expresses aggregate personal consumption (C_t) as a function of aggregate income (Y_t). The second equation expresses expenditure on imports (M_t) as a function of aggregate expenditure (E_t). The first identity defines aggregate expenditure as the sum of its components, respectively, personal consumption, government expenditure (G_t), investment (I_t) and exports (X_t) minus imports. The second identity expresses the equality between aggregate income and aggregate expenditure (each of which is a way of looking at Gross Domestic Product, GDP). The subscript, t, is a time index. In this model, all variables are expressed in terms of other variables for the same period.

$$C_t = 10 + 0.8 \times Y_t$$

$$M_t = -15 + 0.3 \times E_t$$

$$E_t \equiv C_t + G_t + I_t + X_t - M_t$$

$$Y_t \equiv E_t$$

This is a model with seven variables and four equations. It contains each of the three main elements of a proper macroeconometric model: firstly, *endogenous* variables, which are those determined by the model (in this case C_t, M_t, E_t and Y_t); secondly, *exogenous* variables, for which numerical inputs are supplied by the modeller (in this case, G_t, I_t and X_t); and thirdly the *parameters* in the behavioural equations (in this case 10 and 0.8 in the consumption equation and −15 and 0.3 in the import equation).

This is a 'macro' model because the set of endogenous variables in effect includes GDP. Its claim to being an 'econometric' model is based on it having numerical parameters (in the behavioural equations) that have been estimated statistically from data. In fact, the mere use of econometric formulas to *estimate* the coefficients is not a sufficient basis for describing a model as 'econometric'. If the empirical model is to enjoy the enhanced prestige conferred by that tag, it is necessary to show that it is in conformity with various assumptions, mainly of a probabilistic nature, on which such statistical validity depends.

We could use this model both to make forecasts and to give advice on policy. To make forecasts for 1995 say, we would need to come up first with values for the exogenous variables (government expenditure, exports and investment) for 1995 and then solve the equations to obtain the corresponding value of the endogenous variables. As this shows, model forecasts usually depend on forecasts of the exogenous variables, which necessarily have to be made outside of the model (that is, they are, in the jargon, 'conditional' forecasts). For example, if we believe that these variables will take the values 10, 20 and 10 respectively, then solution of the models will yield values for consumption, imports and GDP of 114, 24, and 130. These figures appear in the first column of table 1.1.

The only variable in this model that can reasonably be thought of as a policy variable is government expenditure, G_t. Policy advice concerning this variable broadly comes in one of two forms. The first involves answering a question of the following type: 'What happens if government expenditure is increased by (say) 5?' To obtain the answer, we solve the model again, inserting a value of 15 for government expenditure and leaving exports and investment at 20 and 10 respectively. The second column of table 1.1 shows the results for the endogenous variables, and, by comparing the first two columns, we can see that the effect on GDP is an increase of 10. Consumption and imports also rise, by 8 and 3 respectively.

Table 1.1 Results for three simulations

	1	2	3
Exogenous variables			
Government expenditure	**10**	**15**	25
Exports	**20**	**20**	**20**
Investment	**10**	**10**	**10**
Endogenous variables			
Consumption	114	122	138
Imports	24	27	33
GDP (*E* and *Y*)	130	140	**160**

Figures in **bold** are those that are given for each simulation. Usually these are the exogenous variables but, in the third simulation, GDP is given (the target) and the model is solved to find the value of government expenditure (the instrument) that will satisfy that target.

The second form of policy advice would come in response to a question of a slightly different type: 'What must the level of government expenditure be in order that GDP equals 160?' Strictly, what we would do to answer this question would be to alter the status of E_t and G_t, making the first an exogenous ('target') variable and the second an endogenous ('instrument') variable. Solving the model, given expenditure of 160 and exports and investment, yields a value for government expenditure of 25. The results appear in the third column of table 1.1.

The thing to note about these answers is that they are sometimes qualitative but *always* quantitative. It is this quantitative dimension that is the special contribution of the econometric model.

2

MACROECONOMETRIC MODELS
A panoramic view of their history

Multi-equation econometric models of national economies were an invention of the 1930s, and the first models of the British economy, among the earliest built anywhere, date from the last years of that decade. Although the building of econometric models in Britain did not recommence until the late 1950s, the ten or so years that followed, to 1968, represent a period in which British model-building was rich in innovation and diversity. Thereafter, however, one type of model – the income–expenditure model – dominated the scene until the end of the following decade. During this time, the income–expenditure model underwent an enormous amount of development, but it was not until the 1980s that it first faced a serious challenger. Even so, the modern mainstream macroeconometric models of the UK economy can trace their ancestry to the original income–expenditure models.

The principal theme of this book – the transition from Keynesianism to Monetarism – is concerned overwhelmingly with the late 1960s and the 1970s. But, as is clear from even the barest outline of the macroeconometric modelling in the UK, given above, this is a focus that misses over a quarter of a century of the activity! The purpose of this chapter is to correct that imbalance, by means of a description and discussion of all of the major UK models from the very beginning.

I shall deal with the models in four chronological groups: models of the business cycle (1930s); alternative approaches to modelling (1957–68); the consolidation of the income–expenditure model (1967–72); and the consensus shattered (1973 onwards). With the exception of the first of the new 'supply-side' models, I do not deal with any of the models of the 1980s because, although they have added much refinement, the fundamental lines of development were already laid down.[1]

A TABULAR SUMMARY

A panoramic view of over forty years of macroeconometric modelling must necessarily be selective. Firstly, it is not practicable to mention every model because there have simply been too many of them. The main reason for this over-abundance is that a model that is used for many years inevitably passes through a number of distinct stages; for example, there have now been more than a dozen generations of the model of the National Institute. The cast of principal models (which includes some multiple entries for these multi-generation ones) numbers fourteen. Lesser models that do not attract a separate billing are also mentioned in passing. Secondly, selection is even more necessary when looking at the models themselves: we can afford to attend only to the essential features of each model – those features, in other words, that make it fundamentally different from (or indeed similar to) another. My judgement of what is essential forms the basis for the selection of data shown for each of the fourteen models in table 2.1.

As its title ('A tabular summary') implicitly acknowledges, the table bears some resemblance to Marc Nerlove's famous 'tabular survey' of macroeconometric models, which was published over a quarter of a century ago. Nerlove's survey was a catalogue of twenty-five macroeconometric models for nine national economies. At the time this came close to being a comprehensive worldwide survey of all such models. The data that Nerlove gave for each model included the number and names of both exogenous and endogenous variables, the method of estimation, the pattern of lags and the principal institutional, technical and behavioural equations. Nerlove's survey is a rich database but, in the end, it is perhaps hard to grasp a clear appreciation of what is most important about a model amid the wealth of detail that is provided.[2] My approach, which is intended to help convey an overview rather than provide precise and copious detail, is therefore somewhat different.

To begin with, the models in the table are arranged in the four groups that have already been mentioned. The data provided on each model are arranged in five categories. The first details the frequency of the data used (quarterly or annual), the method of estimation and the approximate period from which the data were drawn to estimate the model. Secondly, the table shows the number of exogenous variables and names the chief ones among them. From the viewpoint of the model as a tool (the user's perspective), the exogenous variables

17

show the causes whose effect the model can represent. Of course, by no means all exogenous variables are policy instruments, because variables can also be treated as exogenous if the model builder believes that the influence of forces represented *within* the model on the variable is negligible (for example, the volume of world trade).

Thirdly the table presents a classification of the relationships within each model, by both the type of relationship and the type of the endogenous variable. This is at the same time therefore a classification of the endogenous variables. There are two types of relationships: 'equations' (whether 'behavioural', such as an aggregate consumption function, or 'technical', such as a function to determine income tax from income) and 'identities' (such as the one that expresses GDP as the sum of its aggregate expenditure components). There are up to six types of variable: 'expenditure', 'income', 'output' (or 'supply'), 'financial', 'labour' and 'costs and prices' (including wage rates, interest rates and exchange-rates). The distinction between equations and identities is standard, albeit coarser than normal, but the attempt to portray the broad balance of the model between various blocks is perhaps unusual. Obviously, there is an element of arbitrariness about it (for example in the allocation of savings to either income or expenditure), while the qualitative importance of a block is not always reflected by its size within the model. However, it does show where the bulk of the model lies and gives clues to the broad type of theory that underpins the model's structure.

Fourthly, the table reports the measure used for the overall level of economic activity; apart from the earliest models, this is always GDP but the question is whether it is built up from the expenditure (GDP(E)), income (GDP(I)) or output side (GDP(O)). This is reviewed in greater detail in chapter 3 but I believe that the answer to this question is probably the key to understanding the model's essential characteristics. Almost as important – and closely related – is the question of how the model ensures that the different measures of GDP, particularly the income and expenditure measures, are reconciled. Again the table records this information. Fifthly, the table reports any other striking features of the model. This includes information such as whether it was static or linear, as well as some of the principal instances of where price variables depended on one or more quantity variables.

Lastly, I should emphasise that by no means all the numbers appearing in this table are beyond dispute. Clearly this applies to those numbers that depend on a judgmental classification; but it is true even of the totals wherever they have been gleaned from model listings. It is the overall impression – the scale of the thing – and not the precise numbers, that matters here.

MODELS OF THE BUSINESS CYCLE

E. A. Radice's model of 'A Dynamic Scheme for the British Trade Cycle 1929–37' was the first macroeconometric model of the British economy and only the second (after Tinbergen's model of the Dutch economy) of its kind anywhere.[3] Containing only six equations, the model was very small and, although certainly innovative, its objective was strictly limited. In contrast, Jan Tinbergen's *Business Cycles in the UK, 1870–1914* was (and is) quite breathtaking, not only for the work involved in designing, estimating and solving a model containing thirty-nine relationships without the aid of an electronic computer, but also for the ambitious scope of the project.

Both models were an application of the theory of the business cycle, which itself had emerged from the new work in mathematical economics carried out in the 1930s. This theory had shown how a set of *linear* difference or differential equations could yield a *non-linear* path through time for the variables. Depending on the values of the equation coefficients, the non-linear path could be both cyclical and stable. Radice built his model in order to see if equations estimated on British data would yield such a damped cyclical path; if so – and Radice found that it was so – it would be possible to view the mathematical business cycle theory as an explanation of the British trade cycle. Tinbergen built his model of the UK business cycle only a short while after his famous League of Nations study of the US business cycle, which itself had followed the pioneering model of the Dutch economy.[4] Tinbergen's UK work as whole was an exercise in quantitative economic history: quantifying the UK cycle before the First World War was therefore no more than a first step. The model was used to explore the linkages through which the British trade cycle influenced, and was influenced by, developments elsewhere in the world for a period during which Britain's economic weight within the world was still very significant. As is clear from the entry in table 2.1, the model was made up of relationships of all types, and in particular it contained a high proportion of equations for monetary or financial variables as well as price variables. In keeping with its international perspective, the model also contained many variables

Table 2.1 A tabular summary of fourteen macroeconometric models
of the UK economy

Model & reference	Frequency; method & period of estimation	Exogenous variables: number & most notable
Models of the Business Cycle (1935–40)		
Radice: 'A Dynamic Scheme for the British Trade Cycle 1929–37' (Radice 1939)	Quarterly OLS 1929–37	0
Tinbergen UK: 'Business Cycles in the UK 1870–1914' (Tinbergen 1951)	Annual (9-year moving average) OLS 1871–1914	15 (UK): import price indices; notes in circulation; gold reserves; world gold stock; foreign short-term interest rate; world trade; world production of pig iron.
Alternative Approaches to Macro-modelling (1957–68)		
Oxford: 'An Econometric Model of the UK' (Klein *et al.* 1961a)	Quarterly (mainly unadjusted) LIML & OLS 1948–56	36: current and capital government expenditure; tax rates; bank rate; sterling balances; indices of foreign prices & foreign production.
CGP: 'A Computable Model of Economic Growth' (Stone 1964; Stone *et al.* 1970)	Annual 2SLS 1900–60	2091: total consumer expenditure; trade balance; government expenditures; prices; industrial demand for replacement of fixed assets.
SEM: 'An Econometric Model of the UK & Trading Partners' (Heathfield and Pearce 1975)	Quarterly OLS No estimates reported	20+: government expenditures, exchange-rate, tax rates & subsidies.
LBS1a (1966): 'An Economic Model for Control' (Ball 1967)	Quarterly (unadjusted) OLS 1955/7–64	15: government expenditure; income taxes; world trade exports.
Byron (1968): 'A Simultaneous Model of Income, Expenditure and Output' (Byron 1970)	Quarterly (adjusted) 2SLS 1958(1)-1968(3)	28: government expenditure (various categories); income taxes; price deflators; exports; agricultural output; trading profits and surplus.

Endogenous variables by block:	Equation	Identity	Measure of overall level of activity & how determined	Comments
Income (inc. Saving)	3	2	Gross National Income.	Linear.
Expenditure	1	–		
Total	4	2		
Output	1	2	Total national expenditure;	Linear.
Income	2	1	non-labour income	
Expenditure	7	7	(profits) defined to make	
Financial	6	1	national income equal	
Labour	2	1	national expenditure.	
Costs & Prices	9	–		
Total (UK)	27	12		
Output	4	1	GDP(O) inferred from	
Income	–	2	industrial production index;	
Expenditure	13	2	gross company profits	
Costs & Prices	10	1	defined to make GDP(I)	
Labour	3	1	equal GDP(O).	
Total	30	7		
Output	–	92	GDP(E); GDP(O) defined	Static.
Expenditure	423	267	equal to GDP(E).	
Total	423	359		
Output	15	–	GDP(O); inventories adjust	Unplanned change
Income	14	30	to make GDP(E) equal	in inventories
Expenditure	112	56	GDP(O).	influences output
Costs & Prices	99	33		and pricing
Labour	17	30		decisions in next
Total	257	149		period.
Income	3	2	GDP(E).	
Expenditure	9	1		
Financial	1	–		
Costs & Prices	5	1		
Labour	2	–		
Total	20	4		
Output	5	9	GDP(E); GDP(O); GDP(I).	Linear.
Income	2	6	Nothing within the model	
Expenditure	10	29	to make the three measures	
Costs & Prices	2	2	equal.	
Labour	3	5		
Total	22	51		

Table 2.1 Continued

Model & reference	Frequency; method & period of estimation	Exogenous variables: number & most notable
Income-Expenditure Models: Consolidation (1967–72)		
NIESR1a (1969) (Surrey 1971)	Quarterly OLS 1958–67	12: government expenditure; investment; exports.
HMT (1972) (Shepherd *et al.* 1975)	Quarterly OLS	73: government consumption; direct, indirect & employment tax rates; world trade; exchange-rate.
LBS1b (1972) (Ball *et al.* 1975a)	Quarterly OLS 1958/63–71	50: government expenditure; tax rates; world trade in exports; exchange-rate; money stock.
The Consensus Shattered (1973 onwards)		
CEPG (1976) (Fetherston 1976)	Annual OLS; AR; MA. 1962–74	65: rate of sales tax; real value of wage bargain; effective exchange-rate; degree of import restriction on finished manufactures. (NB: all model instruments)
NIESRIII (1977) (National Institute of Economic & Social Research 1977)	Quarterly OLS & IV 1963–76 (max)	70: world trade & prices; government expenditure & direct & indirect taxes; nominal money supply.
LBS2 (1978): 'An exercise in International Monetarism' (London Business School 1978)	Quarterly OLS 1963–78 (max)	106: government expenditure; tax rates; world industrial production & prices.
Liverpool (1983): 'A macroeconomic model of the UK' (Minford *et al.* 1984)	Annual SLIML; modified least squares 1959–83 (max)	7: working population; trade unionization rate; tax rates; world trade and price level; real unemployment benefit.

Endogenous variables by block:	Equation	Identity	Measure of overall level of activity & how determined	Comments
Income	5	2	GDP(E).	
Expenditure	4	4		
Costs & Prices	1	1		
Total	10	7		
Output	2	2	GDP(E); gross trading	
Income	13	11	profits defined to make	
Expenditure	16	18	GDP(I) equal GDP(E).	
Financial	–	12		
Costs & Prices	15	3		
Labour	2	1		
Total	48	47		
Output	5	2	GDP(E); undefined	Exchange-rate
Income	31	19	elements of public sector	exogenous.
Expenditure	23	24	income implicitly adjust to	
Financial	6	14	make GDP(I) equal	
Costs & Prices	17	5	GDP(E); GDP(O) defined	
Labour	3	4	equal to GDP(E).	
Total	86	68		
Income	12	18	GDP(E). Private sector	'North Sea' treated
Expenditure	14	33	profits, rents and self-	as a separate sector.
Financial	3	5	employed income together	Model solved under
Costs & Prices	17	15	adjust to make GDP(I)	a regime of targets
Labour	2	3	equal to GDP(E).	and instruments.
Total	48	74		
Output	12	19	GDP(E); other output	Exchange-rate &
Income	9	17	defined to make GDP(O)	money stock
Expenditure	12	26	equal GDP(E); profits	endogenous.
Financial	4	13	defined to make GDP(I)	
Costs & Prices	16	27	equal GDP(E).	
Labour	5	2		
Total	58	104		
Output	5	8	GDP(E); components of	Exchange-rate &
Income	34	42	GDP(I) not constrained to	money stock
Expenditure	25	46	sum to GDP(E); GDP(O)	endogenous.
Financial	10	29	defined equal to GDP(E).	
Costs & Prices	27	27		
Labour	2	1		
Total	103	153		
Output	–	3	GDP(E); but natural rate	Rational
Expenditure	5	2	determined on output side	expectations.
Financial	2	6	where expenditure	
Costs & Prices	7	7	components therefore	
Labour	1	1	adjust to permit GDP(E) to	
Total	15	19	accommodate to GDP(O).	

representing economic conditions in the rest of the world, including a number of world monetary variables.

The mode of analysis for these business cycle models involved reducing the system to a single equation by a process of substitution and elimination. This was possible because all equations were linear. This 'final equation' in one endogenous variable reflected the dynamic properties of the whole system. Tinbergen's system cycled with a period of about seven years and was considerably damped.[5] The final equation also provided the focus for the analysis of policies that might have ameliorated the business cycle. For example, Tinbergen analysed the effects of reducing consumption and investment propensities (to be effected through compensating public expenditures) on the coefficients of the final equation; this showed that such measures would lead to both shorter and more stable cycles.

In view of the model's true vintage (that is, dating from the very beginning of the 1940s), anyone so disposed could easily attack the model simply by repeating the criticisms that had been levelled, by Keynes among others, at Tinbergen's earlier US business cycle model.[6] One such assessment of the UK model, published in the *Economic Journal*, cited spurious correlation and problems with the data as part of an all-round attack on the 'uncompromisingly econometric' approach that Tinbergen had adopted.[7] What is most notable about this review is that its author, Alec Cairncross, later Chief Economic Adviser to the Treasury, was one of the key figures in the economic establishment during the period when macroeconometric modelling was struggling to gain official approval in the 1960s.

ALTERNATIVE APPROACHES TO MACROECONOMETRIC MODELLING

In spite of these two early attempts, macroeconometric modelling in the UK remained in abeyance through the 1940s and the first half of the 1950s. The UK was by no means unusual in this for, as Nerlove's survey records, model-building in that period was taking place only in the Netherlands and in the United States, where the leading role was being played by Lawrence Klein. It is not surprising that when modelling did resume it was through a model of the UK that was built by Klein with colleagues of his. Other models, developed at Cambridge, Southampton, the London Business School and the National Institute, followed over the next decade. What is most striking about them is the extent to which they differed from each other.

The 'Econometric Model of the UK', which was constructed at the Oxford Institute of Statistics in the late 1950s by Lawrence Klein, James Ball, Arthur Hazelwood and Peter Vandome, occupies a pivotal position in the history of UK macro-modelling.[8] This is so, not only for the model itself but also for the people who were involved in its construction, with Klein being the link from the earlier US work and Ball being the link on to much of the future modelling in the UK.

Klein in fact has been the pivotal figure in the worldwide spread of macro-modelling and *A History of Macroeconomic Model Building*[9] gives a measure of his influence. The episode with the UK model is quite typical of the way in which his influence has spread: collaborative work that served to create a network of economists many of whom went on to occupy and maintain influential positions in macroeconomic modelling in their own country for many years.

The model had thirty-seven equations, thirty-one of which were stochastic. It was quarterly and was the first model of its size of any economy to use data of that frequency.[10] The model contained a detailed treatment of the international links to the UK economy, with six export and three import volume equations, two export price equations and sixteen exogenous international variables. It was estimated by Limited Information Maximum Likelihood (LIML) as well as by least squares. LIML was used, rather than FIML (Full information), firstly because the computing load[11] would be lighter and secondly because LIML, unlike FIML, allowed the system of equations to be built up in stages, that is, experimenting with the form of some of the equations without having to make any assumptions about the forms of other equations.

There were not, in the second half of the 1950s, quarterly national accounts data in sufficient quantity to estimate a model such as this and the compilation of suitable data was therefore a major task, which the modellers had to undertake themselves. The consequence of the lack of readily available data and the accounting framework that defines it is that the model builders had a greater degree of freedom in designing the model. So, although this model is a clear forerunner of the later 'mainstream' macro models, it is still strikingly different in a number of ways. In particular, the central aggregate variable that reflected the level of economic activity was an index of industrial production. This is conceptually different from GDP in that it excludes services, but its key implication is that the overall level of activity was modelled from the output (or supply) side.

The model was used to prepare a forecast for the first two quarters of 1959 and was later re-estimated and used to prepare a forecast for 1961.[12] Beyond this, however, the model was not maintained. Difficulties with the data were severe but the forecasts, which were the first to be made for the UK economy using a computer model, were a disappointment in that they were judged worse than the forecasts, using informal methods, that were already being carried out by the Treasury, the National Institute of Economic and Social Research and the London and Cambridge Economic Service.[13]

'A Computable Model of Economic Growth', the macroeconometric model of the Cambridge Growth Project was not at all vulnerable to such adverse comparisons for the simple reason that it was neither intended as, nor remotely capable of being used as, a forecasting model at all. Indeed, in its earliest manifestation, this model was least like any other UK model either before or since. Launched in the early 1960s within a research programme – 'A Programme for Growth'[14] – led by Richard Stone, the model passed through a number stages of evolution and continues, in a much modified form, to be used to this day. This evolution, perhaps inevitably, brought it closer to the mainstream UK models, and in the 1980s its multiplier properties were the subject of regular scrutiny and comparison with other publicly funded macroeconometric models.

The model, which was annual, was in use by 1965, at which time it contained nearly 800 relationships, divided approximately half and half between equations and identities, and it used more than 2000 exogenous variables. This scale is enormous and the reason for it was that the model was highly disaggregated. Organised around a Leontief input–output matrix, it contained forty categories of consumers' goods and services, thirty-one industrial categories and twelve categories of government expenditure. Apart from industry outputs and supplies (these differing by imports of the appropriate good), which were in any case determined by identity from the expenditure side, the endogenous variables in this model were entirely expenditure variables. This was unusual, but the thing that made the model unique was the fact that it was static.

The type of question that the model was designed to answer was as follows: given targets for the aggregate level of consumption in some future year and for steady rates of growth of consumption in subsequent years as well as a target balance of trade, what levels of output and therefore assets would be required, industry by industry, to achieve those targets? *Exploring 1970*[15] used the model in this way.

The starting point comprised a figure for total consumption in 1970, a vector of prices for 1970 and a vector of growth rates for the individual components of consumption for subsequent years. A set of demand equations – a version of the Linear Expenditure System – turned the first two inputs into a vector of demands for the various categories of consumption goods. The future rates of growth translated into a requirement for investment goods. These final demands were then transformed into total demands via an input–output matrix. The share of these going to imports depended on the amount of money available from export sales after allowing for net transfers abroad and also for imports of items (such as raw materials) that were not produced in Britain.

This cannot in any meaningful way be described as a macroeconomic forecast in the sense of a calculation of the position of the economy conditional on the values of the exogenous variables. Instead it is better conceived of as being a calculation of the levels of output (and capital) that would be required in each industry in order actually to produce that desired macroeconomic position. A separate, but related, question was whether or not the economy as it actually existed at the time of the calculation could be adapted so as to achieve those requirements. At an early stage, a separate, but related, model was envisaged to address this question. However, although plans for this 'transient' model existed, it was never developed.[16]

In adopting this level of disaggregation, the Growth Project was not motivated by the belief that more disaggregation would make for a better, or more realistic, model. Rather, as Alan Brown explained, the Growth Project was built around an input–output matrix because 'we want to discuss our results with people in industry in terms of their inter-industry as well as final demand and primary input transactions'.[17] This touches on two crucial ideas: firstly, that the Growth Project saw industry and not just government as a recipient of the model's output and, secondly, that a model must be built in a way that is consonant with its objectives.

Disaggregation was the one thing that the 'Southampton Econometric Model of the UK and Trading Partners',[18] begun in 1965, had in common with the Growth Project. The Southampton model, which was the inspiration of Ivor Pearce, was organised around fourteen industrial sectors, and contained about 250 equations and 150 identities.[19] The great claim made for the model was its deep roots in neoclassical economic theory: 'with a suitable choice of parameters', Pearce had written, the model would 'settle down into a nice "equilibrium" position which is static save for a persistent price inflation and which, apart from inflation, may be described by an equation system familiar to any economic theorist'.[20]

There were two reasons for the degree of disaggregation of the Southampton model. The first was the importance that was attached to being close to economic theory. The second was that Pearce thought that macroeconomic effects ought to be analysed in much more detail than was possible in a purely macroeconomic model. For the Cambridge Growth Project, in contrast, disaggregation was an end in itself, industry-level results being needed for the dialogue with industry.

The primary problem with the Southampton model was its enormous appetite for data, the disaggregated nature calling for some 1500 series, many of which were not routinely available. This in itself was a reflection of the way in which the model specification was drawn up, with economic theory accorded overwhelming priority; practical questions concerned with the availability of data or econometric questions concerning the identification of such a system were regarded as being of secondary importance. In contrast, the Cambridge model had grown out of an earlier piece of applied econometric work concerning the Linear Expenditure System.[21] Thus, although the blueprint was admirable in intent and clear in exposition, the Southampton model barely managed to leave the ground.

As a working model, the Southampton model was an almost total failure; but the thought that went into the economic problems associated with a truly simultaneous model has continued to prove suggestive even to the builders of models in the last decade. It is therefore worth looking at the blueprint. As table 2.1 shows, the expenditure block was, as in every other model, the largest in terms of the number of relationships but it was not here of primary importance. Firstly, GDP was determined directly in the output (supply) block. Total expenditure, at the level of both the sector and the economy as a whole, was brought into equality with total output by using the (unplanned) change in inventories as the accommodating variable. Since this variable – stockbuilding – is defined as a category of expenditure within the national accounting framework, expenditure in the Southampton model adjusted to output. Secondly, prices occupied a central position in the model, with the price in each sector being set in response both to the unplanned changes in inventory and to unplanned changes in profits. Prices therefore played the role of moving the economy towards equilibrium. Equilibrium was, however, a long-run or steady-state phenomenon only; although the economy always satisfied the accounting identities, its general character was one of disequilibrium.

The model produced at the London Business School by James Ball and Terry Burns in 1966 could hardly have been more different from the Southampton and Cambridge models. It was closer to the Oxford model, on which Ball had worked, although simpler. It was small, highly aggregated and contained only twenty-four equations, of which twenty were stochastic. Of these, no fewer than fifteen determined components of either aggregate income or aggregate expenditure. It was therefore the first model devoted primarily to modelling the key elements of the income–expenditure matrix that provides the framework for the UK national accounts. The variable that reflected the level of economic activity was Gross Domestic Product calculated from the expenditure side, that is, it was built up as the sum of the aggregate expenditure components: personal and government consumption, exports less imports and investment. Each of these components (apart from government expenditure) was endogenous and the model treated private sector investment on housing separately from other private sector investment.

From the very outset, the Business School model was used to provide short-term forecasts (over six quarters) of the future course of the UK economy. For different reasons, neither the Growth Project nor Southampton models were capable of doing this; the Business School model was therefore unique in this respect. Moreover, these forecasts were published in the *Sunday Times* newspaper with a supporting discussion of the implications. The first appeared in November 1966, and articles appeared thereafter three times a year without interruption through to the late 1970s.

These articles provide valuable insights into the development of the thinking of the Business School modellers over the next decade and a half, and we shall exploit them as a source for the story to be told here. In a way, however, their very existence sheds a different light on the role of the model, because, although Ball and Burns were restrained for some time in the advice that they presumed to give on policy, the platform that they acquired to discuss and predict what was happening to the UK economy just as it was moving from the tranquillity of the 1950s and early 1960s to the turbulence of the 1970s was one that could only be highly influential. 'The first analysis based on an econometric model and processed by computer – a technique widely used in the U.S.' was how the first article was advertised and whether deliberately sought or not, the cachet that the association with the computer conferred on what Ball and Burns had to say can only have helped in their acquisition of this public platform.[22]

The model that was built by Ray Byron at the National Institute of Economic and Social Research during 1968 and 1969 is probably the least familiar of all the models here. Although development reached the point where preliminary computer simulations were performed with it, the model was never used for forecasting; and it was certainly never *the* model of the National Institute. It is included here because it identified as central the issue of simultaneity that is inherent to the very notion of Gross Domestic Product as both aggregate income, aggregate expenditure and aggregate output. As is clear from table 2.1, Byron's model had income, expenditure and output sides in roughly equal proportion. From these, each of the three measures of GDP was built up *independently*. One advantage of this, in Byron's view, was that it utilised 'a great deal of information which might otherwise be neglected'; another was that it allowed 'for three forecasts of GDP, thus providing an internal check on the specification of the model'.[23] The only way in which the simultaneity was directly addressed was through the use of a method of estimation (two-stage least squares) that was appropriate to such situations. In spite of this, the model certainly did not work satisfactorily; in particular it seems as if the measures of GDP responded quite differently to a change in the value of an exogenous variable – which is probably as unsatisfactory as it is possible to get.

This model may seem – was, even – naive, but in its attempt to tackle the fundamental simultaneity it was addressing a matter that the income–expenditure model of the Business School (and, later, the National Institute) simply ignored. In this, Byron's model is a complement to the Southampton model but, whereas Pearce tried to deal with the problem through the proper application of economic theory, Byron tried to deal with it through the proper application of econometrics. Simultaneity was, moreover, a real problem and, as the income–expenditure model began to develop, the question of how to tackle it could not be avoided.

INCOME–EXPENDITURE MODELS: CONSOLIDATION

The London Business School's income–expenditure model was openly admitted to be no more than a prototype.[24] Once established, the task therefore was one of expanding and developing the model, and this period of growth stretched over six or so years into the early 1970s. As well as growth, however, this period was also marked by propagation of the model type to such an extent that the income–expenditure model rapidly became 'the' UK macroeconometric model. This experience is unique within the UK for, both prior to this time and subsequently, new model types have invariably been one-off affairs. I shall discuss in the next chapter the reasons for the successful spread of this model.

Table 2.1 contains an entry for the Business School model as it stood in 1972. I have labelled this 'LBS1b', but it should be understood that it is simply a snapshot taken at a particular point in time of a model that had been evolving continuously since 1966. If we measure a model's size by the number of relationships (or endogenous variables) that it contains, then the 1972 version, with over 150 relationships, was over six times as large as the prototype. The number of identities had multiplied particularly rapidly and in terms of equations alone (that is, the behavioural and technical relationships) the growth had been about fourfold. Data on block size show that the overwhelming majority of the relationships modelled variables in the income or expenditure blocks. In contrast there were few labour equations (the ones present being for hours, the wage rate, employment and unemployment) and few output equations (output and productivity trends against time). The model's size had grown but its character was little changed.

This point can be seen even more clearly when we consider the exogenous variables. Compared with 1966, they had increased three-fold but the majority of them (even excluding the nearly forty dummy variables) were economically insignificant. The few significant ones were to do primarily with government expenditure and tax rates. The most notable addition to the exogenous variables was the exchange-rate. Six years of growth and development had therefore been directed principally towards refining the effects of the policies that the model was capable of representing rather than extending the range of those policies.

The most important place where the income–expenditure model was propagated was the Treasury. Although the government had been publishing forecasts of the economy since 1947,[25] the first forecast that was made using a fully computerised macroeconometric model was in the summer of 1970. At this point, the model contained about forty equations. The previous 'manual' forecasts had themselves been based on some econometric relationships and the model therefore was primarily a pulling together of these existing relationships supplemented by a small number of new ones to determine variables that were strictly endogenous but that had previously been treated as exogenous. One such new relationship was an 'accelerator' equation to determine private sector non-housing investment. Ball and Eaton from the Business School had written this model (including the provision of the new relationships) for the Treasury. Within two years, the model had doubled in size to ninety-five equations, about half of which were behavioural. However, of the forty-eight behavioural relationships in this version of the model, only fourteen actually used the coefficients obtained from free estimation of the equations.

Although the Treasury model was only about half the size of the Business School model in 1972, the overall balance was very similar. One small but notable difference concerned the way in which the different measures of GDP were reconciled. An unchanging characteristic of the income–expenditure models was that GDP was always built up from the expenditure side through the sum of the components of aggregate expenditure. Reconciliation between the expenditure and output measures was achieved simply by defining the latter as equal to the former. Such an approach was also available for reconciling income and expenditure, but since many of the components of income were themselves defined by relationships within the model this procedure would, whether explicitly or not, involve defining some category of income as the residual. The Treasury model overcame this problem by defining companies' gross trading profits as the difference between the expenditure measure of GDP and the sum of the other factor incomes including the public sector trading surplus. Nothing then depended upon gross trading profits; it was a purely passive variable that simply accommodated to the other variables in the model. The Business School model did not explicitly reconcile the two measures; certain components of public sector 'disposable' income remained undefined and were implicitly therefore the accommodating variable. To some extent, the different choices here reflect different priorities. Inevitably, the Treasury model was focused on the public sector account; something else had therefore to 'give'.

The Business School was clearly instrumental in getting a computer model going at the Treasury through the help that Ball and his colleagues gave in providing the relationships needed to complete the construction. The most direct piece of model propagation occurred at the Bank of England, where research into, and use of, a macro-econometric model began as a result of the acquisition of a copy of the Business School model as it stood in 1973. The only income–expenditure model that appeared independently of the Business School's effort was the model at the National Institute of Economic and Social Research.

The model described by Michael Surrey was the first computerised model that the National Institute used for the preparation of its quarterly forecasts of the UK economy. The Institute had been publishing such forecasts since January 1959; the first forecast for which the model described by Surrey was used appeared in August 1969.[26] At the beginning, the model was extremely small (smaller even than the first version of the Business School model), containing only seventeen equations, of which seven were identities. By 1972 it still contained just twenty equations and, although it trebled in size around 1974, its character was little changed.[27] The structure of this Institute model was very similar to that of the first Business School model in that the measure of overall economic activity was GDP built up from the expenditure side. Unlike the Business School model however, two of the major categories of expenditure – exports and private investment – remained exogenous. This was explained as being due to the fact that, firstly, the forecasting of these variables involved not only econometric relationships but also other guides such as intention surveys and, secondly, the feedback to these variables from other variables in the model was deemed to be quite small.[28] In contrast, the Institute model was better developed than the original Business School model in its treatment of personal income, which was constructed from three equations for pre-tax, nominal income (wages and salaries; income from rent and self-employment; dividends and net interest) and two tax equations. Table 2.1 records that the Surrey/Bispham model was estimated by ordinary least squares but, in practice, freely estimated coefficients were relied upon to only a limited extent. Both the Surrey and Bispham versions of the model contained equations whose co-efficients were either entirely freely estimated, or entirely imposed, or a mixture of the two.

This model was clearly primitive; even when it first appeared it was less developed than the Business School model had been three years earlier. Yet, as I shall explain in chapter 3, the interest in this first Institute model lies in this very primitiveness, for what this model in fact provides is the clearest evidence of how forecasting and policy analysis were conducted in the period before the advent of the computer models pioneered by Ball.

THE CONSENSUS SHATTERED

By 1973, the short-term income–expenditure model dominated UK macro-modelling. Of the surviving alternatives, the model of the Cambridge Growth Project was undergoing alteration in a direction that was to make it much more similar to the mainstream models, while Southampton had still failed to produce any results or output of substance.[29] In spite of the difficulties that had been experienced during the period of consolidation, the consensus amongst practitioners of the art within Britain about what a macroeconometric model should be and do had never been stronger. This consensus was to be shattered by the economic crisis that struck in 1973.

The first challenge to this orthodoxy came from the model of the Cambridge Economic Policy Group led by Wynne Godley, who had spent much of the 1960s as an economist at the Treasury and, for a period, at the National Institute. The Policy Group model in fact had two minor forerunners: the Policy Group's own 'Par' model, which appeared in 1972, and the medium-term model of the Department of Economic Affairs in the middle 1960s.[30] The Par model showed where the Group's focus was directed: firstly towards the assessment 'of alternative public expenditure programmes in relation to the total availability of resources'[31] and secondly towards the medium term.

Both of these marked a move away from the concerns of the short-term forecasting model but, of the two, the first was the more novel. This was because it shifted attention firstly to the need to consider the competing claims of all sectors of the economy – public, personal, company and overseas – simultaneously, and secondly to examine each sector's total expenditure in relation to its total income. The difference between these totals, the sectoral net acquisition of financial assets, was the key Policy Group identity.

The whole problem was still contained within the income–expenditure framework and the Policy Group's model, which was first used for forecasting in 1976, was therefore entirely conventional in this respect. What was unconventional, from a Keynesian perspective, was the inclusion of an expenditure equation for the private sector as a whole. The use of such an equation was quite consistent with a preoccupation with the sectoral totals but, in the case of the private sector, it meant that the traditional distinction between

34

consumption and investment faded into the background. It was the Cambridge critics of this who dubbed the approach 'new Keynesian',[32] although others, including the London Business School economists, had come to recognise that it was also quite consistent with the portfolio balance approach of the monetary theorists.[33] The Policy Group's proximity to this position was in spite of the fact that it was avowedly anti-Monetarist.

The move to Monetarism (to be precise, 'International' Monetarism) was made by the London Business School. Although the Business School's model had by 1975 been altered in such a way that it reproduced some of the properties of the Policy Group model, it was not the income–expenditure nexus that provided the focus for research and development but rather the exchange-rate. Two questions were fundamental: firstly, what determined the exchange-rate and, secondly, what was the effect of changes in the exchange-rate on domestic prices? These two questions – the cause and the effect of the exchange-rate – had preoccupied the Business School economists at least since the demise of the fixed exchange-rate system in 1971; indeed, the problem of the effect of exchange-rate changes on the domestic economy went back to the 1967 devaluation. During this period, Business School thinking had run the full range of possibilities on the exchange-rate and in due course (although beyond the proper end of this story) came back to where it had started. The tale of the Business School model is at bottom an 'exchange-rate odyssey'.

The feature that really marked out the 1978 version of the Business School model from its predecessors concerned the cause of the exchange-rate, since the question of its effect had been resolved by 1975 in favour of the view that, in the long-run, exchange-rate movements led to equi-proportional changes in domestic prices. Although the precise mechanism that gave rise to this effect was different in 1978 from that in 1975, the effect itself was the same. But whereas the exchange-rate itself had still technically been an exogenous variable in 1975, it was by the 1978 version endogenous, determined according to the mechanism proposed by the International Monetarist School. In this view, the exchange-rate adjusted, all else being equal, so as to maintain the ratio between domestic and world money stocks. It was part of a chain of relationships that linked the public sector borrowing requirement at one end, via domestic credit expansion, the money supply and the exchange-rate to the domestic prices and wages. Thus what was still an outwardly Keynesian model had had built into it a Monetarist design for the determination of the price level, a design in which the key component of the transmission mechanism was the exchange-rate.

At this time, deep disputes surrounded not only the economic theories within the models but also the way in which the model coefficients were estimated. In 1978, the seminal paper of the new time-series econometrics on the aggregate consumption function was published.[34] This set out what was to become the new econometric orthodoxy (within the UK at least) and the Business School economists had signalled their acceptance of it by choosing an error correction-form for one of the key price equations. In contrast, Francis Cripps and Martin Fetherston had asserted that, for the Policy Group, 'time-series estimation on its own must ... be considered something of a last resort and should be constrained as tightly as possible by other types of evidence'[35]. However, the attitude towards econometrics as a body of theory and recommended practice was not necessarily the same as the attitude towards the importance of equations 'conforming' to the historical patterns within the data. Cripps and Fetherston had insisted that the major relationships of the Cambridge model were based on the data, rather than being drawn from *a priori* economic theory, and that the relationships had moreover exhibited stability (in the sense of parameter constancy) over the estimation period, that is, from 1960. The Business School model, notwithstanding a supposed adherence to the new econometrics, had many of its key equations in extremely poor conformity with the data on which they were estimated, even according to the old econometric criterion of the Durbin–Watson test.

Around this time, the Business School became involved in research on the application of control techniques, which had been developed in engineering, to macroeconometric models. The work had originated in the 'Programme of Research into Econometric Methods' at Queen Mary College, London (and later at Imperial College). The work had initially centred on a model, developed especially for the purpose, that was small and linear, estimated by maximum likelihood methods and to whose dynamic structure considerable attention had been paid.[36] Later, the research shifted to working with a version of the London Business School model. The high point of interest in the application of control techniques came with the 1978 report of the Committee on Policy Optimisation, a committee chaired by James Ball.[37]

By somewhat different routes, the Cambridge Economic Policy Group and the London Business School had both come to the conclusion by the late 1970s that the old instruments of government policy were incapable of restoring the sustained rate of growth of the British economy necessary to return unemployment to, and maintain it at, the levels that had prevailed for much of the post-war period. The Business School still believed that something could be done about inflation, and its model showed how. The Policy Group denied even that much because its model showed that the way to lower the rate of inflation was by raising the rate of growth; but this, by the old methods, was now impossible. For those who thought in terms of trade-offs of the Phillips curve variety, there could hardly have been a more perverse view.

The substantial alterations in the properties of the 1978 vintage of the London Business School model compared with earlier versions were attributable to changes in a small number of key relationships; but in terms of the overall shape and balance there was, as table 2.1 reveals, little difference, with the 1978 model still being an income–expenditure model with just a small output sector. In contrast, the model that the National Institute began to use in 1977 did look quite different, not only from its predecessors (which was surprising since the original Institute model had undergone few changes during the period in which other income–expenditure models had expanded) but also from its contempories. This was because the Institute's 1977 model was a model with a supply side.

In fact, this 1977 model was less radical than it might have been, for this version, which the Institute called model III, was a compromise between an expanded version of the Surrey/Bispham model (model I) and an entirely new model (model II), which underwent development over a three-year period from 1972.[38] This model II represented the first attempt since the Southampton model to incorporate a proper supply side within a UK macroeconometric model: not only was output modelled via a production function but so too, and consistently with it, were pricing, investment and employment decisions. Simulation and tracking exercises conducted during 1975 and 1976 revealed, however, that the new model was by no means superior to the old; indeed, in certain areas, it was clearly inferior. Model III (details of which are shown in table 2.1) represented a compromise between the two, the output, employment, stocks and financial blocks of model II being incorporated with the pricing and investment relationships from model I.

In spite of this compromise, the Institute's model III still had a different overall balance, not only from the models of the early 1970s but also from those of the Policy Group and the Business School. In particular, pricing and output relationships accounted for nearly half the model. In fact, though, the appearance of being radically different is deceptive, the clue to which is to be found in the way in which the output measure of GDP was reconciled with the expenditure measure, a reconciliation that was achieved simply by defining 'other output' as equal to the difference between GDP built up from the expenditure side and the sum of the various output relationships. It is not that quantitative adjustment to maintain accounting identities is inconsistent with a (dis-)equilibrium framework – the Southampton model relied on quantities adjusting – but rather that there was then no feedback from this adjustment, via price or future output decisions, which tends to push the economy towards equilibrium. In that regard it is significant that the model III price equations did not in general respond to quantities. It should also be added that these observations were not problems resulting from the compromise, for much the same characteristics were to be found in the defunct model II.

The first model that had a supply side that really mattered (and the last model to be considered here) was the one developed by Patrick Minford and his colleagues at Liverpool. Although the fully articulated model did not emerge until the early 1980s, work on the model began in 1976.

Even superficially, as a glance at table 2.1 reveals, the Liverpool model was quite different from its predecessors: it was small; it was not built around the income–expenditure framework; it contained a singular collection of exogenous variables; it was an equilibrium (new classical) rational expectations model. As a consequence, the means by which the model yielded results tended to be very different from those of its predecessors. The result that the model gave for the standard simulation of an increase in government expenditure was quite categorical: in response to increases in either the money supply or the public sector borrowing requirement the model showed no sustained effect on real GDP whatsoever.

The model also appeared to be different in that a serious effort had been made to employ methods of estimation that were appropriate for simultaneous equations. In truth, however, the real feature of the Liverpool model's econometrics is quite different, for although the equations of the model were estimated by subsystem limited information least squares (SLIML) and modified least squares, the coefficients so produced were not the ones that appeared in the model; instead, the actual model coefficients were imposed by the model's authors. Minford and his colleagues explained this in terms of their maintaining 'intellectual command' over the model, which was, they stressed, 'intended to represent what we believe; it has not been our intention to *test* its structure against past data, rather to use this data to help parameterize the model'.[39] What we have here then is a model that was openly admitted to be ideological – to represent a view – which, while it nodded towards econometric theory, nevertheless abandoned it when it did not suit its purposes.

It is, however, its supply side that provides the deepest reason for regarding this model as something apart from its predecessors. The supply-side or 'natural rate' part of the Liverpool model was not simply some set of equations for output and employment tacked on to an otherwise conventional model; neither, as in the Southampton model, was it one of the pair of blocks, along with demand, that between them determined the level of GDP. Instead, the natural rates of output and employment were the underlying, or equilibrium, values to which the economy would return, quite quickly in the Liverpool view, following some shock. The real point about this is that the model also included exogenous variables that between them determined (and that between them could therefore *alter*) those natural rates. These variables, listed in table 2.1, either were explicitly economic policy instruments or could perhaps be influenced by more general government action. The inclusion within the model of the natural rates of output and employment along with a mechanism for permanently changing their positions was a tremendous innovation with a potentially great appeal for what it amounted to, no more and no less, was both an explanation of the steep rise in unemployment since the late 1960s and a representation of the way to do something about it. However odious the message and however little empirical support it had at the time or has had since, a computer econometric model that purported to show how something lasting could be done about the otherwise seemingly inexorable rise in unemployment was bound to command attention. Although the Liverpool model itself was held in low esteem by other economists in this field, the ideas that it introduced have penetrated to the very core of UK macro-econometric modelling in the 1980s and beyond.

THE BROADER PERSPECTIVE

The account of the transformation from Keynesianism to Monetarism that is going to be the subject of the remainder of this book will begin with income–expenditure models of the late 1960s and trace their development over the next decade and beyond. The focus on these models in accounts of the development of macroeconometric modelling in the UK is not unusual; but the point that stands out here is that the models of the 1960s made up a spectrum of which the prototype model of the London Business School occupied only one small part. Some of this diversity lived on (the Cambridge Growth Project model); another part bloomed in the 1970s (the Cambridge Economic Policy Group's model as the final flowering of the medium-term approach to modelling); while yet other parts (notably Southampton) have provided a fertile source of ideas for later model builders.

Why, then, did the rather insignificant creature that was the London Business School's prototype come so rapidly to define what constituted 'the' UK macroeconometric model?

Part II

THE RISE AND FALL OF THE KEYNESIAN INCOME–EXPENDITURE MODEL

3

KEYNESIAN DEMAND MANAGEMENT

The emergence of the model as the formalisation of a view

The income–expenditure macroeconometric model did not make its appearance until 1966, yet, before the end of the decade, this model type, pioneered in the UK by Jim Ball and Terry Burns, was established as the paradigmatic UK macroeconometric model. The first task for this chapter is to explain why this model type was so successful in propagating itself, the key to which is shown to lie in the manual procedures for macroeconomic forecasting that had preceded it. The model that was closest to this procedure was the one that was built at the National Institute. A quick study of this model and the way in which it fitted together provides a good introduction to the model type. This in turn leads to a consideration of the wider income–expenditure framework around which the UK national accounts are built and which provides the fundamental underpinning to all the models in subsequent chapters.

EXPLAINING THE SPREAD OF THE INCOME–EXPENDITURE MODEL

There are three levels at which we can answer the question why the income–expenditure model succeeded in spreading from its initial base at the London Business School to the Treasury, the National Institute and later the Bank of England. Firstly, through their work in completing the Treasury model and later through the transfer of their own model in its entirety to the Bank, the Business School economists evidently exercised a direct influence at the formative stage in model-building in three of the four institutions in which such models flourished. This, however, has more to offer as an explanation of how the type of model introduced by the Business School spread rather than as an explanation of why it spread, and we need therefore to look deeper.

From a practical perspective, the model was attractive for the reason that, from almost the very beginning, it 'worked' in the simple functional sense of that word. This was achieved by developing the bare minimum of a model, using the simplest estimation technique and employing quarterly data which, by 1966, were regularly available. The obvious cost attached to this was that the model's capability was limited. This strategy of beginning with a small, even rudimentary, model, which nevertheless worked, was a quite deliberate one that Ball had enunciated previously in a review of the first paper produced by Stone and Brown on the model of the Cambridge Growth Project. In this review, Ball described the Cambridge model as one 'conceived in the grand manner' but it should not therefore, he cautioned, be thought of as simply a single model; instead,

> it must be considered in the context of a systematic project which is organic and which has great possibilities of growth and development over time. The present writer has for some time advocated the strategy in model-building of the construction of an initial model followed by intensive work on its less satisfactory components, rather than that of attempting to perfect all the components before assembly. To take this latter course often results in no model at all, for one never achieves such a degree of perfection in components as to make one entirely happy about leaving them alone. Furthermore, the adequacy of particular types of relationship can never be properly judged in isolation, but should be evaluated in terms of their role in the complete model. The former strategy appears to underlie the Cambridge project.[1]

(Ball 1963: 189)

This strategy had its advantages. Firstly, by avoiding a long gestation period during which the 'ideal' model was under construction, but for which there was nothing to show save an elegant blueprint, the pronouncements of the Business School model could be in the public eye from the very beginning. The telling contrast here is of course with the Southampton model. Secondly, a living model could develop in response not only to economic and econometric advances but also to changes in economic conditions. With the benefit of hindsight it is clear that, for a model conceived in the relative tranquillity of the early 1960s, there could be no more valuable an attribute than the flexibility to address new problems in very different circumstances.

Functionality was essential but not alone sufficient; in plain terms, just because something works is no reason to go out and buy it. The reason why the income–expenditure model spread was that short-term forecasting, in which GDP was calculated as the sum of forecasts of the principal categories of aggregate expenditure, was something that had been going on for years; the Business School model was therefore just a computerisation of a well-established process.[2] Unlike Stone and Brown at Cambridge,[3] Ball and Burns were not trying to model something that had not been the object of attention before; neither were they proposing a fundamentally different set of economic relationships with which to model it. Provided their model worked, proponents of such computer models had really to win an argument only about means and not about ends; about the best way to prepare short-term forecasts and not about the virtues of those forecasts themselves.

What arguments were raised against the use of computerised models in the forecasting procedure? A good starting point is Alec Cairncross's review of Jan Tinbergen's UK model,[4] firstly because this review consciously followed the criticisms that Keynes had made of Tinbergen's US model a decade earlier and, secondly, because of Cairncross's central position in the British economic establishment during the period prior to the adoption of computer-based modelling and forecasting. Of Tinbergen's model, Cairncross made two types of criticism, one econometric and the other related to the construction of several key data series.[5] On the first, Cairncross suggested that the correlations in the model could well be spurious since the data showed strong and common cyclical patterns that would allow correlations to be established between quite unrelated variables. He also queried the interpretation that the model made of certain phenomena. For example, Tinbergen has estimated an investment demand curve containing a low price elasticity. Cairncross challenged this on the grounds that the pattern of movements between the quantity of investment and its price (the latter fluctuating much more than the former) on which this equation had been estimated could more plausibly be seen as a reflection of the low elasticity of supply of investment goods. These types of econometric concerns are fundamental, and there is no evidence to suggest that they were addressed by Ball or any other pioneers of the income–expenditure model. The point is, however, that in the Business School's project, the task of which was the computerisation of relationships previously employed, there was no need to address these econometric concerns since the model was no more vulnerable on this score than was the activity that it sought to automate.

On the face of it, the Business School model avoided Cairncross's second criticism of Tinbergen concerning the construction of some of his data series. This is because Ball and Burns could, for the most part, rely upon the quarterly data supplied by the government's Central Statistical Office, data that by the middle 1960s were available in sufficient quantity for econometric purposes. The availability of official statistics is one of the factors that distinguished the Business School model from the earlier Oxford model on which Ball had worked, where certain series, for example for profits, had had to be constructed by the model builders themselves. In fact, however, the availability of official data by no means exhausted Cairncross's views of the difficulties that were presented by the data.

Over a decade after his review of Tinbergen, by which time he was established in the Treasury, Cairncross was still pointing to such difficulties as a reason for not relying exclusively on econometric methods – or on a computer programme alone. The difficulties mentioned fell under three headings.[6] The first related to the considerable effort that had to be devoted to the construction of the series of future values of the exogenous variables; in other words, although a model may be *estimated* on officially supplied data, forecasting still relied upon extensive data *construction*. Secondly, Cairncross doubted whether much confidence could be placed in formally produced econometric relationships that were based on data that had been drawn from a brief period of observation, during which 'the system itself may have been changing'.[7] Thirdly, forecasting was concerned not only with predicting the future but also with interpreting the present and near past. This was deemed to be a special problem whenever different series pointed in different directions. One instance of this related to the problems created when the different measures of GDP – income, expenditure and output – moved by very different magnitudes;[8] another concerned the reliability of data, particularly data of a recent vintage, which were often subject subsequently to substantial revisions. These views can be summarised as saying that judgement is the most important ingredient of a forecast. In such circumstances, the forecaster cannot merely let the figures speak for themselves in conflicting voices. He must assemble all the economic intelligence available and relevant and weigh the evidence offered by different statistical series in inverse proportion to their known limitations, whether these arise from the particular method of collection or from knowledge of past quirks.

(Cairncross 1965: 123)

By the end of the decade, however, Cairncross had reached the conclusion that there was a role within the forecasting process for a formal, econometric model and that the ideal approach would be one involving a synthesis between that and the informal method.[9] David Worswick, who became Director of the National Institute in 1965, explained how this synthesis had been achieved in practice. He explained that his initial concern had been that the use of a model would reduce the forecasting process to something merely mechanical, thereby precluding the introduction of a certain amount of judgement into the forecast. The problem, however, was overcome to his satisfaction by the simple expedient of introducing an intercept adjustment term (or 'add factor') into each behavioural equation,[10] which 'avoided the risk of introducing the rigidity which I had feared would might be one of the consequences of "going econometric". On the contrary, this device has ensured the maximum flexibility.'[11] As he went on to observe, the advantage of introducing judgement into the forecast in this way (rather than simply amending the figures produced by the computer) was that it ensured that all the figures produced were consistent with the national accounting identities embedded within the model. The sense of this is that the flexibility that computers allowed more than offset the rigidity imposed by using a fully formalised model. Treasury economists were making exactly the same point, albeit in a slightly different way, when they noted that there was 'nothing in the present procedure to constrain any component of the forecast to be consistent with the behavioural relationships in the model'.[12] This quote comes from a passage that emphasised that the move to forecasting with a model did not represent the (sudden) adoption of a rigid forecasting process. 'There is', they continued, 'no necessary conflict between the use of a formal model and the extensive consultation and exercise of judgement which is put into the forecasts.'[13]

With the benefit of hindsight we can see that the key to the acceptance of the computer-based model in the UK in the late 1960s was the realisation that it did not preclude a role for judgement in forecasting but could, on the contrary, accommodate it with comfort. The importance of this to the forecasters can be seen in the fact that, to this day, computer-generated forecasts of the UK economy are invariably not pure model forecasts but instead include manual adjustments based on judgements made by the model proprietors.[14]

These concerns, which related to the way in which a model was used, are evidently of a quite different weight from Cairncross's original objections to Tinbergen's model, which related to the way the model was constructed and to the interpretation of events that the model represented. The emergence of modelling in the late 1960s in the UK owed nothing to the belief that these difficulties had been resolved. This is in notable contrast to the experience in the USA, where such models first emerged in the 1940s. The stimulus there came from the work of the econometricians, associated with the Cowles Commission in Chicago, who had developed methods of estimation appropriate for *systems* of equations. The stimulus for their work had been the statistical problems inherent in Jan Tinbergen's pre-war US model, problems that overlapped with those mentioned later by Cairncross in connection with Tinbergen's UK model.[15]

HOW THE MODELS WORKED

Now let us turn to the models themselves. By virtue of their simple structure and small size, it is possible to convey a sense of the way in which these early income–expenditure models worked through the use of a diagram in the form of a flow chart. Figure 3.1 is such a representation of the earliest model used for forecasting by the National Institute.[16]

The diagram shows each of the seventeen endogenous and twelve exogenous variables contained within the model along with the connections between them. These connections represent the structural equations (and identities) of the model and they have been drawn on the principle that a line running down from one variable to another means that the higher variable appears as an explanatory variable in the relationship that determines the lower variable. Exogenous variables are therefore naturally shown as variables to which no lines flow from above. A line running from a variable to

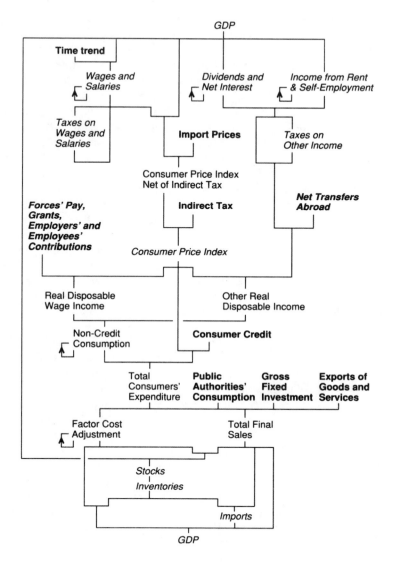

Figure 3.1 Flow chart for first version of NIESR model showing the connections between all variables

Notes: Variables in bold are exogenous while those in italics are at current prices. Functional causality is always downwards; the model would have to iterate until the top and bottom values of GDP were equal. A small loop from a variable to itself indicates that the variable depends on its own past value.

itself indicates that the lagged value of the variable enters directly into the determination of the current value; this was the only way in which lagged variables entered into this model (that is, the dynamic equations of this were invariably of the partial-adjustment kind). Intercept terms are not shown. Variables in italics are measured in nominal terms.

As an example of how to read the diagram, consider wages and salaries: from the lines running to it from above, we can see that wages and salaries are modelled as a function of GDP, a time trend, wages and salaries lagged one quarter and (not shown) a constant. In their turn, wages and salaries enter into the determination of taxes on wages and salaries, real disposable wage and salary income and the consumer price index net of indirect taxes.

By starting at the top and assigning values to each of the exogenous variables, the diagram shows the sequence in which the equations must be solved in order to solve the model as a whole, finishing up at the bottom with a value for GDP. However, since the routine requires that a 'trial value' be supplied for GDP at the top of the diagram, solution requires iteration using different trial values each time, until the final value is deemed to be sufficiently close to the trial value.

Looking in more detail, the upper part of the diagram shows how incomes and the general level of prices are determined while the lower half shows how GDP is built up as the sum of its expenditure components. Working downwards, given a starting value for GDP the model calculates three categories of nominal income – wages and salaries; dividends and net interest; and income from rent and self-employment – and then two categories of tax. At the same time, two indices of consumer prices are determined, one excluding, and the other including, indirect taxes. These variables, together with various exogenous components of aggregate income, combine to determine two categories of real disposable income. On the expenditure side of the model (in which all endogenous variables are denominated in real terms), the main elements are a consumption function giving 'non-credit' consumption; an identity yielding total consumption; a function for stocks (responding directly to GDP as a proxy for output); a function for imports that depends on total final sales and stockbuilding; and a number of identities including that for GDP. Since a solution of the model involves iteration, everything (endogenous) in the model depends indirectly on everything else.

THE AFFINITY BETWEEN THE MODELS AND
THE MANUAL FORECASTING PROCESS

The relationship between this model and the Institute's manual forecasting procedure that it superseded was extremely close: what this model did, according to Worswick, 'was to put on to a formal basis and on to the computer the iterative procedure previously adopted and which used to take several days'.[17] That iterative procedure – an 'arduous and exhaustive routine'[18] evolved by Wynne Godley – worked thus:

> Given the exogenous variables – for example, exports or public authorities' current expenditure – the task was to find a set of numbers for the next six or eight quarters which would: (a) satisfy the accounting identities; (b) be consistent with those equations already estimated and considered to be satisfactory; and (c) make good sense in areas where no such equations existed. The actual method was iterative, and it could take several days of very hard work. The iteration was done by successive trials, the calculations being done on a desk machine by Godley with an assistant.

> (Worswick 1975: 67)

The first part of this statement might as well be a verbal description of the procedure represented in the flow diagram in figure 3.1!

In drawing attention to the formative influence that Wynne Godley had exerted over forecasting at the Institute, Worswick also mentioned the extensive attention that was paid by Godley to data series, their construction, their revision and whether such revisions seemed to be systematic or not. With Godley's disciplined approach to the regular scrutiny of data becoming an established part of its practice, we see in the Institute's forecasting procedures precisely the synthesis that Cairncross had advocated.

The relationship between the Institute's model and the manual forecasting procedure that it replaced is the key link in the more general argument that the income–expenditure models were fundamentally just computerisations of the old procedures. To complete the argument, we have to look at the old Treasury procedures on the one side, and the Business School model on the other. The forecasting procedures of the Treasury and the Institute were very close to one another in the middle 1960s, focusing on the same objects – the expenditure aggregates – over the same forecast horizon of up to eighteen months.[19] The main difference between the two was that, whereas the Institute forecasts were made public, those of the Treasury had for the most part remained private.[20] Although it had insisted on its independence from departments of government,[21] the Institute was nevertheless very heavily influenced by the Treasury; for example, Godley had joined the Institute in 1963 on a two-year secondment from the Treasury, while, up until 1965, the preparation of forecasts at the Institute had been 'planned and supervised under the leadership of men[22] intimately acquainted with Treasury proceedings'.[23]

And as the manual routines of the Institute and the Treasury were similar, so too were the models of the Institute and the London Business School. This affinity can be seen in the flow diagrams of the two models. Figure 3.2 is the flow diagram for the first Business School model. This diagram has been drawn on principles similar to those used for figure 3.1, with two exceptions: the first concerns time trends, which entered into the Business School model at a number of points and which have therefore been omitted from the diagram for the sake of simplicity; the second concerns lagged variables, which, although still only few in number, nevertheless entered into various equations and not just the equation for the corresponding current endogenous variable. Thus, whereas the diagram for the Institute model shows the connections between *all* variables, the one for the Business School depicts only the connections between variables for the *current* period.

The relationships represented in this diagram that made up the Business School's model came from a number of sources. Some, especially those pertaining to prices, were developed specifically as part of the process of building the model; others, however, had been developed prior to the model and had been published as free-standing applied econometric studies of single equations. Most of the relationships that determined components of aggregate expenditure fell into this category; thus, in the few years preceding the first appearance of the model, Ball, in conjunction with fellow researchers, had published papers on equations for aggregate consumption, expenditure on consumer durables, stock adjustment and export performance, all of which found their way into the model. The consumption function was of the permanent income variety and its ancestry could therefore be traced back to Friedman, while the import equation was based on a paper by Godley and Shepherd.[24] There are three aspects to the way in which this model was put together, each of which is highly characteristic of the London Business School's approach during that

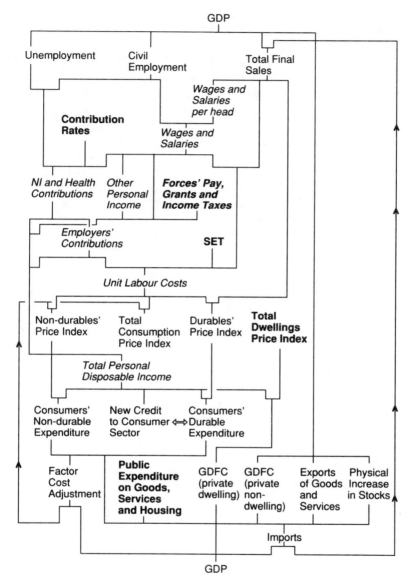

Figure 3.2 Flow chart for first version of LBS model showing the connections between current variables

Notes: Variables in bold are exogenous while those in italics are at current prices. Functional causality is downward except where shown otherwise. The model would have to iterate until the top and bottom values of GDP were equal.

period. Firstly, it is reasonable to describe the model as an assemblage of previously existing relationships. Secondly, the Business School approach was an eclectic one, drawing on diverse sources of research. Thirdly, we can see that the model, small though it was, was not in fact the first step; the first step, rather, had been taken years earlier with the publication of the single-equation studies. This was wholly consonant with the model-building philosophy that Ball had enunciated earlier, in his review of the Growth Project model.

Although there are many differences of details, the overall shape of the two models depicted in figures 3.1 and 3.2 is very similar. The upper part of each diagram shows how nominal incomes and prices are determined and the lower part shows how GDP is built up from its expenditure components. The main difference between them would appear to arise from the more developed and sophisticated nature of the Business School model. One aspect of this is to be found in the somewhat greater degree of simultaneity on show in figure 3.2, where consumer credit and durable expenditure are modelled jointly, factor-cost adjustment feeds back into the price indices and, thanks to the key role of total final sales, imports influence many of the variables in the model directly, rather than indirectly via GDP.

It would also appear that the Business School model contained a number of equations for variables of considerable importance that were nevertheless absent from the Institute model, these equations being those for private sector investment, exports, employment and unemployment. This, however, is more a superficial difference, relating simply to the question of what was contained within the iterative procedure represented by the model, since econometric equations for all of these 'missing' relationships were fully reported by Michael Surrey in his account of the Institute's model. One of the reasons for omitting these relationships from that model was that there was in general little feedback *from* the rest of the model *to* these variables. In other cases, for example exports, the econometric equation was omitted because it had been found to forecast poorly, although it was nevertheless still consulted as a check on the reasonableness of the informal forecast of exports.[25] In the case of investment, on the other hand, the reason was that the formal relationships embodied effects that operated with a considerable lag. This was particularly the case in the equation for private sector non-residential investment, which was a function of lagged changes in GDP, the most recent of which was the lag three quarters earlier.[26]

For the purposes of forecasting over twelve to eighteen months, it is not surprising that the Institute relied upon surveys of investment intentions rather than a model. And this, in fact, was exactly what the Business School did too when it came to forecasting because, instead of using the relationship for investment in plant and equipment reported in the model listing, Ball and Burns built up an off-model figure for it based on information gleaned from the investment intentions survey data published by the Board of Trade.[27] Thus, for forecasting, the two models' treatment of this major component of investment was to all intents and purposes the same. There was a difference, however, for the purposes of policy analyses conducted via comparative simulations since, for these, the Business School investment equation was employed.

THE CHARACTER OF THE MODELS: INCOME–EXPENDITURE OR IS–LM?

This treatment of investment raises an issue of wider significance concerning the proper characterisation of these models. It is evident from figures 3.1 and 3.2 that to label them as 'income–expenditure' models can be justified on the grounds that it describes their structure and content. What, if any, though was their relationship to the more familiar textbook concept of a 'Keynesian' model, namely that of the IS–LM framework? Were they also special cases of that framework or were they, instead, something subtly different from it?[28] Superficially, it is tempting to regard them as mere special cases, because by dealing simply with the goods market they can be seen as models just of the IS curve. To the extent that the Institute model excluded the interest rate altogether, it could be seen as the special case of the vertical IS curve. The Business School model did include an interest rate as an exogenous variable in the equation for residential fixed investment,[29] but its effect would have been weak overall, meaning that the implied IS curve would still have been 'almost' vertical.

However, it would be fundamentally wrong to characterise these models as special cases of the IS–LM framework.[30] Firstly, the way in which investment was forecast, on the basis of a survey of investment intentions rather than as a function of the rate of interest, is quite at odds with the IS–LM approach. Of course, investment intentions themselves may be influenced by the rate of interest; behind this income–expenditure approach must therefore lie the view that, if interest rates influence investment at all, they do so only over the medium or long term, rather than the short term of eighteen months to two years for which forecasts were published.

The second reason why it would be incorrect to treat the income–expenditure model as a special case of the IS–LM is to be found in the limitations of the IS–LM framework itself. One aspect of this is that the framework is static; in even the most rudimentary income–expenditure model (that of the National Institute), the equations were generally dynamic. Another limitation of the IS–LM is that it operates in real terms with a fixed price level. Again, as the presence of italicized and non-italicized variable names in figures 3.1 and 3.2 shows, even the earliest income–expenditure models were more complex than this, containing an amalgam of both nominal and real variables.

Thirdly, the early income–expenditure models embodied channels of monetary influence different from those of the IS–LM set-up. Instead of relying simply upon the rate of interest, figures 3.1 and 3.2 show that the principal short-term financial influence on expenditure is the availability of credit to the private sector. Indeed, even where the interest rate did appear (in the Business School equation for residential investment), the rationale that was given for its inclusion was as a proxy for credit conditions.[31] In that respect, the income–expenditure model stood much more in the tradition of the type of Keynesianism embodied in the 1959 Radcliffe Report – the official government report of the Committee on the Working of the Monetary System – with its emphasis, as Victoria Chick put it, on whether money was 'easy or tight' rather than the textbook IS–LM view in which what mattered was whether money was 'cheap or dear'. Chick went on to characterise the Radcliffe Report by its method, as being a 'process analysis covering a variety of time horizons'. Figures 3.1 and 3.2 show the income–expenditure models to be very clear representations of a sequential process in time and in this, therefore, we can see another and perhaps more fundamental similarity between the approach adopted in that report and the income–expenditure model. Chick added that Radcliffe's method was 'at variance with the postwar conception of respectable economic theory'.[32] Much the same could be said of the income–expenditure model.

Although the income–expenditure and IS-LM models both treat the goods market and therefore have important points in common, the IS-LM's simplifications, along with its different view of the route by which monetary factors influence the remainder of the economy, preclude any possibility of it being viewed as containing the income–expenditure model as a special case.

As with almost every aspect of these early income–expenditure models, the treatment of credit and money was underdeveloped. It may be the case that the model proprietors held to the view that the finance necessary to support any increase in expenditure would appear automatically and that the maintenance of expenditure was therefore the appropriate focus for macroeconomic management of the economy. Certainly by their choice of variables, the first income–expenditure models would seem to be consistent with that view. The point is, however, that, without any further disaggregation than that already explicit in these earliest models, the task of building a more complete income–expenditure model naturally tended to direct model makers' attention towards the question of finance and the financial counterparts to the real flows.

4

KEYNESIAN 'NORMAL SCIENCE'

The elaboration of the income–expenditure model

The half decade that followed the introduction of the income–expenditure model in 1966 was one devoted to the elaboration and enlargement of the model. In retrospect we can see it as having been something almost of a 'golden' age: earlier critics of formalised model-building had been stilled or even won over to the new approach, while the storms of the middle 1970s that were to engulf macroeconomic policy making and the models with it were still some years in the future. The programme of work with which modellers were occupied these five years was essentially a positive one. It is true that even in this period a good deal of it had had to be directed towards repairing parts of the model that had been found to be faulty, but this was counterbalanced by other work that was directed towards the development of new sides of the model.

In order to make sense of this developmental phase of macro model building it is helpful to recognise that, with one exception, the forces guiding that development were internal to the basic project of computerising an income–expenditure model. This contrasts sharply with chapter 3. The story told there concerning the establishment of the model type was that the choice of the short-term forecasting model was determined above all else by the practices and views of the economy that predominated in official and semi-official circles before 1966. The initial direction taken by these models was therefore entirely predetermined – the first push came from outside, as it were – and the models were innovatory only to the extent that they constituted a new way of accomplishing an old task. That account forced us to look back and outside of the models themselves, to the forecasting that had been practised for nearly two decades by the Treasury before the advent of these models and even to the view of the way in which the economy operated that had been embodied in the Radcliffe Report. In contrast, in the next phase that is the subject of this chapter, the new computing power, which in one sense was 'all' that the model brought to the old process, nevertheless opened up a range of new issues. The germs from which these issues grew lay always there, latent, within the body of the income–expenditure framework; they were not introduced by the computerisation but rather brought to life by the computing power unleashed. In this chapter therefore I shall look basically at two things: firstly, at the actual nature of the model development over the period and, secondly, at the opportunities for new kinds of exercises that the models provided. In each case, however, we shall find that the internally logical developments led to an end point that, as well as constituting a completion, marked also the opening of a whole new set of questions.

One more characterisation of this period in the history of macro-econometric models that suggests itself is that of Thomas Kuhn's well-known concept of 'normal science'. 'Normal science' – the articulation, or elaboration, of some paradigmatic object[1] – was the name that Kuhn gave to the activity that he regarded as the norm for the great majority of scientists for the great majority of the time. One of Kuhn's examples of normal science was the search, which was still being conducted in the late nineteenth century, for the elements that were missing from the periodic table of the chemical elements.[2] This example, in which a table serves as the paradigm or framework and where the activity of normal science involves the filling-in of the still empty spaces in that table, is an excellent image of the development of the macroeconomic model over its first half decade. The table was the income–expenditure framework and the model builders' normal science was the development of equations to model the 'missing' variables.

THE INCOME–EXPENDITURE FRAMEWORK OF THE NATIONAL ACCOUNTS

We must naturally begin, therefore, by looking at the framework of the United Kingdom 'national accounts'. This framework forms the skeleton on which the income–expenditure macroeconometric model is built. It plays this role not simply because such models are estimated on data drawn from it – were that its only role it would be no more than a source for the models – but because it serves to define a very large part of the model. It does this in two ways. Firstly, as the count of identities in table 2.1 shows, a good proportion of the economic variables of interest contained within a model are simply defined in terms of the other economic variables: GDP as the sum of the categories of aggregate expenditure, or saving as the difference between personal disposable income and expenditure are two examples. These basic definitions are contained and first made in the national accounts framework. Secondly, that framework is responsible for defining the great majority of the variables that actually appear as endogenous variables within the model. As a result, it is quite reasonable to regard an income expenditure model as being a model of part, or even all, of those accounts. For our purposes two consequences follow: the accounting framework is common to all macroeconometric models within this tradition and, unlike the specification of the behavioural equations, it is not subject to dispute from either economic or econometric points of view. The accounting framework is therefore one of the very few constant points of reference to which all models and model developments can be related, and a concise representation of it can therefore serve as a kind of map on which to locate the key features of these models and the differences that distinguish one model from another. A simplified version of the framework is shown, in the form of a matrix, in table 4.1.[3]

The columns of the matrix represent sectors: firstly, the two parts of the private sector, namely the personal sector and company sector (the latter of which is made up of industrial and commercial companies on the one hand and financial institutions on the other); secondly the public sector (made up of public corporations, central and local government); thirdly the overseas sector; and, lastly, the total for all sectors added together, that is, the economy as a whole.

The rows of the matrix are organised as three blocks: the top block contains the components of GDP measured from the income side; the middle block contains the components of GDP measured from the expenditure side; the bottom block shows the financial surpluses or deficits by sector and how they are financed. Strictly speaking, the income–expenditure framework proper contains the two top blocks only; the financial block is included here to emphasise the position of the sectoral financial surpluses at the interface between the income and expenditure blocks on the one side and the flow of funds on the other.

Entries in the 'total' column in each of the top two blocks add up to yield GDP: in the top block, GDP measured on the income side –

GDPY – is shown as the sum of the factor incomes (such as wages and salaries and gross trading profits), while in the middle block GDP measured on the expenditure side – GDPE – is shown as the familiar sum of the components of aggregate expenditure (consumption, investment, exports less imports, stock building). As well as the factor incomes (in rows 1 – 5), the income block contains a sub-block of transfer incomes (such as dividends and income taxes), which do not contribute to GDP. Both the income and expenditure measures of GDP are of course equal to the sums of the sectoral incomes and expenditures (in rows 11 and 18 respectively).

The table contains 117 cells (row and column intersections); however, twenty-nine cells are not defined as economic variables, leaving a total of eighty-eight variables. These undefined cells are blacked out in the table. The table also contains a number of cells joined together. This has usually been done where it is the resulting combination of cells that corresponds to the economic variable. This applies particularly in the flow of funds block, where both the money supply and the public sector borrowing requirement (PSBR) are variables of this type.

But, although the table contains eighty-eight variables (note that this count ignores the joining of cells just mentioned), it contains too no fewer than forty-one definitional constraints, which therefore reduce the number of free variables to forty-seven. These constraints are of four types. The first is the simple identity that determines the elements of the 'total' column, the 'total' rows (11 and 18) and the row of sectoral financial surpluses or deficits (row 19). The second type of constraint is that required to ensure that a row representing an inter-sector transfer sums to zero. The third type of constraint is that required to ensure that the sum of each sector's flow of funds (rows 20 – 26) adds to the sector's financial surplus or deficit (row 19). The fourth constraint is the requirement that GDP measured from the income side (GDPY) must be equal to GDP from the expenditure side (GDPE).[4]

The matrix does not, of course, contain all of the variables that appear even in income–expenditure models. Some of the other variables can be deduced from the variables in the matrix (for example, the personal sector savings ratio using personal sector disposable income and consumption); many others represent subdivisions of variables in the matrix (for example, net dividends and interest is the difference between gross payments and gross receipts). The most important variables that do not appear at all are employment and

Table 4.1 The income–expenditure framework and the flow of funds by sector

	Personal	Company	Public	Overseas	Total
I GDP (INCOME MEASURE)					
(a) Factor incomes					
1. Income from employment	W&S				W&S
2. Income from self-employment	YSE				YSE
3. Gross trading profits & surplus		*PROFITS*			
4. Rent	YOP	YOC			
5. Capital consumption less stock appreciation	YOP	YOC			
(b) Transfer incomes					
6. Net direct overseas income	YOP	OIC		YOO	
7. Net dividends and interest	YOP	DIC		DIO	
8. Taxes on income	–TAXP	–TAXC			
9. Net social security	YEC+YCG –ENIH	YOC		YOO	
10. Other current grants and transfers					
11. Total disposable income	PDI	CDI		ODI	(GDPY)

II GDP (EXPENDITURE MEASURE)

(a) Current expenditure

12. Consumption
13. Exports of goods and services
14. less Imports of goods and services
15. Adjustment to factor cost

(b) Capital expenditure

16. Gross domestic fixed capital formation
17. Physical increase in stocks
18. Total expenditure

III FLOW OF FUNDS

19. Financial surplus (income less expenditure)

Made up of:

20. Net direct and portfolio investment
21. Miscellaneous financial transactions
22. Credit and lending (not public sector)
23. Treasury Bills and government securities
24. Notes and coin
25. Sterling bank deposits
26. Change in official reserves

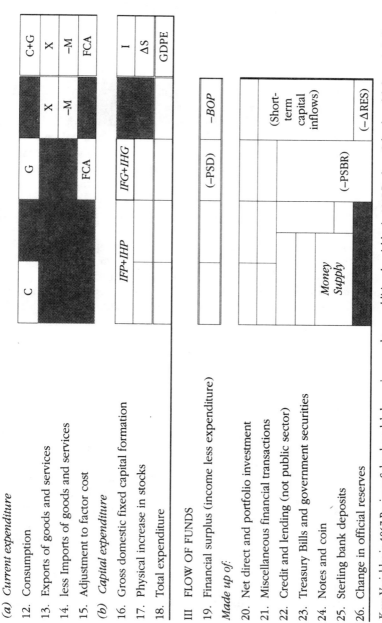

Key: Variables in 1967 Business School model shown in normal type; additional variables in 1967 Business School model shown in italics; other variables of interest shown in parentheses.

unemployment as well as various price indices, including rates of interest and the sterling exchange-rate.

A SCHEMATIC REPRESENTATION OF MODEL DEVELOPMENT, 1967–72

Many of the cells contain the name of an economic variable. Mostly, these conform to basic economic usage (especially in the expenditure block) and will therefore mean something in their own right, but even where they do not they are defined by their row and column labels. However, these names are there only to mark the cells: what matters in looking at the body of the table is therefore firstly, whether a cell is empty or not and, secondly, if it is not, how the contents are printed. With the help of this scheme, the table can be used to convey a sense of the development of the London Business School's model from 1967 onwards.

We begin with the variables that went to make up the first London Business School model, described in detail in the last chapter. The variables that appeared in that model are shown in table 4.1 in ordinary, non-italic type not enclosed within parentheses. As can be seen, the majority of them appear in the expenditure block, which is, even in this rudimentary model, more than three-quarters completed, missing only the sectoral disaggregation of stockbuilding. In contrast, the income block remains largely empty, with the only factor income appearing being that for income from employment (wages and salaries) while the only category of sectoral disposable income is for the personal sector (determined through the use of an 'other personal income' variable to cover the missing factor and transfer incomes).[5] No sectoral totals for either expenditure or income appear; there are therefore no sectoral financial surpluses or deficits and there are, in turn, no financial transactions corresponding to those totals.

Now look again at table 4.1, but this time at the variables printed in italic type. These variables represent the additional variables that had been introduced by 1972; together with the original set, they therefore denote the extent of the coverage of the income–expenditure model by that date. It will be noted that a number of the italicised names appear more than once in the income block; this designates the fact that the corresponding variables were treated by the Business School as a single category of 'other' income for the sector.

As can be seen from the disposition of the italics within the table, the main direction in which the coverage of the framework was extended during these years was in the area of the income side of the accounts, particularly for the company and overseas sectors: a search, in other words, for formal relationships to fill in the many gaps in the framework left in the original model. For the overseas sector this represented a completion of the income–expenditure account, as a result of which that sector's financial surplus (or deficit), equivalent to the negative of the current account of the balance of payments, was also modelled. None of the other sectors had quite reached this point, although for the personal and company all that remained to be done was a disaggregation of the capital expenditure variables, that is, gross domestic fixed capital formation and stockbuilding. Some categories of income were modelled together, as 'other' income, but this was of minor significance. The major remaining gap concerned the income side of the public sector, which, at this level of aggregation, remained almost completely unmodelled. As a result, the model did not contain either the public sector deficit (PSD) or the PSBR – eloquent testimony to the low importance attached to those variables even in the early 1970s. The model did contain the money supply, but only as an exogenous variable and with no direct linkages to other variables within this framework.

According to the data presented in table 2.1, both the Business School model as a whole and the income and expenditure blocks within it underwent a sixfold increase in size over the period 1966 – 72. In terms of the variables in table 4.1, however, the later vintage was no more than double the size of the earlier one. These different rates of growth highlight the fact that the development of the model over this period had two aspects to it: firstly, a tendency towards completion – that is, the modelling of a greater proportion of the variables within the income–expenditure framework – and, secondly, a tendency towards greater refinement and disaggregation. Since table 4.1 portrays only the effects of completion, we can see that the tendency towards disaggregation accounted for by far the greater quantity of new relationships. It is certainly this aspect of model development that normally attracts attention, most of it unfavourable. This is not the point to review in detail the arguments against the ever greater size of models, which prompts critics of macro-econometric models, particularly those proposing a different approach, to argue that a small, sometimes very small, model may nevertheless be superior. Ball and his colleagues were by no means supporters of disaggregation for its own sake. They expressed the view that, while there was no technical limitation to the size of a model, the practical limitations imposed by the cost of maintenance, as well as the need to maintain both an understanding of the model and a control over it, argued against ever larger models;[6] indeed, they regarded the 1972 model considered here already to have reached the desirable maximum size.[7]

The pertinent point here, however, is that there is a fundamental difference according to whether the growth is to do with disaggregation or whether it is instead to do with completion. Given a model that is adequate for the purposes for which it is to be used, the decision about how to model a variable – either directly or alternatively as the sum of its components, which are themselves modelled directly by separate equations – is less a matter of principle than one of trading off the costs incurred in a more refined approach against the loss of accuracy, if any, in a less refined way (or one that is refined in a different way, for example through the greater attention paid to the time-series properties of the economic series involved).[8] But where growth and a larger model size result not from disaggregation but from completion, in the sense used here, then the matter is rather different because completion itself raises questions of a new kind.

THE CONSEQUENCES OF 'COMPLETING' THE FRAMEWORK

The simplest way into this matter is via a consideration of the 1972 version of the Treasury's model. Here the problem is not yet one of the consequence of completing the sectorally disaggregated accounts shown in table 4.1 but instead just the problem of modelling GDP from both the expenditure and income sides. Were we to represent that version of the Treasury model in the form of table 4.1, we would find that the expenditure block looked very similar to that shown for the Business School model. The income block on the other hand would look rather different. It would lack the complete disaggregation of company sector income shown in table 4.1, but it would show that the Treasury model contained all five components of aggregate income (in the total column), namely income from employment and self employment, gross trading profits and the public sector trading surplus, rent and stock appreciation. GDP was therefore modelled from both the expenditure and income sides, as the sum of both aggregate expenditures and factor incomes, but these two sums are of course required to be equal to one another. The Treasury model achieved this equality simply by *defining* company sector profits as the difference between GDP determined on the expenditure side and the sum of the other factor incomes. Profits, in other words, acted as the 'buffer' category, adjusting in order to accommodate the other variables in the model.

This raises two questions: firstly, is it reasonable to determine profits in this way and, secondly, what consequences, if any, should there be on other variables within the model of changes in the level of profits? It is at moments like this that the elaborate blueprint of the Southampton model can be illuminating. Recall from chapter 2 that a central issue in the Southampton model was that of ensuring *ex post* equality between output and expenditure. This was achieved by defining stockbuilding as the buffer category, a variable that does seem a reasonable choice for this role. But the point in the South-ampton model is that this buffer was not a just 'sink' that went on swallowing without complaint whatever discrepancies arose between the planned, *ex ante*, levels of output and expenditure. On the contrary, the previous quarter's unanticipated change in stocks was one of the two major determinants of the next quarter's production and pricing decisions. Clearly there is always room to debate the merits of the particular variable chosen to play the role of the buffer; there can be little doubt, however, that it is unsatisfactory to treat it also as a sink, without feedback to the rest of the model. This, however, is precisely what the Treasury model did with profits. It may be, of course, that for any reasonable range of forecasts (determined by the choice of values for the model's exogenous variables) the buffer is found to behave in a way that is not judged to be unreasonable or inconsistent with other aspects of the situation forecast by the model. This underlines the need for the careful scrutiny of the results produced by the model but, in a process that all the time is seeking to formalise the informal, the very need for this is indicative of a new problem.

What was the buffer in the 1972 Business School model? Both within the body of the income block and from the point of view of the factor incomes, the answer to this is not clear cut. Profit was certainly not the buffer (since it was modelled explicitly), while quite a large number of sectoral and total variables on the income side were not modelled. These included components of rent and stock appreciation for the personal and public sectors and the public sector gross trading surplus. However, we can also look at the matter from the point of view of the sectoral 'disposable incomes' (row 11) that sum to GDP. The model did not include GDPY explicitly but it is there implicitly of course, equal by definition to GDPE. Since the model included three of these four sectoral disposable incomes (for the personal, company and overseas sectors), the fourth – public sector 'disposable income' – was therefore the buffer that ensured that the sum of these sectoral totals equalled GDP. Unlike profits in the Treasury model, this variable was not explicitly defined as the buffer – indeed it did not appear explicitly in the model at all – but implicitly it was there nevertheless.

Again, the same questions are posed: firstly, is it reasonable to treat public sector income as the buffer and, secondly, what consequences are there (or should there be) on the rest of the model as a result of the discrepancies between *ex ante* (planned) and *ex post* (outturn) public sector income? The answer to the first would require a full articulation of all elements of public sector income, although it certainly seems plausible to treat something such as tax receipts as a passive variable that would accommodate to the rest of the model in the manner of a buffer. The answer to the second is that there are no consequences on the rest of the model, which is in keeping with the basic philosophy of the model, showing as it does the effect of government action on the rest of the economy, rather than the subsequent effect from the rest of the economy back onto the government.

But the most interesting point to be made in connection with this treatment of public sector income as the buffer is that the matter does not remain within the confines of the income and expenditure blocks. It is true that public sector expenditure is not quite complete in the model, but it lacks only the physical increase in stocks. Were that to be included, giving public sector total expenditure (row 18), it should be clear from table 4.1 that the implication of treating public sector income as a buffer is that some financial flow is also being treated as a buffer: for the sake of simplicity (that is, ignoring the public sector's direct and portfolio investment and miscellaneous transactions in rows 20 and 21), say the public sector borrowing requirement. That in turn has to be financed; since it contained the money supply as an exogenous variable, the model came close to treating, again implicitly, the demand for Treasury Bills and government securities (row 23) as a buffer. In short, an explicit model of the expenditure categories of GDP and three of the four sectoral disposable incomes comes close to being an implicit model of the bond market.[9]

In this specific example are represented two general points. Firstly, a complete model of the income and expenditure blocks that contains too perhaps just one or two financial variables is implicitly a model of some other financial variable: a demand for bonds or, with a different selection of exogenous variables, a demand for money. Secondly, and as a consequence, the very process of completing the income–expenditure model pushes the erstwhile 'Keynesian' to attend more closely to the 'monetary' side of the economy. This does not make for Monetarism, but it does mean that the variables that typically sit at the centre of the Monetarist view come increasingly into focus for the 'Keynesian'. This raises new questions and, to the extent that Monetarism and Keynesianism are seen as polar opposites, it shows the place at which their concerns meet.

Table 4.1 shows that place of meeting precisely: at row 19, the sectoral 'balances', which are both the difference between sectoral incomes and expenditures and also the totals to which each sector's financial transactions must sum. It is clear from the table that the development of the Business School model over the period to 1972 had taken it to the very brink of being obliged to grapple with the financial consequences of the income and expenditure flows. All that was preventing the modelling of those sectoral balances, was the lack of the sectoral disaggregation of the physical increase in stocks. The logical first step in addressing these financial consequences would be to investigate what constituted reasonable behaviour for the sectoral balances, and this would be both a theoretical and an empirical matter. I shall take up this matter at the beginning of chapter 6.

'WHAT IF?' SIMULATIONS

I have already indicated that the two major developments in macro-econometric model-building that took place during this period were both made possible by the great increase in computational power afforded by the electronic computer over the old manual method. One of these developments was the sheer increase in model size discussed above. The other was the preparation of far more ambitious forecasts than were previously possible. This ambition extended in two directions.

Firstly, it was possible to produce not only a 'base' forecast, corresponding to the continuation of the present macroeconomic policies, but also any number of alternative forecasts corresponding to different settings of the (exogenous) policy variables. Descriptions of the old manual forecasting method had emphasised that the forecast was prepared on the assumption of unchanged fiscal and monetary policies.[10] Of course the logic that lay behind the manual forecast would also have lain behind the formulation of the advice that would have been given to government ministers on the nature and magnitude of any changes in policies that seemed desirable. But, in view of the length of time involved in the preparation of a forecast, few if any of the policy options would have been presented as a full-scale alternative forecast. Once the process was computerised, however, this drawback no longer existed. Secondly, and for exactly the same reason, the sheer weight of calculation involved no longer restricted the forecast to the traditional eighteen-month horizon. All that was required to produce a forecast for, say, five years was series providing the values for the exogenous variables over that time-scale.

The great increase in computing power did not, however, simply result in a proliferation of forecasts over far longer time horizons than those employed previously. In practice, the number of plausible scenarios for which a forecast was required would be small, while the original decision to restrict the horizon to eighteen months was based on the view that forecasts were insufficiently reliable beyond that point to make their preparation worth while. There *was* a lengthening of the forecast horizon, from eighteen months to approximately four years, but this change in forecasting practice did not come until the second half of the 1970s, long after the increase in computing power that was necessary for it had become available. Instead, the way in which that power was first utilised was to get the models to produce answers to questions of a 'what if?' nature. Although there were exceptions, questions of this type normally referred to a 'typical' change in either government policy or external economic circumstances, for example: 'What would happen were government expenditure to be raised by x million pounds?'; 'What would happen were tax rates to be increased by y per cent?'; 'What would happen were the annual rate of growth of world trade to increase by z per cent?'; and so on. The answer to this type of question required that a comparison be made between two 'projections' from the model over a period longer than eighteen months. As such, we can see that they therefore combined the two developments that the greater computer power afforded: firstly, the ease with which more than one projection could be produced and, secondly, the ease with which projections over a longer term could be made.

Figure 4.1 is a typical instance. Drawn using figures that were produced from the Business School model in 1972, it shows the effect

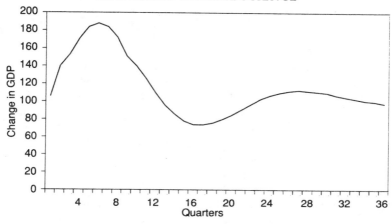

Figure 4.1 LBS model (1972): effect of sustained £100m increase in government expenditure
Source: Ball *et al.* (1975b), table 7.2.

on GDP of a sustained increase in current government expenditure of £100 million per quarter. All figures are measured at 1963 prices.[11] The way this effect is shown is via a comparison of the path followed by GDP in a 'base' projection with the path followed in an 'alternative' projection. The two projections differ only in the values taken by (exogenous) government expenditure, being £100 million per quarter higher in the second than in the first. Since the Business School model was non-linear, the result was sensitive to the values of the exogenous variables in the base projection.[12] However, since this sensitivity was judged to be a second-order effect only, the precise values adopted for the two projections would not have been crucial. As a consequence, although there was no particular reason why it *should* not, the base projection *need* not have corresponded to the base forecast and indeed, as we shall see in a moment, there was no need even for such projections to involve the future. In short therefore, 'projection' and 'forecast' stand for slightly different things even though there is no difference between them in terms of the manner of their execution through the computer model.

Images like that depicted here in figure 4.1 have become the leitmotif of the macroeconometric model: the appearance of such a diagram in an article published in a journal, book or newspaper is a sure sign that a macroeconometric model is being used to support the argument expounded therein. Translating figure 4.1 into words, we can see that in the first quarter (that is, the period in which the increase in government expenditure first takes place) GDP is increased by a fraction more than the size of the initial stimulus of 100. Over the next five quarters, the size of the response increases, peaking at a value that implies that the initial 100 boost brings forth a further rise in GDP of 88; a GDP multiplier, in other words, equal to 1.88. Thereafter, however, GDP falls away from this peak, dropping back to 100 (in the thirteenth quarter) and falling as low as 75 (in the sixteenth). A further cycle of rise then fall follows. The results for the projection cease at the thirty-sixth quarter, but were they to have continued for longer we could guess that they would probably have shown a further, more damped cyclical movement settling towards a level close to the 100 level, corresponding to a multiplier of around 1.0.

Although there is nothing in an exercise of this sort that could not in principle have been produced via the old manual method, the projection beyond eighteen months took the models into uncharted territory. What status did the modellers give to it? Was it presented as a new 'finding', which had been obtained by applying a familiar model to a new situation, or was it, alternatively, treated as something that was open to critical appraisal, appraisal that could in turn feed back and add to an assessment of the original model in its original short-term domain?[13] Broadly speaking, the modellers' stance was very much closer to the former position than to the latter, but the model results were in no way presented uncritically.

In commenting upon the results depicted here in figure 4.1, Ball and his colleagues described as 'striking' both the 'degree of fluctuation produced by the system and the relatively small magnitude of the equilibrium solution to which the [GDP] multiplier seems to be approaching'.[14] What is most interesting about this is that no reason was given for this judgement. A possible basis for it could certainly be found in the *contrast* between the behaviour in the first six quarters and the behaviour subsequently. Given that the sixth quarter was the previously accepted limit up to which the model (or its informal predecessors) was regarded as valid, this contrast is indeed 'striking' because, apart from the fact that the effect on GDP is always positive, these first eighteen months are really rather atypical of the whole picture. Were we to see just these first six quarters, we would surely suppose that GDP would continue to grow, albeit ever more slowly, to finish up at a level perhaps around 200, implying a multiplier with a value of about 2.0. Instead, we see some large oscillations and a finishing value that is closer to half that value.

However, rather than devote time and space to a justification of why this or that feature of the projection might be 'striking', the model builders directed their attention towards investigating which parts of the model were responsible for the observed behaviour. Thus the oscillations were traced to the particular form of the function that had been used to model inventories, and the point was demonstrated via projections obtained from an amended version of the model that used a different stockbuilding equation. The small equilibrium multiplier was traced to movements in the foreign balance in which exports had declined and imports risen. The former was accounted for in terms of the rise in export prices, which itself was explained in terms of the higher wage costs following from increases in overtime payments. When overtime was held to its path in the 'base' projection, exports and the multiplier turned out higher. The rise in imports was qualified by the observation that the model did not discriminate between the different components of final expenditure; in view of the lower than average import content of government expenditure, it was concluded that the projection overstated the true effect on imports and therefore understated the multiplier. This general assessment of too low a multiplier was supported by some simple calculations based on the average ratios to output of consumption, imports and stock-building over the period from 1960. Also reported were simulations demonstrating the effect of alternative assumptions about earnings.[15]

This approach to the assessment of the 'what if?' projections was by no means confined to Ball and his colleagues but was, rather, the general mode in which builders of macroeconometric models discussed the properties of their models at that time.[16] Its full significance becomes clearer when we examine the way in that the basis for such assessments was to shift later in the decade. We can characterise this earlier approach as one that devoted very little attention to identifying or justifying what was 'right' behaviour for the model as a whole. Instead, it preferred to demonstrate how that behaviour would alter as different parts of the model were altered. Implicit within this approach is the view that the behaviour of the model as a whole should and could be judged by reference to its component relationships. These were the things about which definitive judgements could be made – the things about which economists 'knew' – and the role of the model was to show the consequences of some particular assembly of such relationships. There was a feedback from

73

the whole model to the individual equations (for example, the stockbuilding equation), but such 'whole model' criteria were at this stage under-defined. In one sense, we can see this as a natural consequence of the approach to model-building that Ball had outlined in his review of the Cambridge Growth Project model nearly a decade earlier. In another, and I think more profound sense, we can also see that this approach was consistent with a view that gave the building of macroeconometric models a purpose: if previously the work of applied econometrics had been the development of single equations to explain the behaviour of this or that variable, then the purpose of building a model was to show the consequences of assembling and solving a set of these equations simultaneously.

5

KEYNESIAN REFORM
Kaldor's radical critique and the
exchange-rate

Among the 'what if?' projections from the 1972 version of the
London Business School model was one that addressed the question
of what would have happened had there been no sterling devaluation
in 1967. This was unusual in being historically specific – a counterfactual – but its real interest here is that it marked the arrival of the
exchange-rate as an instrument whose effect could be represented
within a macroeconometric model. The importance of this event
comes from the fact that the exchange rate and its use as an instrument
of policy have been at the very centre of almost every major policy
debate and economic crisis in the UK for the past quarter-century
from the 1967 devaluation onwards.

SIMULATING THE EFFECT OF THE 1967 DEVALUATION

The 14 per cent sterling devaluation of November 1967 occurred less
than one year after Jim Ball and Terry Burns had started to write what
was to become their regular column in the *Sunday Times* on the short-
term prospects for the British economy. The devaluation was therefore an event of great topicality that could be expected to affect the
performance of the economy in a profound fashion. Inevitably, the
builders of UK macroeconometric models had to take account of this
event.[1] There was, however, a choice to be made concerning the
manner in which this was done. This lay between adjusting the
parameters of the model to reflect the new situation and incorporating
the exchange-rate as an exogenous variable within the model. The
Cambridge Growth Project followed the first route to reach the
conclusion, published in *Exploring 1972*,[2] that the devaluation would
permit a higher sustained rate of growth of GDP to be consistent with

a satisfactory balance of payments position. In contrast, the London Business School altered its model in order to introduce the exchange-rate into it as an exogenous variable. As a result, the model could be used to show how a change in the exchange-rate would affect the behaviour of the economy.[3]

One difference between the devaluation simulation and the others was that, whereas the latter were in effect showing what would happen were the policy change to take place now, the devaluation exercise was arranged so as to show what would have happened had there been no devaluation in 1967. It was therefore strictly a counterfactual exercise, a re-running of history under a different policy regime. The effect of devaluation was obtained by comparing two projections from 1967: one, the 'control', included a devaluation equal to that which had actually taken place, while the second proceeded on the assumption that the exchange-rate had remained at its pre-1967 level. This gave the modellers an additional perspective from which to assess the exercise, since the 'control' projection could firstly be compared with the actual outcome. The discrepancies were examined to see if they contained any implications for the devaluation exercise itself. Both projections were carried out on the basis that the exogenous variables were set to their actual historical values.

Figures 5.1 and 5.2 trace out the main effects of the devaluation according to the Business School's 1972 model. Figure 5.1 shows the effect of the devaluation on GDP, measured as a percentage of its level in the third quarter of 1967 (that is, the last complete quarter before the devaluation). As can be seen, GDP increases gradually, achieving a level in 1970 and 1971 some 3 per cent above the level it would have attained had there been no devaluation. Figure 5.2 shows the effect in millions of pounds on the current account of the balance of payments. After an initial deterioration, this improves to the extent of something near to half a billion pounds for 1970 as a whole. Thanks to the devaluation, unemployment (not shown) was calculated to be some 335,000 lower on average throughout 1970. By the end of 1970, consumer prices still stood no more than 2.5 per cent higher as a result of the devaluation even though import prices had risen 13 per cent and export prices over 9 per cent. This is an impressive result. Taken at face value, it implied that the devaluation had accounted for some four-tenths of the total growth actually recorded between the third quarter of 1967 and the fourth quarter of 1970. Unemployment, which averaged a little over half a million in 1970, had been reduced by a similar proportion.

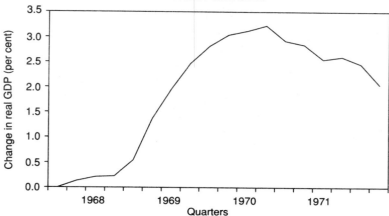

Figure 5.1 LBS model (1972): calculated effect of 1967 devaluation on GDP
Source: Ball *et al.* (1975b), table 7.13.

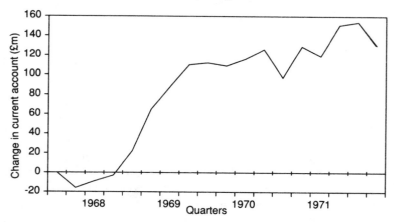

Figure 5.2 LBS model (1972): calculated effect of 1967 devaluation on balance of payments
Source: Ball *et al.* (1975b), table 7.13.

Some reservations were recorded: the effect of the rise in import prices on final expenditure was likely to be underestimated; the initial downward impact of devaluation on the current balance was thought to be too small; export prices should perhaps have risen less rapidly; and, above all, devaluation was assumed to have no impact on wage rates. Wage rates, in fact, were set at their actual levels in both projections, the relationship that determined wage rates having been removed from the model. The implication of this treatment of wage rates was that wage rates did not change in response to price changes. Of course this called for the results to be qualified, but the qualification was hardly severe: the estimates were to be 'regarded as being at the upper end of the likely range'; and, in spite of the problems noted, 'the calculations [were] about the right order of magnitude'.[4] Ball and Burns were later to conclude that the limited feedback from price inflation to wage inflation that they had detected in the period following 1967 was attributable to the presence of the (effective) policy of income restraint that the then Labour government had first introduced in 1966 and maintained for some three years.

As a technical exercise, the role of the model in this simulation was no different from that in any of the others. This role was to show the effects that arose from the interaction of various specific assumptions embodied in individual structural equations. In this case, the particular assumptions of interest related to the points through which the consequences of a devaluation would enter the rest of the economy. In the Business School's model, these points were the obvious ones of export and import prices as well as overseas property income credits along with other 'invisible' transactions. What the model did here was to show 'how the various changes induced by the devaluation work through the system',[5] which was exactly its role in other simulations.

However, this simulation of the 1967 sterling devaluation was much more than a mere technical exercise. It was path-breaking, in two senses: firstly, none of the other income expenditure models was capable of being used in this way at that time; and, secondly, the exchange-rate had not previously been viewed as an instrument of policy. Hitherto, changes in public expenditure or tax rates had enjoyed a quite different status as policy instruments from that attached to a devaluation. Under a Keynesian regime that gave the priority to fiscal measures as the means by which the government should affect the level of aggregate demand within the economy, there were no questions of principle associated with the use of changes in government expenditure or tax rates. The only questions concerned the magnitude of such changes and their timing. Devaluation, in contrast, was in no way an accepted instrument of government policy, to be used or not as the circumstances required. It was, rather, a one-off event that had happened when it had only because it had been forced on the government.

To have succeeded in treating devaluation in a manner identical to that in which wholly accepted policy instruments were treated – and to have shown it moreover to have such positive effects – can only have served to promote the claim of the exchange-rate to be numbered among the ordinary instruments of policy, to be used as and when needed, rather than one whose use was regarded as wholly exceptional. One thing that it certainly did was to provide Ball and Burns with a basis from which to advance an argument on the use of the exchange-rate. The model was a systematic representation of their thoughts on this matter and its properties in this regard were distilled from the experience gained since 1967.

While their conclusion from the purely academic discussion, noted above, was somewhat restrained, their tone in the *Sunday Times* had been altogether more enthusiastic. In January they had called on the Chancellor of the Exchequer, Anthony Barber, to be prepared to 'adapt the exchange-rate to the needs of growth as the occasion arises'.[6] When, in his Budget statement in the spring of that year, the Chancellor announced that an inappropriate exchange-rate would not be allowed to constrain growth, Ball and Burns were willing to interpret the statement as representing – at last – a commitment to economic growth. 'Barber', they opined, would be remembered for 'sweeping away the exchange-rate shibboleth'[7].

In these arguments, Ball and Burns were embracing what we can see, with the benefit of hindsight, was the last great attempt to reform the practice of Keynesian demand management 'from within'; a reform, in other words, that had been proposed by those who remained fully committed both to the goal of full employment and to the means of attaining it through the management of effective demand by the government. The reform was associated above all with Nicholas Kaldor.

KALDOR'S CRITIQUE OF DEMAND MANAGEMENT

Nicholas Kaldor's proposal for the active use of the exchange-rate as an instrument of policy derived from his reflections on the difficulties that had beset British economic policy since the Second World War. He set out his case in his presidential address to Section F of the British Association in 1970.[8]

Kaldor was well placed to take such a long view. He had been involved in the preparation of Sir William Beveridge's *Full*

Employment in a Free Society, published in 1944, which had set out both the case for full employment and the means by which it might be achieved. Kaldor was one of the authors of the memorandum entitled 'The Quantitative Aspects of the Full Employment Problem in Britain', which later appeared as an appendix in Beveridge's book. His association with the conduct of economic policy in Britain was a long one. In 1964, he was appointed Special Adviser to the Chancellor of the Exchequer on the Social and Economic Aspects of Taxation Policy. For four years he used this as a base from which to try to influence many aspects of government economic policy.[9] His presidential address came only a few months after the defeat of that government in the 1970 general election.

The root of the difficulties, according to Kaldor, could be traced to the fundamentals of the policy regime that had been in place since the Second World War. This regime 'relied on internal demand management through fiscal measures and a system of fixed exchange-rates';[10] an adjustment to the exchange-rate (which occurred in 1949 and 1967) was only a measure of last resort. This was a flawed regime because it failed to take account of the fact that

> the main autonomous factor governing both the level and the rate of growth of effective demand of an industrial country with a large share of exports in its total production and a large share of imports in its consumption is the external demand for its exports; and the main factor governing the latter is its international competitiveness, which in turn depends on the level of its industrial costs relative to other industrial exporters.
>
> (Kaldor 1971: 7)

The flaw itself was traced to the thinking of those (including himself) who had laid out the groundwork in the Beveridge memorandum. Their collective error had been to fail to take proper account of the implications of translating Keynes' argument from its original 'closed' economy setting to the more appropriate setting of the 'open' economy.

The consequence of relying on internal demand management was that personal consumption became the channel through which the overall level of economic activity was controlled. Of course, it would be far better were it possible to use investment as the channel but in a capitalist economy this is not possible. Incentives such as tax breaks, subsidies or even interest rates had little influence on investment in Kaldor's view; what mattered was the demand in prospect for the goods that would flow from that investment. Personal consumption, in contrast, *was* amenable to direct government control through the exercise of fiscal policy and credit controls. Consumption, not investment, was therefore the 'prime mover' of the economy. Under the policy regime that had been in place since the end of the war, economic growth in the UK was 'consumption led'.

Kaldor's proposed remedy was to switch the focus of demand management from consumption to exports: 'export-led' growth should replace 'consumption-led' growth. The way in which the government could influence exports was by adjusting the exchange-rate, usually (although not necessarily always) in a downward direction so as to maintain international competitiveness. The old regime of 'internal' demand management was to be replaced by a new regime of 'external' demand management. The new regime would continue to employ all the old policy instruments, but these would be supplemented by, and subordinated to, the instrument of the exchange-rate.

It is possible to view this argument as being no more than an application of Jan Tinbergen's theory of economic policy that the number of policy instruments must in general be equal to the number of targets that a government is seeking to achieve.[11] Kaldor recognised that, but his argument was more than just a case for 'one more policy instrument'. Instead, as an argument that showed the benefits that were to be had from treating exports as the 'prime mover' of the economy, it made the specific case for the exchange-rate since it was the use of that instrument that opened up the possibility of treating exports in that way.

The case for export-led growth had two parts to it. The first part of the case rested on the fact that manufacturing demand formed a far higher share of export demand than it did of consumption demand. Manufacturing demand would therefore increase by a larger amount from a boost in exports than it would from a boost in personal consumption of equal size. The full significance of this depended in turn on the special benefits that flowed, in Kaldor's view, from manufacturing as a result of its strongly increasing returns to scale.

The second part of the case for export-led growth rested on the practical difficulties that consumption-led growth had faced. Its central deficiency was that it contained no mechanism by which to transfer resources from consumption to investment. Reductions in consumption would release resources for investment but, since growing consumption demand provided the incentive to invest, a slowing in that growth, let alone a fall, might in fact serve to lower investment, notwithstanding the greater availability of resources. With export-led growth in contrast, the growing export demand would serve to sustain investment while consumption could be cut back so as to release resources for that investment. The regime of internal demand management targeted on consumption also faced a particular problem of timing. The problem was that import growth would precede export growth. This was because, while exports would only follow the growth in productive capacity, imports would lead it. The boost to imports would occur not only as a direct result of the boost to home consumption but also as an indirect result, as business acquired a certain amount of its investment goods from abroad in order to meet that new consumption. A balance of payments problem would therefore be endemic to internal demand management. The avoidance of such a problem would call for a good sense of timing on the part of those responsible for managing the economy. This would in turn depend on accurate and timely short-term forecasts.

At least as important as the specific proposals and their rationale is the spirit in which this argument was made. Kaldor's argument was for the reform of demand management and not for its overthrow; he never once sought to diminish the achievements of the previous twenty-five years. Thus, although the whole case was based on a critique of that quarter-century, the policies that had been pursued were never described as having been harmful, or even ineffective, but simply described as second best, the reward for which had been 'relatively meagre'.

> But in saying this, I do not wish to imply that the post-war attempt at 'managing the economy' was a failure in the sense that we could have been better off without it. On the contrary, I am convinced that in comparison to the restoration of the pre-war system of *non*-management – which would have meant operating under a system of fixed exchange-rates with a 'neutral' fiscal policy – we have achieved higher employment and also more stability of employment; a higher level of investment, a faster rate of economic growth and also a faster trend rate of growth of exports.
>
> (Kaldor 1971: 14–15)

The fundamental argument, for a move away from a fixed exchange-rate, was made historically specific. He did not condemn the original adoption of the fixed exchange-rate system that formed part of the Bretton Woods Agreement. On the contrary, he noted that the willingness to accept Bretton Woods, notwithstanding the commitment to fixed exchange-rates about which misgivings were expressed, was in large part due to the prospect that it held out for the dismantling of controls on international trade. This was something that was judged at the time to be very much in Britain's interest, more than outweighing the risks associated with fixed exchange-rates.[12]

Above all else, Kaldor's critique and the conclusions that he drew from it never for a moment abandoned the goals of demand management, first among which was the goal of an almost-full level of employment. I have already mentioned the objectives of post-war policy at the beginning of this book. But the goals, or targets, and the interpretation that Kaldor put on their very existence, are worth repeating because they serve to draw attention not only to the essential nature of Keynesianism but also to his continued commitment to those goals. The very existence of such targets, not only for employment but also for growth, wage increases and the balance of payments, testified to the acceptance, by politicians and people alike, of the fact that governments could, and therefore should, be responsible for such matters and that as a consequence they should be judged by the degree to which they succeeded in attaining the targets. It was this, Kaldor believed, that was the most important political legacy of Keynes' *General Theory*.

THE AFFINITY BETWEEN THE VIEWS OF KALDOR AND THE BUSINESS SCHOOL

I have reported Kaldor's views here at some length for the same reason that I discussed UK pre-model economic forecasting in chapter 3 and will discuss certain Monetarist ideas in chapter 7. The macroeconometric computer-based model is a means by which to represent a view of how the economy functions. Each of the major steps in the development of modelling has been associated with a new idea on how some aspect or other of the economy functions; either old models have been amended or new models have been introduced specifically to represent a theory of how some action by the government (or central bank) will affect the rest of the economy. Such acts of representation are necessarily partial since models can never portray the richness and subtlety of thought that has been expressed verbally. But, at the same time, such acts also bring precision since there is less room for ambiguity in both the quantitative and algebraic modes of representation than in the verbal.

It is in this light that we should see the relationship between the ideas that had been spelled out by Nicholas Kaldor and the London Business School economists' advocacy of that policy. The model had been amended in order to illustrate the benefits of devaluation, but in no sense had it become either a direct or a complete embodiment of Kaldor's views. For example, although growth, employment and the balance of payments responded strongly in the simulation to the devaluation, albeit after some time had elapsed, investment responded weakly. Since increased investment (in manufacturing) was the key to the all-round improvements in productivity and productivity growth that Kaldor had argued would flow from export-led growth, this weak response meant that the model was failing to reproduce an effect of crucial importance.

In view of this gap between the model and Kaldor's theory, it is therefore particularly interesting to note that, in commenting on these results, Ball and his colleagues suggested not only that the investment response was possibly an underestimate but also that the underestimate could be blamed on the model's failure to take account of the change in the composition of final expenditure on investment. Such a comment must have a basis that is apart from that on which the model was built and Kaldor's theory provides just such a basis.

We can also find a close affinity between the Business School's model simulation and Kaldor's argument in the key matter of the effect of devaluation on the wage rate and the level of domestic prices. As we have seen, the model showed wage rates as quite unaffected by the devaluation. This was a direct result of the manner in which the simulation had been conducted, wherein wage rates were simply fixed at the actual levels that had been observed. The devaluation did cause the index of consumer prices to rise but by no more than 2.5 per cent after three years. In consequence, the simulation showed that the devaluation lowered both the real wage rate (the nominal wage rate divided by the consumer price deflator) and the 'efficiency wage' (the nominal wage rate expressed in foreign currency). The former marks a shift from wages to profits, while the latter marks an improvement in international competitiveness. Kaldor can provide a justification for the Business School's whole treatment of this matter:

This is not to deny that the rate of increase in money wages – with or without an incomes policy – is influenced by the cost of living, so that money wages will tend to rise faster as a result of a falling exchange-rate and rising import prices; if the movement in wages is controlled, or moderated, by an incomes policy a flexible exchange-rate will put greater strain on this instrument. But there is no reason for supposing that the 'efficiency wages' of a country, in terms of international currency, cannot permanently be lowered by a downward adjustment of the exchange-rate, even though the change in the exchange-rate necessary to secure a given reduction in 'efficiency wages' will be greater than it would if money wages did not react to the change in the cost of living.

(Kaldor 1971: 8n)

Now, as before, Ball and his colleagues did not cite Kaldor in support of their approach, even though this passage, and especially the crucial conclusion contained in its final sentence, accords very well with the model results as they were presented. But this passage *would* be cited some five years later, not in support and not with approval, but rather to serve as a statement of the effect of devaluation that was diametrically opposed to the London Business School economists' later belief.[13]

A COMMITMENT TO SUSTAINED GROWTH

As a model, that of the London Business School in 1972 has no claim to be a direct embodiment of Nicholas Kaldor's theories. A better claim to that inheritance can be made for the prototype 'Par' model and its successor, the model of the Cambridge Economic Policy Group, since these models flowed from work that was being undertaken at that time by economists at Cambridge who were closely associated with Kaldor. The Policy Group model is the subject of the next chapter, a reflection of the fact that I see it as a part of the reaction against Keynesianism. The affinity that I assert exists between Kaldor's ideas and the Business School economists is, in the last instance, based less on the model than on the policies that Ball and Burns were to advocate for at least two more years, their continued espousal of the values of Keynesianism[14] and the critical but nevertheless still resolute support for demand management that they expressed.

Inevitably, any attempt to summarise the half-dozen articles that Jim Ball and Terry Burns wrote in the crucial years of 1972 and 1973, and to place them in the context of the fifteen or so that had been written during the previous five years, is bound to be impressionistic. As a starting point, however, it is helpful to recognise that 1970 marked a distinct change of tone. Until then, the articles were devoted to explaining the forecast of GDP and its expenditure components over the coming eighteen months. The economic problems confronting the government were discussed. Some articles pronounced on whether the government should take action to expand or contract demand. The level of unemployment was a concern. For example, a forecast that unemployment would rise through 1970 from 600,000 at the beginning of the year to 650,000 at the end was accompanied by a call for a relaxation of policy to stimulate growth in order to prevent the rate of unemployment from reaching 'socially unacceptable levels in the winter of 1971'.[15] Although some more profound policy changes had been discussed before the devaluation, once this had occurred it was necessary to wait some time for clear evidence of its effect to emerge.

The change in tone that took place in 1970 was caused by the fact that the beneficial effects of devaluation were seen to weaken. In particular, the surplus on the balance of payments was falling, even though the economy continued to suffer slow growth.

> 1969 and 1970 taken together will have been a period of wasteful under-utilisation of resources that should not be allowed to continue. The rate of growth of investment in private industry has been hopelessly inadequate.
>
> (*Sunday Times*, 23 August 1970)

This presaged the return of the old dilemma that had bedevilled UK macroeconomic policy – growth and employment or the balance of payments? – a dilemma that devaluation had been supposed to banish. By 1970, the policy problem had been made that much worse by the rise in inflation, to the 'extraordinarily high rate' in 1970 of 6 per cent.[16] To some, this seemed to introduce a second dilemma – growth and employment or inflation? Ball and Burns dismissed this second dilemma as groundless since the relationship on which it was supposedly based, between wage inflation and unemployment had, in their view, broken down.[17] Whatever the extent of these dilemmas, the key point here is that they were urging a course that would avoid such unacceptable trade-offs altogether.

'What is required is a shift in emphasis away from policies of manipulating demand to protect us either from balance of payments deficits or high rates of inflation, towards policies designed to protect the rate of growth.

(*Sunday Times*, 3 January 1971)

The principal aim of economic policy should be the maintenance of a steady rate of growth equal to the rate of growth of productive potential. To avoid the two dilemmas they advocated a statutory incomes policy to deal with inflation and a more flexible exchange-rate to create the room for growth by relaxing the balance of payments constraint.

The message was repeated throughout 1971. The 'central objective' of economic policy should be growth; 'the rate of inflation and the balance of payments are means to an end that cannot be dealt with in the longer term by holding back the rate of growth itself'.[18] Intervention was required on prices and incomes. The balance of payments position had worsened, fundamentally because, while exports were almost flat in 1970, import volumes had risen substantially. The balance of payments remained favourable thanks only to favourable movements in the terms of trade.

But events were providing new hope. In August 1971, the Bretton Woods system, which had provided the framework for currency stability since the end of the Second World War, collapsed as the United States suspended the convertibility of the dollar into gold. After a week, during which the foreign exchange markets were closed, the pound was allowed to float along with the other leading currencies, all of which had previously been pegged to the dollar.

With luck, the present monetary crisis will enable politicians to clear their minds of their instinctive belief that changes in the exchange-rate are national disasters. Then the foundation may be laid for the Chancellor, in his next Budget, to appear totally committed to a growth policy on which to bring the nation into the Common Market.

(*Sunday Times*, 29 August 1971)

By the beginning of 1972, the signs were that the tide was turning. Growth was expected to be at 4 per cent and unemployment was forecast to be down to 900,000 by the year end. Even so, they continued to call for higher growth on the grounds that unemployment of 700,000 by the end of 1973 would still be too high 'on social grounds', 500,000 being 'more sensible in view of the colossal wastage of such high levels of unemployment'.[19] It was possible that the new exchange-rate was unsuited to providing a current account consistent with that level of unemployment, in which case the Chancellor should not hesitate to

> adapt the exchange-rate to the needs of growth as the occasion arises, nor to seize any initiative towards a more constructive approach to an incomes policy than at present exists. With these attitudes finally established, we have every reason to believe that we are at the beginning of a period of more rapid and sustained growth than we have experienced since the war.
>
> (*Sunday Times*, 2 January 1972)

When the Chancellor announced in March that growth would not be constrained by an inappropriate exchange-rate, Ball and Burns welcomed it as being (at face value at least) the long called-for commitment to growth.

With this commitment to both growth and the exchange-rate flexibility deemed necessary to achieve it, the articles enter a period in which, although surrounded by difficulties, support is given to the policies and priorities in force. Inflation was worsening and the balance of payments in the middle of the year was considerably worse than it had been during 1971. Ball and Burns predicted that the latter would improve in 1973, thanks to the devaluation. But, at each point, the forecast itself got worse. Thus in August, they predicted a surplus for 1973 of £340 million. In December, when they foresaw a rate of growth of 5 per cent in 1973, the current account was forecast to be heading for a £135 million deficit – but with improvement through the year as the benefits of the devaluation came through. By April 1973, the forecast had worsened to £500 million, again with a better second half than first and with an improvement stretching into 1974. This figure was notably more optimistic than the £1 billion foreseen by the Cambridge Economic Policy Group and the £900 million foreseen by the National Institute. Growth over the two years, 1973 and 1974, was forecast at 5 per cent.

Unemployment was by now falling fast and Ball and Burns therefore turned to the question of whether such a rate of growth (4 per cent) was sustainable beyond 1974. Once again, they found themselves facing the twin dilemmas. On the balance of payments, they continued to urge a floating pound in order to provide the room for continued growth. They anticipated pressure from EEC countries for either a fixed rate or a joint float of the European currencies against the dollar; both, they urged, should be resisted. Yet at the same time, the exchange-rate could be left to do the job of maintaining competitiveness, thereby alleviating the balance of payments problems, only if inflation were kept under control. If it were not, the strain that a falling exchange-rate would impose on domestic prices would be too severe; yet to maintain the exchange-rate would be to 'return to the socially wasteful policies of deflation'.[20]

The arguments for sustained growth reached a climax in September of 1973. Once more, the forecast for the 1973 balance of payments deficit had been revised upwards, this time to £1,300 million. This coincided with a growth forecast for the year of 7 per cent.[21] Ball and Burns went to considerable lengths to explain their failure to forecast the deficit. Although the higher rate of growth naturally meant that imports would be higher than in previous forecasts, this error was offset by the performance of exports, which were also much higher than had been anticipated earlier. Instead, the problem lay with the explosion in commodity prices (especially the price of oil) and the short-term adverse effects of the exchange-rate depreciation, which had led to a rise in the import price index of no less than 20 per cent. Moreover, they emphasised that balance of payments forecasts were highly sensitive to the likely range of assumptions that were made about the future course of import prices.[22]

In spite of the enormous deterioration in the balance of payments, Ball and Burns still pressed the case for growth. This was not just because they were 'for' growth (as if in some mindless kind of way) but because of their analysis of the situation in the short term. Thus they noted that the present situation was one that had occurred on a number of earlier occasions: a sharp rise in consumers' expenditure had been followed by a subsequent pick-up in investment, which this time had been accompanied by a sharp rise in exports too; the balance of payments had deteriorated (although the reasons this time were different); the absolute level of unemployment was higher than in previous cycles. In the past, this sort of situation had been handled by introducing deflationary measures, but such a response could be (and had been) criticised on the grounds that the economy was already moving into recession just as the measures were being applied.

In our view we could be poised to make the same mistake again. If our forecast of the main components of national output is roughly correct, from the point of view of securing and maintaining full employment the problem at the next budget will not be one of how much to deflate the economy, it will be one of how much more to pump into the system in order to ensure that unemployment does not begin to rise again in 1975.

(*Sunday Times*, 2 September 1973)

This of course is an argument – even *the* argument – for short-term forecasting, to help see what is 'around the corner' and act accordingly, instead of simply assuming that the near future will be no more than a continuation of the present.

In advising against a sharp deflation, Ball and Burns cited not only the employment goal but also the goal of keeping demand growth in line with the growth of capacity. Without this, investment would fall back. Sustained growth – and only sustained growth – would allow the UK to launch itself onto a higher growth path. The 'critical question', therefore, was whether the UK could, for very long, afford to sustain the current balance of payments deficit. If not, then neither could the UK afford full employment.

It is a matter of risking employment and the rate of growth against the balance of payments. In the past, it has always been jobs and growth that have been sacrificed. On this occasion we think the risk should be taken the other way.

(*Sunday Times*, 2 September 1973)

By the end of the year, they had abandoned this position.

6

KEYNESIAN CRISIS
New Cambridge and the attack on
short-term demand management

The worldwide economic crisis of 1974 and 1975 was of necessity a crisis for Keynesianism. The objective of steady growth necessary to maintain full employment was simply overwhelmed by the twin problems of an unprecedented balance of payments deficit (over £3 billion in 1974) and an explosion of prices during which the annual rate of retail price inflation peaked at almost 27 per cent in August 1975.[1] The effect that this crisis had on UK macroeconometric modelling was to shatter the consensus that had prevailed since the appearance of the first London Business School model in 1966. Although recognisably Keynesian models of the 'old' type continued (most notably at the National Institute, where the simple model of the late 1960s was finally given a thorough overhaul), two new types emerged 'from within', as it were. These two types were a 'new' Keynesian model, associated with the Cambridge Economic Policy Group, and an 'International Monetarist' model, associated with the London Business School. The evolution of the Business School model is the subject of chapter 7. This chapter is devoted to the model of the Cambridge Economic Policy Group, whose central figure was (and still is) Wynne Godley.

The ideas that were to become crystallised in the econometric model of the Cambridge Economic Policy Group took shape during the economic boom of 1972–3 and came to maturity during the recession that followed. In order to understand the Policy Group's model and the way it was used, we have to trace the development of the thinking that lay behind it during this formative period. The reason for this is that the development of the ideas that went into the model is more important than the model itself. There are two senses in which this is true.

The lesser sense is that the model was secondary for the Cambridge economists themselves; it did not make its appearance until 1976, by

which time all the significant policy criticisms and theoretical innovations had already been made, and, when it did appear, the role
accorded to this 'comprehensive econometric model' was that of
providing 'reinforcement' to the 'verbal argument'.[2] The model represented a view. That view was to change little over the second half of the
1970s and, as a result, the model changed little. This is in sharp contrast
to the models that had existed hitherto and that have occupied us to this
point, all of which, and especially the London Business School model,
had *evolved* through time. But the Cambridge pattern, of a model
representing a view of how the economy worked, was to be repeated in
the 1980s, most notably in the Liverpool model of Patrick Minford.

There is, however, a greater sense in which the development of the
ideas of the Cambridge Group in that period is more important than
the model that came to represent them. That sense stems from the
historical significance of those ideas. Although the ideas contained
elements of both continuity and discontinuity with what had gone
before, my judgement is that the elements of discontinuity predominated; the ideas were therefore more 'anti-Keynesian' than
'Keynesian'. There was then, as there is now, no shortage of anti-
Keynesian views; what makes the anti Keynesian views of the 1970s
Cambridge Economic Policy Group so significant is that they grew
out of the very heart of Keynesianism itself.

The position of the Group in relation to the development of
Keynesianism was therefore a complicated one. On the one hand, as
far as the *goals* that it espoused are concerned, of full employment, of
steady growth and of the government's responsibility to pursue these
ends, the Group's commitment to Keynesianism never wavered. But,
on the other, as far as the *practice* of Keynesianism was concerned and
especially the conceptualisation of the reasons for the increasing and
evident failure of that practice, the Policy Group not only was part of,
but in some respects actually led, the revolution against Keynesianism in the UK. This position gives rise to particular difficulties, since
sharp differences in one area sit side by side with deep similarities in
another. It also, however, makes the Group and its thinking crucial to
an understanding of the shift away from Keynesianism.

FORESEEING THE CONSEQUENCES OF THE 'BARBER' BOOM

The ideas that were to characterise the Policy Group's model and the
use that was made of it appear, in rudimentary form, in two pairs of

articles that were published in *The Times* newspaper in January and July 1973. The articles, which were written under the auspices of the *London and Cambridge Economic Bulletin*, were concerned with the consequences of the government's economic policy and, in particular, its commitment to an annual rate of growth of 5 per cent. The first pair, by Wynne Godley and Francis Cripps, foresaw that this policy would lead to a balance of payments deficit of no less than £1 billion for 1973. The second pair, by Robert Neild, asserted that the policy contained the 'seeds of a classic inflation'.

Before examining these ideas further we should look first at their context. The *London and Cambridge Economic Bulletin* went back to the 1920s. Among the first members of the editorial committee were John Maynard Keynes and Sir William Beveridge. Twice-yearly economic assessments had been published in *The Times* for many years.[3] Although each article was written by just one or two authors, this was normally 'after consultation' with the *Bulletin*'s editorial committee, among whose number, in the early 1970s, was Sir Alec Cairncross, who had joined the committee in 1969 after giving up the post of head of the government's economic service. Typically, a *Bulletin* article was discursive and indicative: it would outline the prospects for the economy and it would set out the options facing government, but it was neither centred on a formal 'forecast' – still less on a formal model – nor devoted to urging some particular course of action. It was, in short, the discourse of the insider, published (during the period of interest here) in the newspaper of the British establishment.

Godley and Neild were certainly insiders themselves. Neild had been Economic Adviser to the Treasury during the early years of the Labour government that came to office in 1964; earlier, he had been the first editor of the *National Institute Economic Review* in the late 1950s, when the Institute first began to publish short-term forecasts that were arrived at in the informal manner. We have already dealt, in chapter 3, with the part that Godley had played in economic forecasting in the early and middle 1960s. Seconded to the Institute from the Treasury in 1963, he had been responsible for three major innovations: firstly, for devising some of the key behavioural relationships that later were to appear in the Institute's model; secondly, for initiating the practice of regular scrutiny of the latest data and the (often significant) revisions to which they were subject; and, thirdly, for devising the informal but regular routine by which forecasts were prepared in the period prior to the emergence of the computerised model.

The articles, firstly by Godley and Cripps and secondly by Neild, were very much in keeping with the traditions of the *Bulletin*. Most notably, although each article was saturated with economic statistics, the study and discussion of which formed the raw material from which the arguments were crafted, there was no sign of any formal, econometric model. Neither was the forecast itself the ultimate object of the exercise. Instead, the purposes were to reveal the inconsistencies within current policy and to indicate the means by which these inconsistencies would resolve themselves were no corrective action to be taken: through either an enormous balance of payments deficit on the one hand, or a jump in inflation on the other. Neild, in particular, had emphasised that he did not expect things to work out in that way, because the government would be forced to adopt some 'fairly drastic new measures before very long'.[4] Each article proposed policy changes, common to both being an argument for higher taxes.

But Godley and Cripps also introduced a number of innovations. Firstly, the analysis was conducted within a medium-term framework; instead of just concentrating on the standard eighteen-month time-frame, they looked ahead over the following four years to 1976. Secondly, the basis of the calculations was quite different from that which was normal; instead of forecasting GDP as one of the 'outputs', the calculations were conditional on an assumption about the GDP growth rate, this assumption being the 5 per cent figure for each of the years 1973 and 1974 that had been published by the government in the autumn of 1972 along with projections for government expenditure. Thirdly, alongside the conventional policy advice for higher taxes to restrain consumption, they argued, albeit tentatively, for some unconventional policies to deal with the balance of payments: either wage subsidies financed by value-added tax as an aid to exports (an idea attributed to Kaldor), or quantitative restrictions on the growth of imports.

At *this* point in time, the novel aspects of the analysis had only a restricted impact on the conclusions reached. In particular, they were not responsible for the eye-catching balance of payments deficit of £1 billion forecast for 1973. This forecast, made at the beginning of 1973, was indisputably a short-term forecast, while the actual figure forecast for the deficit would appear to have been arrived at simply by applying an import propensity to the GDP growth and combining this with a likely figure (based on past performance) for exports. It is not clear that they were, in fact, doing anything different from what a conventional forecaster would have done here. Although they succeeded, in this article, in giving a good indication of the scale of the deficit at a time when the London Business School was forecasting £135 million,[5] this almost certainly was thanks to their appreciation of the already very adverse short-term trends in the balance of payments. Godley and Cripps had compared the first stage of expansion, in 1971–2, with three similar stages of the business cycle over the previous two decades, and had shown just how badly things were going, even before the sharp increase in the rate of growth of GDP in 1973.

The one area where the appreciation of the trends over the medium term did have an impact was in the unconventional measures that were proposed to deal with the balance of payments problem beyond 1973. The most significant thing about them is simply that they were put forward at all, for what this showed was a loss of faith, even at the very beginning of 1973, in the efficacy of devaluation as a means by which to achieve the Kaldorian goal of increased competitiveness. The fundamental difficulty was that, in view of the deficit that was foreseen for 1976, the size of the devaluation that would be necessary would be 'impossibly large'.

> Repeated depreciation of the exchange rate would probably lead to unemployment and inflation on an unprecedented scale. This danger is sufficiently real to warrant serious consideration of new and unconventional measures.
>
> (Godley and Cripps 1973)

This assessment, it should be noted, was made even though there was only 'limited evidence' about the effects of devaluation on exports and imports. Nevertheless, 'any devaluation will add to inflationary pressures on domestic costs which will reduce the effectiveness of the devaluation itself'.[6] What matters here is not the precise measurement of the effect of devaluation on inflation or GDP but rather a calculation to determine an 'order of magnitude', from which it is possible to conclude that devaluation does not match up to the scale of the problem that it was supposed to address. We shall return to this in due course.

Neild's articles six months later took the Cambridge Group's argument a step forward. In making their case for higher taxes, Godley and Cripps had shown that the government's policies were inconsistent: consumption would have to be restrained by higher taxes in order to leave sufficient resources for the growth in private investment and stockbuilding that could be expected in the strong upswing phase of a boom. This was a criticism of the conduct of economic policy, but its tone was muted. Neild's criticism, in contrast, was explicit and it was moreover directed at the (as he put it) 'official' forecasts of the Treasury and National Institute that provided the basis for policy choice. What Neild advocated was a new approach by which it would be possible 'to cross-check the implications of present policies',[7] and the way that he proposed to do this was to examine the forecasts from the point of view of their impact on the financial balance – the net acquisition of financial assets (NAFA) – of each of the principal sectors of the economy, namely the public, personal, company and overseas sectors. This was an innovation within Keynesian forecasting and policy analysis of the first order.

Any such innovation must necessarily have two aspects to it: one is the choice of some new variables as the focus of attention; the other is the identification of some pattern in the past behaviour of these variables. The variables themselves and their place within the income–expenditure framework can be seen if we turn back to table 4.1: each sector's net acquisition of financial assets, shown there in row 19, is equal to the difference between the sector's disposable income (row 11) and expenditure, both current and capital (row 18). As can be seen (from the fact that there is no entry in the 'total' column for this row), the sectoral balances sum, by definition, to zero. Having identified the variables of interest, much of Neild's article was devoted to an informal but nevertheless careful scrutiny of the behaviour of each of the sectoral balances over the previous two decades in order to identify patterns. Among the features he noted were the (positive) constancy of the personal sector balance[8] and the cyclical nature of the company and overseas sector balances. Both these latter balances mirrored the pattern of the public sector balance over the cycle; their magnitude, though, was about half that of the public sector.

This historical analysis implied that, by virtue of its position as a year of economic boom, 1973 should see a diminishing or even negative balance for the company sector as investment and stock-building advanced rapidly. The cross-check of the official projections, however, revealed that they implied not a deficit for the company sector but a surplus. This conclusion was reached by combining the projected public sector deficit of £2,300 million with the (favourable) assumption of an unchanged personal sector surplus of £1,250 million and an overseas sector surplus (current account deficit) of £750 million. Since the four sectoral surpluses must add to zero, this implied that the company sector should be in surplus to the extent of

£300 million, yet at that stage in the business cycle such a surplus was most unlikely. Thus, when they were examined from this overall perspective, the official projections appeared quite implausible. Subsequent analysis of the company sector capital account indicated that profits would need to rise by some 40 per cent in the second half of 1973 in order to achieve such a surplus. This rise in profits could be achieved only by a substantial rise in prices. As I have already noted, Neild did not expect this to happen; instead he believed that the government would be forced to change course, and his article included proposals as to how that should be done.

It is impossible to overstate the importance of the shift of focus introduced by Robert Neild: it was the culmination of not one but two traditions within the body of British economic thought and practice and it marked the turning point for Keynesianism.

What were these traditions? Firstly, by focusing attention on the net acquisition of financial assets of each sector, Neild can be seen as having taken the modelling of the income–expenditure framework to its logical conclusion. As I showed in chapter 4, the standard Keynesian models of the London Business School and the Treasury had been working towards the position where they modelled sectoral income and expenditure, but neither model had properly reached this point. The Business School had done so implicitly, with the public sector income in effect acting as the buffer that ensured equality between the income and expenditure measures of GDP. The Treasury model did not include such a sectoral disaggregation, explicitly or implicitly, but, as was noted earlier, company sector profits played the role of the buffer to bring the two measures of GDP into equality with one another. Neild looked past these details to see how the sectoral financial balances should behave. This was the logical endpoint of the long development of the income–expenditure models, but the implausibilities that Neild uncovered indicated that that development contained significant and perhaps serious flaws. Indeed, to the extent that Neild traced the flaw in the official projections back to their implications for company sector profits, it is possible that the very structure of the Treasury model and the part played in it by profits (not only as 'buffer' but also as 'sink') was one of the basic reasons for the implausibilities in those projections.[9]

Secondly, by insisting on the stability of the sectoral balances and by asserting that there existed a clear pattern to the fluctuations, Neild was calling into question the tradition of short-term management itself: had demand management helped stabilise the economy or had it, in fact, been the cause of the instability? Neild discussed this question with regard to the specific experience between 1967 and 1972 – during which time the Labour Chancellor, Roy Jenkins, had tightened the public sector balance by 8 per cent of GDP only to be followed by the Tory, Anthony Barber, who had relaxed it by a similar amount – but he did not broaden his observations into a general attack. But when Cripps and Godley wrote again six months later, in January 1974, when the phenomenal boom of the previous year was turning into the worst recession since the 1930s, they developed the attack to take in the very principles on which economic management had hitherto been conducted.

THE FALLACY OF SHORT-TERM FORECASTING AND DEMAND MANAGEMENT

It is not surprising that, at such a time, economists should look for deep-seated reasons for the kind of crisis that Keynesianism was supposed to have banished for ever. The Cambridge economists did not restrict themselves to chiding their fellow economists in the Treasury, the National Institute and the London Business School for failing to forecast what would happen; indeed, although occasionally they were prepared to blame official incompetence,[10] the kernel of their argument was that the fault lay in a fundamental misunderstanding of how the economy worked. The macroeconometric models, based on quarterly data and used to peer some two years into the future, embodied that misunderstanding.

> From one quarter to the next, the conventional assumptions largely hold good. The immediate impact of changes in taxation and public expenditure falls mainly on domestic income and output while the immediate impact of changes in the value of exports or in import prices falls mainly on the current balance of payments. But in the longer run, as the whole chain of adjustments in domestic output, spending and income follows through, here emerges a very different pattern of ultimate effects.
>
> (Godley and Cripps 1974b)

These 'ultimate effects' were that

> the public sector's budget deficit fully determines the current balance of payments: given the size of the budget deficit,

changes in exports, import prices, etc. make a lot of difference to real income and output but none at all to the balance of payments, however paradoxical this may at first sight appear. It also implies that the balance of payments is no harder to forecast and control than domestic output.

(Godley and Cripps 1974b)

These views can easily be summarised in a simple table (figure 6.1), which shows why even their authors admitted that such views could be thought of as 'paradoxical'. The immediate impact of changes in taxes and public expenditure would fall on the level of domestic income and output, whereas their ultimate effects would be wholly on the balance of payments. In contrast, the immediate impact of changes in export and import prices would fall on the balance of payments, while the ultimate effects would be wholly on income and output. (Export and import prices are not, of course, 'policy variables' themselves, but they could be influenced indirectly via changes in, for example, the exchange-rate.)

| | | Effects of policy changes | |
		Immediate impact	Ultimate effect
Policy changes	Changes in tax and public expenditure	Domestic income and output	Balance of payments
	Changes in export and import prices	Balance of payments	Domestic income and output

Figure 6.1 Summary of the 'New Keynesian' view

In focusing on the budget deficit of the public sector and the balance of payments on current account, Godley and Cripps were following Neild in placing the sectoral surpluses at the centre of the analysis, but whereas he had examined the matter in terms of four sectors – personal, company, public and overseas – Godley and Cripps reduced this to three by treating the first two together as a single private sector. This was done, it would seem, because the Cambridge economists believed that the surplus of private sector income over private sector expenditure, including investment, tended to be small and stable. This was in contrast to the orthodox view, which assumed, implicitly, that the surplus varied sharply with variations in the level of income.

If we speak loosely for a moment, the implication of a small and stable private sector surplus is simple: since the surpluses of the private, public and overseas sectors must sum to zero by definition, a 'small and stable' private sector surplus means that a change in the public sector deficit will 'ultimately' induce a corresponding change in the overseas sector surplus (balance of payments deficit). In one sense – and provided we are prepared to overlook the point that the three surpluses do not, *in practice*, add to zero but instead leave a residual whose size is by no means insignificant – the conclusion follows trivially once the original proposition regarding the private sector is accepted. But although this serves as a useful sketch of the Policy Group's central proposition and the logic behind it, it is quite insufficient as a basis on which to examine the questions and doubts that surround the position. This is because such disputes emerge only once we try to define and clarify the meaning of the central concepts involved and the conditions under which they are supposed to hold. Before exploring this, we need to look at the conclusion that was reached regarding the conduct of forecasting and policy analysis.

In the summer of 1974, Cripps, Godley and their Cambridge colleague Martin Fetherston submitted written evidence to the House of Commons Select Committee on Public Expenditure. The cornerstone of their argument was once more the behaviour of the private sector, and one of the main features of the memorandum was that it reported an equation that for the first time cast the relationship between private sector income and expenditure in a formal, econometric manner.

Their immediate target was the 'record of demand management' during the previous twenty years, which, they asserted in their opening sentence, 'had been extremely poor'. The whole period had been marked by a series of sharp changes in fiscal policy: two-year spells of demand expansion, in 1953–4, 1958–9, 1962–3 and 1971–2, had been followed by two-year spells of demand deflation, in 1955–6, 1960–1, 1964–5 and 1973–4. To some extent, these reversals of policy were the result of changes in the government's policy objectives. But they were also down to the fact that

> some of the outcomes were not properly foreseen – in particular that the conventional forecasting systems on which policy is based may underestimate the full effects of changes in policy.
>
> (Cripps, Godley and Fetherston 1974: 1)

What were the consequences of this failure 'properly to foresee the outcomes'? An implication of the stability of the relationship between private expenditure and income was that the only sources for instability were either the government's own actions (on fiscal or credit policy) or foreign influences, notably export demand and world commodity prices.

> It appears to have been the case that during the past twenty years or so, purely by chance, the fluctuations in UK exports, to the extent that these were induced by changes in world trade, have been roughly offset by changes in import prices attributable to the same cause. To the extent that this is true, fluctuations in world trade have generated very little disturbance either to the U.K. balance of payments or to real output in total, and the observed fluctuations in output have, to this extent, been *entirely* the consequences of the stabilisation measures!
>
> (Cripps, Godley and Fetherston 1974: 5)

What this last sentence, and in particular its last two lines, is saying plainly enough is that Keynesian demand management during most of the 1950s, the 1960s and the early 1970s, far from helping to stabilise the economy through counter-cyclical measures, was in fact wholly responsible for the instability that had been observed. Indeed, there might have been greater stability, in demand, output and the balance of payments,

> had some simple rule been followed through thick and thin such as that a tax yield should be sought such as to cover, as nearly as possible, some fixed proportion of public expenditure.
>
> (Cripps, Godley and Fetherston 1974: 1)

The memorandum had credited Nicholas Kaldor with 'an essential role in the evolution of the ideas' contained within it. Yet what is most striking about these ideas is not their continuity with what Kaldor had said but rather their discontinuity. Writing in 1970, Kaldor (as we saw in chapter 5) had been prepared to describe the gains from twenty-five years of demand management as 'relatively meagre'; yet Cripps, Godley and Fetherston now saw this system to have been positively harmful. Kaldor had gone on at once to emphasise that even such 'meagre' gains were decidedly superior to the fruits that would have been had under the old, pre-war, system of *non*-management. Such non-management was characterised by a fixed exchange-rate and a neutral fiscal policy; yet Cripps, Godley and Fetherston had now suggested that just such a neutral fiscal policy would have been preferable to the extent that it would have brought greater stability. And, although they continued very much to share Kaldor's view that performance in export markets was the key to domestic output and sustained growth, they had abandoned the view that the exchange-rate was the right instrument of policy to achieve that objective. Therefore, although the Policy Group continued to share the goals of Keynesianism, it had come to the point where it rejected the past practice of Keynesianism in its entirety.

With a rejection of demand management went a rejection of the models that had until then been used to assist both in foreseeing the consequences of a continuation of present policies and in assessing the implications of alternatives. Reflecting some months later on what had been said to the Public Expenditure Committee, the Policy Group noted that the objection to the use of short-term forecasts as the basis for fiscal policy was not that they were inaccurate but rather that they were 'the wrong basis *in principle* for budgetary policy'.[11]

The essence of this error of principle can be stated in terms of the multipliers on government expenditure. The standard Keynesian view would be that the multiplier on post-tax income was

$$\frac{1}{(m+s)}$$

where m and s are the marginal propensities to import and save respectively. The implication of the private sector expenditure equation was that, irrespective of the form in which it was paid out, nearly all the government's current account expenditure (other than the part that flowed back to the government in the form of tax receipts) would get spent. As a result, the only leakages from the domestic economy are those to imports, with the consequence that the multiplier was simply

$$\frac{1}{m}$$

This multiplier is, of course, larger than the standard Keynesian one.[12] If the Policy Group's view were correct, a model that reflected the standard Keynesian view would underestimate the effect on the overall level of output of a change in fiscal policy. Fiscal policy that had been planned on the basis of the standard multiplier would turn out be too strong and there would therefore be a need to take action to correct its excessive effects; but this corrective action would in its turn be too strong, provoking a need for a further reversal of policy to correct the correction; and so the cycle would continue. This was the pattern of events that the Cambridge economists saw when they looked back over the previous twenty years, and their story about the multiplier offered an explanation of it.

THE COUNTER-ATTACK ON THE 'NEW SCHOOL'

These propositions, which were described variously as belonging to the 'New School' or to 'New Cambridge', provoked considerable dispute and the Policy Group was attacked from all quarters. From Cambridge itself, Richard Kahn and Michael Posner, styling themselves 'Old School' Keynesians, criticised the propositions through the well-established medium of articles that were published first in *The Times* and later in the *London and Cambridge Economic Bulletin*.[13] Corden, Little and Scott, who in passing questioned the novelty of the propositions, attacked the policy conclusions on international trade.[14] John Bispham, who had long worked on the National Institute's model, attacked the Group's econometric evidence, and in particular the private expenditure equation, which he alleged had broken down 'massively'.[15] For various reasons, the 'New School' doctrines were rejected by almost the entire economics profession.

In some areas, the subsequent debate did succeed in taking the Policy Group's ideas forward; one area where this was so was the private expenditure equation itself. Bispham's assertion that this equation had broken down was accepted by Cripps and his colleagues, and they responded by recasting it in nominal (current price) terms rather than 'real' (constant price) terms.[16] One feature of the new equation was that it made the savings ratio of the private sector depend positively on the rate of inflation, a dependency that they saw as an essential property of any model that purported to account for the experience since 1974.[17]

In other areas, however, disagreements remained unresolved and this was nowhere more true than in the dispute between the 'New School' Policy Group and the 'Old School' Keynesians at Cambridge. This disagreement is important for us here because both the reasoning and the concerns of the old-style Keynesians were very close to those that were embodied in the conventional macroeconometric models and the use that was made of them.

Kahn and Posner's critique[18] of the 'New School' Policy Group sought to scrutinise the logic of its position in order to show the hidden assumptions on which it depended. Their argument examined the case of an economy that was suffering from unemployment that received a boost to its competitive position through a depreciation of the exchange-rate. The Policy Group's position, which was shown in figure 6.1, was that the ultimate effect of such a policy would be a rise in income and output but no change in the balance of payments. Kahn and Posner sought to challenge this by listing the various 'leakages' from the circular flow of income and expenditure that would follow the initial stimulus. The leakages fell into three categories: firstly, leakages to imports; secondly, leakages to personal sector savings and company sector profits; and, thirdly, leakages to and from the public sector, in the form of increased tax revenues, reduced unemployment and insurance payments, and reduced losses of the nationalised industries.

Old-style Keynesians believed that all three categories of leakages were important: imports would certainly rise, but, since there would be an increase in the saving (net acquisition of financial assets) of both the public and private sectors, the current account of the balance of payments would necessarily improve; and this improvement would be sustained. In contrast, the Policy Group's position, as Kahn and Posner saw it, required that the only leakage of any importance should be that to imports; only with this assumption would it be possible to obtain the Policy Group's 'ultimate' effect.

The dispute between the two 'schools' centred therefore on the second and third categories of leakage. As far as the second category (to the private sector) was concerned, Kahn and Posner saw the disagreement as being empirical in nature, relating to the magnitudes of various behavioural parameters that determined sectoral saving. But as far as the third category of leakages (to the public sector) was concerned, they saw the difference as being the altogether more fundamental one of whether the public sector deficit was independent of the overall level of economic activity or not. For this independence to hold, Cripps and Godley's phrase 'given fiscal policy' had to mean that,

> as the level of activity changes, tax rates, public expenditure policy and the pricing policies of nationalized industries are changed in such a way as to prevent the magnitude of the public sector deficit from being altered as a result of the change in the

level of activity. They might perhaps use such a phrase as a 'neutral budgetary policy' to describe such a bizarre policy.

(Kahn and Posner 1974: 23)

FROM CYCLE TO TREND

When we come to examine the Policy Group's model itself, we shall find that Kahn and Posner were correct in their assessment of what was necessary to obtain the Group's conclusions. However, what we are really interested in here is not the detail of the argument so much as the *type of question* that Posner and Kahn were asking. This type was as follows: given that these public sector leakages exist, at least within the realm of the 'immediate impacts' of some change in policy, how does it come about that their ultimate effect is nevertheless zero? The only way that Kahn and Posner could see this working within the Policy Group's argument was through measures taken by the government specifically to achieve the required outcome: immediate impacts turned into ultimate effects because of government action directed towards that end.

Of course, this type of question – of how immediate impacts turn into ultimate effects – was (and still is) a central part of the way in which macroeconometric models are assessed. The distinctive diagrams of the kind shown in figure 4.1 deal with precisely this type of problem: of how, to take one example, an initial increase in GDP following a stimulus administered through a rise in government expenditure is to some extent reversed or at least dissipated as a result of other consequent changes. A conventional model – or, rather, the proprietor of a conventional model – would have been able to give a precise answer to the type of question posed by Posner and Kahn, and the graphical output from a 'what if?' simulation would have been an important part of that answer. This challenge from the 'Old School' pre-dated the appearance of the Policy Group's model by as much as two years, yet even when the model did emerge, in 1976, no such simulations from it were reported. There is no technical obstacle to their production; therefore the failure to do so is evidence that the type of question such simulations answered was not one that was thought important by the Policy Group economists.[19]

Why was this so? One reason is that they seem to have thought that the ultimate effects of the type of policies normally considered by modellers were effects that operated quite quickly. They had spoken earlier of the models being valid in the short term – 'from one quarter to the next' – only; an inference that we may draw from this is that they believed that the immediate impacts would themselves be overwhelmed by the ultimate effects within a space of time that was still conventionally understood as the 'short term'. A second reason for their failure to take this matter seriously is that, once they came to believe that changes in fiscal policy would have no ultimate effect on the level of output, then the question of how the immediate impact turned into the ultimate effect became a problem of merely academic interest. What *did* matter instead was the course through time of the 'position' to which the economy would return once the effects had worked themselves out. This was a shift of focus from cycle to trend, and it was a shift that had been maturing within the Group's work for a decade.

As I explained in the historical overview in chapter 2, the Policy Group's model, and the research out of which it grew, was the result of a long study of the UK macroeconomic data that went back to the paper 'Long-term Growth and Short-term Policy',[20] which Godley had written while on secondment from the Treasury to the National Institute in 1964. The work had been revived after Godley had moved to Cambridge in the early 1970s, where the focus was on what was described as 'medium-term' analysis. In the use that the Cambridge Group made of it, this was a notion with two distinct sides to it. One side concerned the horizon over which forecasts and other conditional predictions were prepared. Beginning in 1972, the Policy Group began publishing an annual assessment of the prospects for the economy over the coming four years. The horizon was stretched to five years in the assessment conducted in 1975 and eight years in that of 1977. In this sense therefore, a 'medium-term analysis' simply meant looking forward four years, in contrast to the conventional short-term analyses, which sought to peer no further than eighteen months into the future.

The other side to their notion of 'medium-term analysis' involved the thing that was being projected four years into the future: it was not simply a question of running an ordinary model (albeit an annual one rather than a quarterly one) further than had hitherto been the practice; rather, the approach involved projecting into the future what the Cambridge economists believed to be the economy's *underlying trends*. The rationale behind this was that, over the four-year period, it was these trends, especially those for productivity and UK export competitiveness in world markets, that determined the 'feasible actual' movement of the principal macroeconomic variables.

It is assumed, therefore, that the actual pattern of economic events which we observe consists of short-term deviations about longer-term trends. In order to project these trends and make inferences about the future prospects for the economy, it is necessary to correct observed past series for deviations from trend in their determining variables and thus extract the under-lying trends.

(Fetherston 1975: 63).

Obviously, extracting the trends from the past data was the practical problem with which the Cambridge economists had to deal in order to implement their medium-term approach. But the fundamental point was their belief that the historical data could be viewed in that way, that is, as short-term deviations around a long-term trend. In itself, this is simply a characterisation of a pattern in the data, but such a characterisation is inextricably linked with a view that the under-lying trend acts as a centre of attraction from which it is possible to deviate but only for a short time.

In terms of the development of the Policy Group view, we can therefore see a shift in attention from one aspect of the decomposed series to the other. When we look back at what was being written by Godley, Cripps and Neild in 1973, we find arguments that draw their strength from an assessment of the behaviour of various macroeco-nomic variables, such as investment, stockbuilding and the balance of payments, during the particular phase of the economic cycle; the arguments therefore relied on the historical pattern of the deviations about the trend. In 1974, beginning with the evidence to the Public Expenditure Committee, the cyclical deviations were of interest only to the extent that they revealed the futility and self-defeating nature of the policies that had been pursued over the previous two decades. From that point onwards, the attention of those, such as the Policy Group, who were still committed to the old Keynesian goals of steady output growth and sustained low unemployment shifted from the deviations around the trend to the trend itself and its deter-minants. And it was to the representation of these trends that the Policy Group's model was devoted.

THE POLICY GROUP'S MODEL AND THE USE OF TARGETS AND INSTRUMENTS

It is in keeping with the chronological sequence of events to treat the model as the final stage of evolution of the Group's economic thinking. Although the Group had used a computer model (the 'Par' model) to support its medium-term analyses since 1972, it was only in 1976, when a number of important amendments were made to this model, that it became recognisable as *the* model of the Cambridge Economic Policy Group. These amendments included the introduction of the private sector expenditure equation as well as changes to the modelling of inflation, which allowed, for the first time, a full and proper treatment of the effects of devaluation.[21] The model also gained a certain independent existence at this point when the first technical manual describing it in detail was published.[22] It is also the case that there were few significant developments to the model after that date; the economics of the Group had reached a certain maturity, and once that stage had been reached there were naturally few amendments to make to the model.

As I explained in chapter 2, the structure of the model was markedly different from that of the conventional income–expenditure models that had preceded it. But the really significant thing about the projections produced from the Policy Group model was less the model itself than the way in which the model was used. In particular, these medium-term projections were constrained to satisfy a set of clearly defined targets, whose attainment was achieved by the use of a (necessarily equal) number of instruments. I shall concentrate on the results that were published by the Policy Group in 1976, since these were the first to appear with the benefit of the fully fledged model; but the pattern laid down at this time was altered little in later years.

The model results took the form of three projections, each one of which corresponded to a different policy regime: the first was deemed to represent a continuation of existing, or 'orthodox', policies; the second was a strategy in which devaluation was the principal means by which to secure certain output and employment targets; and the third used the control of imports as the principal means to achieve that same end. It was suggested that the projections were there to 'reinforce the verbal argument',[23] but in fact the model did a great deal more than merely 'reinforce', since by making explicit things that were previously only implicit it served to clarify some of the previously unresolved disputes that had surrounded the Group's position. The targets that the projections were constrained to satisfy and the instruments that were used to achieve this are crucial here; those that were used in the 1976 projections are shown in table 6.1.

Table 6.1 Targets and instruments in the 1976 CEPG projections

	Targets	Instruments
1.	Balance of payments on current account	Rate of sales tax on income-elastic consumption
2.	UK export cost competitiveness	Effective exchange-rate
3.	Level of money earnings at settement	Real value of the wage bargain
4.*	Numbers unemployed	Degree of import restriction on finished manufactures

* Fourth target and instrument used only for the import restriction projection.
Source: Fetherston (1976).

Although all four pairs of targets and instruments had a deep influence on the results produced by the model, the target for the balance of payments was in a class apart from the other three. That this was so can easily be seen from their respective roles in the different projections: whereas the other three targets differed between projections, thereby distinguishing one from another, the balance of payments target was common to all three projections. It therefore served to characterise the Policy Group's whole approach and it is indeed the key to understanding its conception of how the economy functioned.

The existence of this target reflected the belief that the British economy had, for a long time, operated as though it were constrained by the balance of payments; and this constraint would continue to apply in the future. As far as the future was concerned, this conclusion was based on an assessment of Britain's external financial position and the liabilities that it had already acquired, partly as a result of its borrowings from the International Monetary Fund. For there to be some net repayment of this debt, it was judged that the current account would have to turn positive by 1980. It is absolutely characteristic of the Policy Group that it should have arrived at this balance of payments constraint not as a result of some economic-theoretical analysis but rather as a result of a piece of national accounting.[24]

This target had the profound consequence that the normal sequence of model solution was in effect reversed. Normally (as for example in figure 3.1), GDP (or some similar measure of domestic demand) would determine imports and this, along with exports, would determine the balance of trade, this being the major component of the current balance. In the Policy Group model, however, the sequence was that exports minus the balance of trade would determine imports and this, via the propensity to import, would determine GDP. 'Determine' does not mean the same thing in these two sentences: in the first its sense is the usual behavioural one, whereas in the second its sense is that of determining 'that which is allowable, or permissible'. Given GDP, the Policy Group model would then determine the private sector's surplus; but, since the model had started with the surplus of the overseas sector (current account deficit), the sum of these two sectoral surpluses was equal to the public sector surplus. Public expenditure was treated as an exogenous variable within the model; therefore a variable was needed that would adjust to ensure that public sector income was at the level necessary to achieve the required public sector deficit. This variable - the instrument that corresponded to the balance of payments target – was the indirect tax rate. In the language of previous chapters, we can describe the revenue from indirect taxes as playing the role of the 'sink'.

What this sequence shows, with its use of the indirect tax variable as an instrument of the model, is that the Policy Group had in effect made the behaviour of the government endogenous; although government expenditure was still exogenous, government income was not. This manner of solution sheds light on the neutral tax policy that Michael Posner and Richard Kahn had deduced as a necessary condition of Cripps and Godley's argument; what the model reveals is the reason for that policy, namely the perception of a balance of payments constraint on the action of the UK government. It was not, therefore, that the 'New School' disagreed with the 'Old School' about leakages at the abstract level of reasoning adopted by Kahn and Posner; it was rather that, in the actual circumstances of the UK economy as Godley, Cripps and their colleagues saw them in the middle 1970s, changes in the net expenditure of the government beyond what would be permitted by the balance of payments constraint were simply ruled out as being, in practice, impossible. It is this awareness of the actual circumstances of the British economy, an awareness that pervaded the whole approach of the Cambridge Economic Policy Group and which manifested itself in the form of constraints or targets on the model, that made the Group's ideas seem so alien to other economists who were used to arguing in more abstract, yet more generally applicable, terms.

The other three targets, as I have already mentioned, took different values in the three projections and they therefore served to distinguish one projection from another. The projection of 'existing policies' was defined by a 3 per cent per year gain in export cost competitiveness, money wage settlements falling to 10 per cent per year from 1978 and, of course, no import controls. The 'import restrictions' projection involved no change in competitiveness but restricted imports in order to achieve an unemployment target of 900,000 by 1980. Money wage settlements, for the sake of ease of comparison, were set at the same level as in the 'existing policies' projection. The 'devaluation' scenario also eschewed any quantitative control of imports but set a path for the effective exchange-rate, and hence export competitiveness, that would achieve the same level of unemployment in 1980 as was achieved in the 'import restrictions' projection. Money wage settlements were held at an even lower rate of increase (7.5 per cent per year from 1977) than in either of the other two projections.

By virtue of their being targets, the balance of payments, the rate of money wages at settlement and the number unemployed operate as exogenous variables within the model. But it would be a mistake to infer from this that the Policy Group regarded these as policy levers that the government could set as it wished; quite the contrary, in fact, since the whole thrust of the discussion that surrounded these projections centred on the feasibility of actually achieving the levels for the instruments that emerged from the model. The role of the model was not therefore to demonstrate what would happen were the government to pull this lever or that; nor was it to show what would be possible; rather the role of the model and the status of the projections were to demonstrate what was necessary if certain goals, above all else a goal for unemployment, were to be achieved. The accompanying discussion, much of which was itself typically empirical, was then directed towards an examination of whether or not the necessary changes were actually feasible. It was on this basis that the Policy Group came out against devaluation on the grounds that what was necessary seemed quite implausible.

THE SCALE OF THE PROBLEM AND THE INADEQUACY OF DEVALUATION

Certainly, the inadequacy of 'existing policies', even in relation to the much-watered-down goal of 900,000 unemployed in 1980, was quite evident: from a little over 1 million in 1976, the Group foresaw unemployment rising to above 1.4 million in 1978 and to around 1.6 million in 1980.[25] In 1978 (by which time the forecast horizon had

111

been stretched to 1990), it foresaw 'existing policies' claiming 2 million unemployed in 1981, around 3 million in 1985 and no fewer than 4.5 million in 1990.[26] It is unavoidable that this should now be viewed as a forecast; and it certainly seems remarkably prescient, especially when allowance is made for the fact that, were unemployment measured now in the same way as it was measured in the 1970s, the number unemployed would be around 1 million more than the official figure.[27]

We should not, however, be distracted by the forecast question. What the base projection was intended to do was to show how existing policies were quite incapable of addressing the scale of the problem that would be faced. For a Keynesian committed to sustained low unemployment at even the pragmatic level of around 3.5 per cent, the inadequacy of existing policies was a conclusion that was robust to even quite enormous model errors.

But not only did the Group dismiss existing policies, it also in a similar manner dismissed the radical Keynesian solution of devaluation to secure sustained growth and low unemployment:

> The vital issue, both from the foreign and domestic standpoint, is how large a devaluation would be needed to secure an acceptable rate of growth of output and reduction of unemployment in Britain. As we shall now see, the scale of effective devaluation required is large and almost certainly impossible to implement.

> (Cambridge Economic Policy Group 1976: 15)

Of course, at the heart of the calculation lay estimates not only of price elasticities for exports and imports but also of the impact that devaluation would have on export and import prices. The Policy Group economists seem to have drawn these figures from other models, both within the UK (including the Treasury and the London Business School, circa 1972, as per the last chapter) and elsewhere. The calculation was also conditional on various assumptions about the future growth of world trade and therefore of the market for UK exports. The conclusion was that UK labour costs would have to be cut by up to 30 per cent in foreign currency terms in order to achieve the necessary boost, for which a 40 per cent devaluation of sterling would be required relative to the 1975 level.

Was this feasible? On the one side was the question of whether or not a devaluation on such a scale could possibly be brought off for a freely convertible currency under an international regime of floating exchange-rates. There was no precedent other than the franc devaluation in 1958 after General de Gaulle's accession to power. But even more serious were the domestic implications: import prices would rise 30 per cent and, even with wages growing at the (instrumentally fixed) rate of 7.5 per cent, domestic prices would rise by over 20 per cent in the first year after devaluation. The Policy Group foresaw that this would provoke enormous problems: profits would be increasing rapidly if devaluation was to succeed in delivering both cost advantages and profit incentives, while wages would have to rise by less than half the 20 per cent rate at which prices would be rising. Such a squeeze on real wages was, in the Group's view, inconceivable with the existing wage-fixing machinery; and yet, if wages were to begin to rise at rates approaching the rate of price inflation, then the gains from devaluation would be 'diluted' or even 'possibly destroyed'.[28]

Behind this assessment lay a model of wage-bargaining behaviour that was incorporated within the larger model but that was overridden on this occasion by the wage target and instrument. In later simulations this target was removed. But the treatment here, in which that relationship was used as one element of the basis on which the feasibility of devaluation was assessed, has the advantage of bringing out very clearly the conflict that devaluation posed: to secure even moderately low unemployment by this route, workers would have to sustain a nearly 10 per cent fall in their real wages. Nicholas Kaldor had not thought it impossible that workers would be prepared to accept *some* fall in real wages; this had always been seen as a necessary part of the devaluation designed to secure sustained growth and low unemployment. The validity of this judgement, though, would inevitably depend on the scale of the fall involved. What the Policy Group had done with Kaldor's proposal, as they had done before with the arguments of Richard Kahn and Michael Posner, was to show that what might be right in abstract, and therefore good enough in some circumstances, was no longer good enough in the circumstances of the British economy of the middle 1970s.

If real wages would not give, then even the radical Keynesian reforms of Nicholas Kaldor would not be able to safeguard the values of Keynesianism.

7

KEYNESIAN DEMISE
The rise of Monetarism

In the Cambridge economists' dismissal of devaluation as inadequate to the scale of the problem, all that was new in 1976 was the strength with which this judgement was expressed: after all, Wynne Godley and Francis Cripps had voiced similar doubts about devaluation a full three years earlier, and it was such doubts that had prompted them even at that time to call for a careful consideration of more radical alternatives, including import controls. In contrast, during those same three years the views of Jim Ball and Terry Burns on the role of the exchange-rate underwent a complete transformation.

Throughout 1972 and 1973, as we saw in chapter 5, Ball and Burns had strongly and repeatedly argued that sterling should be allowed to depreciate in order first to gain and then to maintain an improvement in the UK's international competitiveness. This course of action was intended to alleviate the perennial problem of the balance of payments constraint, thereby permitting a sustained higher rate of growth of output. Their advocacy of this policy ceased, abruptly, at the end of 1973 and the Business School economists were obliged to reflect on the failure of the policy that they had publicly urged. By 1975, they had developed an explanation for the failure of the old policy. The model was amended to encapsulate that explanation, and simulations from it were used to illustrate and support the explanation that they had developed.

It is impossible to overestimate the historical significance of this amended '1975' version of the London Business School model. Firstly, it marked the completion of the process of gradual development of the income–expenditure model that UK modellers, and the London Business School in particular, had been pursuing for nearly a decade. Secondly, the Business School's model now stood very close to the model of the Cambridge Economic Policy Group; Ball and Burns had been able to absorb most of the 'New Cambridge' critique of conventional policy making (and models). Thirdly, the new version of the model succeeded in accommodating both the rationale for the old view, which Ball and Burns had been advocating earlier in the decade, and the explanation for why that old view had, ultimately, failed. Fourthly, the model was open to two quite different kinds of interpretation: one negative, explaining the previous failure, and another positive, revealing a whole new prospect for effective government action. This gave this 1975 version of the Business School model a dual character that placed it on the cusp between Keynesianism and Monetarism.

THE INEFFECTIVENESS OF EXCHANGE-RATE CHANGES

The Business School's new view of the effect of a devaluation of the exchange-rate was set out in a paper – 'The Role of Exchange Rate Changes in Balance of Payments Adjustment the United Kingdom Case' – which was published in the *Economic Journal* in 1977. This paper greatly facilitates the task of giving an account of this model's properties and the interpretation that Ball and Burns put on them. Since there is invariably a delay in the publication of papers in academic journals, it should be noted that the model and the views really date from the middle of 1975 when the first version of the paper appeared.[1]

It should be emphasised that the representation of the new view through the medium of the macroeconometric model was accomplished by *amending* the old model rather than *replacing* it.[2] As a result, some of the central features of the older (1972) version were retained in the newer (1975) one and, of these common features, none was more important than the treatment of the nominal exchange-rate as an exogenous variable. Although by 1975 the UK had been operating under a regime of floating exchange rates for some years, the Business School economists were still not ready to incorporate within the model a mechanism that represented their view of how the nominal exchange-rate itself shifted in response to developments in both the domestic and international economies. Since the new version of the model continued to treat the exchange-rate as exogenous, what was at issue (in 1975 as it had been in 1972), was the response of the rest of the economy to an alteration in the nominal exchange rate; the major difference between the two versions of the model concerned that response.

The difference in the response can be stated succinctly in terms of the relationship to Kaldor's view of the role of the exchange-rate, for whereas the 1972 version of the model could be seen as representing that view, the 1975 version was built on an explicit rejection of it.[3] What Ball and Burns now wanted the model to do was to reproduce the result that 'with a fixed exchange-rate domestic prices will follow the world price level and following a devaluation domestic prices will rise by the full extent of the devaluation'.[4] This was explicitly justified as an attempt to replicate conclusions that were characteristic of the monetary approach to the balance of payments.

The way they went about this was to examine three alternative theoretical specifications of the wage–price equations in order to establish the conditions under which each would reproduce the required result: first, a Phillips curve for nominal wages and an equation for consumer prices; second, a Phillips curve for nominal wages and an equation for the GDP price deflator; and, third, the 'Scandinavian inflation model' with separate equations for prices and wages in the traded and non-traded goods sectors. At this stage, the Business School economists opted for the first of these; later they were to switch to the third.[5] They then succeeded in incorporating one of these specifications into the model so that the revised model behaved as required. To cast an abstract construction in quantitative form and incorporate it sensibly into a large, multi-equation model was a considerable achievement.

The natural way to see the consequences of the new thinking is via the quantitative results that were generated by the model and that accompanied the paper. Their chief features are shown here as three graphs, figures 7.1, 7.2 and 7.3, which have been drawn here using data from the paper. The projections, which ran for twenty-four quarters, are 'what if?' graphs in the standard style, showing the difference between a control solution and a second solution corresponding to the change in policy whose effect is to be illustrated. In this case, the policy change was a 20 per cent devaluation of sterling. Figure 7.1 shows the resulting percentage changes in consumer prices, export prices (in sterling) and wages and salaries per employee. Figure 7.2 shows the effect on real GDP. Figure 7.3 shows the effect on the current account of the balance of payments (in pounds sterling) for both this main projection (labelled 'I') and a variant ('III') in which all public sector transfer incomes, including grants and pensions, as well as the pay of the armed forces were indexed so as to rise in line with income from wages and salaries.[6]

We begin with the effect on wages and prices. As can be seen from figure 7.1, the immediate impact, in period 1, is that export prices rise by about half the extent of the 20 per cent devaluation (9.7 per cent), consumer prices rise by about a quarter (4.6 per cent) while wages and salaries rise by less than a tenth (1.3 per cent). Import prices (not drawn here) rose immediately by the full 20 per cent and remained at that level throughout the projection. These effects can be summed up as follows: the terms of trade deteriorate; real wages fall (by about 3 per cent); UK producers are more competitive in both home markets (15 per cent) and export markets (10 per cent). However, as time goes by, the initial advantages conferred by devaluation are gradually eroded. For example, by the end of the third year, further rises in sterling export prices have reduced the competitive gain to exporters to only 4 per cent, while further rises in consumer prices have reduced the gain in home markets to only 7 per cent. What is responsible for the rise in both of these price indices is the fact that workers have been able to secure rises in wages and salaries sufficient to recoup almost entirely the initial fall in real wages suffered as a result of the devaluation. By the end of the sixth year, export prices have risen by the full 20 per cent, while consumer prices and wage rates have risen by about

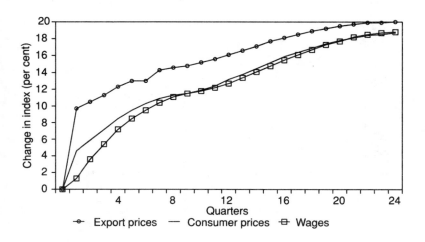

Figure 7.1 LBS model (1975): effect of 20 per cent devaluation on wage and price indices
Source: Ball *et al.* (1977), Simulation I.

18.7 per cent. The export competitiveness has vanished, while the advantage to those selling in home markets is now no more than 1 per cent.

Figure 7.2 shows the effect of the devaluation on GDP. The immediate impact on GDP is in fact negative (thanks to the fall in consumption due to a fall in real income) but, as exports begin to improve, so GDP performance turns positive, reaching a maximum gain of over 2 per cent early in the third year following the devaluation. But thereafter, as the initial gains in competitiveness fall away, so too does the gain in GDP fall away, to such an extent that it returns to its level in the control after five years and even falls below it in the sixth year. The inference that we are supposed to draw from these results is that, although the impact of devaluation on output over the first two years is clearly positive, the long-run effect is to all intents and purposes zero.

A comparison of the results in figure 7.2 with those drawn in figure 5.1 shows how the Business School's view of the effect of devaluation had altered since 1972. Initially, over the first couple of years, the effect is similar, GDP being around 2 per cent higher after two years than it would otherwise have been. Of course, the size of the earlier devaluation was somewhat larger (14 per cent as opposed to 20 per cent) so the effect shown in the 1975 model is correspondingly weaker. Beyond two years, however, the effects begin to diverge markedly.

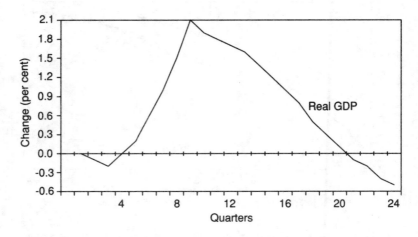

Figure 7.2 LBS model (1975): effect of 20 per cent devaluation on real GDP
Source: Ball *et al.* (1977), Simulation I.

The cause of this difference can be traced to the inclusion within the new model of a feedback from prices to wages, a feedback that was absent from the 1972 version. Ball and his colleagues had observed in 1972 that this absence would inevitably lead the model to understate the true effect of devaluation on prices, but they had nevertheless thought that, in spite of this, the model simulation was of the right order of magnitude.[7] That the introduction of a feedback from prices to wages – by which price increases prompt wage increases, which in their turn prompt further price increases – should lessen the long-run gain to competitiveness is therefore no surprise; but, by 1975, the Business School economists had concluded that even quite substantial initial gains in competitiveness would be eroded *almost completely* after about six years.

However, as figure 7.3 (simulation 'I') shows, the 1975 model continues to record an apparently lasting improvement in the current account of the balance of payments. The diagram displays something of the familiar 'J-curve' shape whereby the initial effect of a devaluation on the balance of payments is negative, the principal reason for which is that, while the increase in import prices is immediate, the changes in import and export volumes take time to come through. Once the effects of the improved competitiveness feed through, the balance of payments improves and remains that way throughout the simulation. In spite of the fact that the initial competitive advantage

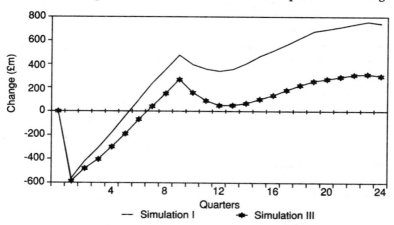

Figure 7.3 LBS model (1975): effect of 20 per cent devaluation on the current account
Source: Ball *et al.* (1977), Simulations I and III.

119

conferred by devaluation has disappeared by the sixth year, the current account is still stronger than in the control to the tune of some £3 billion. The alternative projection ('III'), which is also shown in figure 7.3, was designed to explain why this was so. This projection is characterised by the feature that all public sector transfer incomes along with forces' pay are indexed in line with wages. In the base projection, in contrast, these incomes remain fixed in money terms, with the result that the consumption from those incomes falls in real terms as prices rise. This sustained fall in consumption is what is chiefly responsible for the sustained improvement in the balance of payments. Once these public sector incomes are indexed, this fall in consumption disappears; and, as the alternative projection shows, when this disappears, then the lasting gain in the current account is substantially reduced: for example, the improvement in the final year is now only £1.2 billion, while the cumulative effect, corresponding to the effect on the UK's reserves of foreign currency, turns positive only in the fifth year after devaluation.

Ball and Burns pointed out the inequitable consequences of using this method to achieve a lasting improvement in the current account, for, while wage earners adjusted their earnings to changes in prices,

> those who receive grant income from government are not permitted to do so. In this case, the burden of balance of-payments adjustment is being borne by pensioners, recipients of unemployment benefit, etc. At the cost of inflation the balance of payments is indeed adjusted in the right direction, but the burden of adjustment is most inequitably distributed. In simulation III, when the inequity is corrected, not surprisingly the improvement in the balance of payments is largely con-sumed away.
>
> (Ball et al. 1977: 18)

In order to bring about a sustained improvement in the balance of payments, a devaluation must exert a squeeze on some elements of domestic consumption. If all sections of society are able to offset the initially negative effects on their real income, then the devaluation can have no lasting effect on the balance of payments. 'With free collective bargaining and no fiscal or monetary measures other than indexing government grants, the impact of an exchange-rate change is likely to be temporary.'[8]

We can find these rigorous arguments pre-figured in Ball and Burns' commentary in the Sunday Times. As early as August 1974, they had adopted a position that was the opposite of the one, which they had held less than a year earlier, of relying on exchange-rate depreciation to maintain competitiveness and thereby output and jobs. In the absence of an incomes policy, their calculations suggested that

> the long-term effects of an exchange rate change are primarily on prices rather than the level of economic activity. After a few years the effects of the exchange rate on competitiveness are simply washed away by higher money wages and a faster rate of domestic inflation.
>
> *(Sunday Times*, 25 August 1974)

At the time, this problem was analysed in terms of an imbalance between the number of targets (three, namely growth/employment, inflation and the balance of payments) and the number of instruments (only two, namely the exchange rate and fiscal policy). An extra instrument was therefore required and the Business School clearly favoured an incomes policy as that extra instrument. The message was repeated in a slightly different form in December of that year: the use of the exchange rate to offset different export and import 'income' propensities was possible only if it did not feed through into wages and prices; success therefore required that the domestic price level be controlled independently of the exchange-rate. On this view, the eventual success of the 1967 devaluation was now attributed to the success of the incomes policy that had been pursued between 1966 and 1969.

AFFINITIES BETWEEN THE VIEWS OF THE POLICY GROUP AND THE BUSINESS SCHOOL

There are many points where the Business School's new view and the understanding that informed it resemble the arguments of the Cambridge Economic Policy Group. On occasions, the resemblance was the result of a direct and acknowledged influence, but usually it was more a matter of an affinity between the two groups' ideas rather than a direct influence from one to the other. The affinity is not surprising: both sets of economists were working within the same empirical tradition, seeking to make sense of the events of the previous twenty (and especially the previous five) years through a Keynesian filter. Moreover, the Business School economists were assiduous in reviewing the work of a wide range of economists in order both to borrow from them where that seemed to bring gain and also to relate their own work to that of others. In view of its standing in the middle 1970s, 'New Cambridge' was naturally one school of thought to which Ball and Burns turned. The resemblances are not always quite as close as they might at first seem and it is the subtle differences, just as much as the similarities, that are of interest to us here.

The first point at which the influence of the Policy Group is evident concerns the sectoral financial surpluses. One of the main elements within the Business School's new view was the behaviour of these surpluses, and both the fact that they were now deemed important as well as the particular behaviour that the surpluses were required to display were openly acknowledged legacies of the 'New Cambridge' position. Unlike the 1972 version of the model, the 1975 version modelled these financial surpluses explicitly. In order to do this, a 'buffer' variable had to be selected that would ensure equality between the income and expenditure measures of GDP. Previously, as we saw in chapter 4, it was (implicitly) public sector income that had played this role within the Business School model, but in the new version, the public sector accounts were modelled fully and a different buffer variable was therefore required. Following Treasury practice, the Business School accorded company profits this role, although in the earlier version of their model this variable had been modelled directly via a behavioural relationship.[9]

The implication of company profits being the buffer that brought the income and expenditure measures of GDP into equality is that, in turn, it was the company sector's financial surplus that adjusted to ensure that the surpluses of the four sectors summed to zero. The published projection results included data on all four of these surpluses, and the Business School economists drew attention to the fact that their model replicated the 'New Cambridge' behaviour whereby the public and overseas sector surpluses tended to move together, at least after three or four years.

Secondly, the properties of the Business School's wage and price equations, which imparted to the 1975 model so much of its special character, were very close to the Policy Group's understanding of the determinants of these variables. The Cambridge equation represented trade unions as seeking (and securing) settlements that compensated workers for the erosion of real wages suffered since the last settlement.[10] The Business School wage equation modelled the rate of growth of nominal wages as a constant term plus the weighted sum of the rates of growth of prices in the current and three previous periods.

The weights on these price terms summed to unity, which implied that the long run response of nominal wages to a variation in prices would be sufficient fully to compensate wage earners for any changes in the rate of price inflation. The equation's constant term (which was interpreted as representing the historical average rate of growth of productivity) therefore measured the long-run rate of growth of real wages.[11] This equation could be interpreted as reflecting the fact that workers and their trade unions succeeded in securing increases in money wages that ensured a constant rate of growth of real wages; any increase in price inflation, such as that following a devaluation, would in due course be fully offset by a compensating increase in nominal wages. Domestic prices in their turn were modelled in terms of labour costs and import prices; this approach to prices was acknowledged as being similar to the normal full cost pricing approach used by the Policy Group.[12] When combined with the wage equation, this yielded the result that the long-run response of both consumer prices and nominal wages would be equi-proportional with the rise in import prices.

Thirdly, and as a consequence of the similarity in their handling of wages and prices, it seems as if the two groups both reached the same conclusion about the effect of devaluation, albeit that they presented the conclusion somewhat differently. Here is a case in which the difference is more important than the similarity. The way in which the Policy Group constructed its argument was explained in chapter 6: it began with a calculation of the fall in real wages that would be required to restore the UK's international competitiveness to a level at which unemployment would be returned to an acceptably low level; it then looked at the pattern of past wage-setting behaviour, expressed in the wage equation, to try to decide whether such a fall was plausible; on this basis it concluded that such a fall was 'almost certainly impossible'. The Business School, in contrast, presented the result in terms of the long-run effect of devaluation on prices (which it would affect) and output and employment (which it would not).

Two things are significant about this difference. The first is the weight that each group was prepared to put on behavioural relationships based on past data. Presenting results as long-run results, as the Business School did, gives them a certain air of universality, as if they are applicable wherever and whenever. Cambridge, in contrast, used the equation in a specific, quantified setting. The second difference lies in the fact that the Cambridge analysis was conducted with the particular question – how to restore unemployment to a low level –

clearly in view. For Godley, Cripps and their colleagues, the rejection of devaluation was preparatory to an argument for an entirely new policy – that of the quantitative control of imports – which, it was argued, would be capable of achieving a sustained reduction in unemployment and steady growth. In contrast, Ball and Burns' presentation closed the chapter on the long commitment to the policy of a depreciating exchange-rate to secure lasting improvement in the UK's international competitiveness; but, in so doing, it marked the end of any attempt to attain the goal towards which that policy had been directed. Instead, these goals simply disappeared from view; they ceased, in other words, to be an object to which the means that were represented within a macroeconometric model could be addressed with any hope of lasting success.

Both the Policy Group and the Business School faced this dilemma but they resolved it in quite different ways. Godley and his colleagues proceeded by retaining the old goal (of low unemployment and sustained growth) while abandoning the means (the exchange-rate). Ball and Burns proceeded by abandoning the goal but retaining the means, turning it instead towards a new goal, namely the control of inflation.

The consequences of this shift in the role for the exchange rate have permeated UK macroeconomic policy ever since 1979.

ON THE CUSP: BETWEEN KEYNESIANISM AND MONETARISM

It is not surprising that economists whose primary motivation was to provide policies to solve the problems of the moment should have turned their attention in the middle 1970s to the control of inflation. Between the end of the Korean War and the beginning of the 1970s, the annual rate of inflation in the UK had never risen above 5 per cent. Thereafter, it began to climb sharply, reaching annual rates of some 17 per cent in 1974 and 27 per cent in 1975 before subsiding to the still historically high rate of 15 per cent in 1976. Jim Ball and Terry Burns had always been well attuned to the latest developments in academic macroeconomics and they had long sought to relate their work to a wide range of macroeconomic thought; the paper on exchange-rate changes was just one of a number of papers in which they sought to communicate 'back' to academic economics. But this link to academic economics was not the end itself but rather the means to an end; the end was the advocacy and conduct of economic policy on a coherent, perhaps even a scientific, basis. The whole constellation of their activities points towards this: their base within a 'practically orientated' business school rather than a university department; the centrality of the 'systematic and modern' computer-based model to all of their work; their involvement in the completion of the Treasury's own econometric model; their platform within the pages of the *Sunday Times* from which they sought to address in plain language not just Treasury ministers, or civil servants, but rather a swathe of well-informed public opinion; and, above all, their repeated calls, dating from about 1971, for the vigorous pursuit of radical policies to reduce unemployment and secure strong economic growth. A commitment to putting forward policies to address problems rather than a commitment to a particular theory of how the economy worked is an essential component of the explanation of the Business School's change of view.

But, while the orientation towards policy helps explain what *prompted* the shift, it contains nothing that contributes to an understanding of what *enabled* it.[13] These were not hack economists, mere opportunists simply following fashion. Indeed, their initial public pronouncement following the collapse of the old policy was a sarcastic attack on those who now held that the government budget deficit was the root from which all the UK's problems stemmed. This was a scapegoat, they insisted, which conveniently allowed the nation to pretend that inflation had 'nothing to do with the nation's need to exercise responsibility regarding demands for higher money incomes, or to restrain price increases'. 'This blinding light', they continued, 'has produced converts who would have done credit to Saint Paul on the road to Damascus, such is their uncritical new-found faith; while those who have always adhered to the monetarist variant of this creed have enjoyed the comfort of knowing that they told us long ago.'[14] The Business School economists' whole reputation, the very basis of their participation in the field of macroeconomic policy advice and analysis, was founded on their macroeconometric model. What enabled their conversion was their success in representing both the new and the old within the model.

In their analysis of the effect of an exchange-rate change on output, employment, international competitiveness and even domestic price inflation, the emphasis throughout was on the temporary nature of the effect: following such a change, each of these variables would eventually return to its long-run value. The key point about this model was that it contained a mechanism, simple but nevertheless fully articulated, that explained the long-run rate of domestic (consumer) price inflation in terms of other variables: in the long-run, the rate of growth of domestic prices was equal to the rate of growth of import prices measured in sterling. An implication of this relationship was that in the long-run, under a regime of fixed exchange-rates, domestic inflation would equal external inflation measured by the rate of change of the index of import prices.

Looked at one way this is a negative conclusion in that it implies that the UK authorities can do nothing in the long-run to influence the rate of inflation under a regime of fixed exchange-rates. Looked at another way, however, it is a positive policy prescription for a country that has been suffering from a rate of inflation above that of its international competitors. For such a country, exchange-rate stability is a desirable intermediate objective since its achievement brings with it the promise of an eventual return to the international average. Beneath this lay the belief that the UK's long post-war experience of higher than average inflation had been due to changes in sterling's parity against other currencies, in the two devaluations of 1949 and 1967 and in the experience following the floating of the pound after 1972.[15]

And it is possible to go beyond mere exchange-rate stability. Import prices denominated in sterling are equal, by definition, to import prices denominated in foreign currency divided by the exchange-rate (expressed as units of foreign currency per one pound sterling). In the long-run, that is when all rates of inflation are steady, domestic inflation equals 'world inflation' (as measured by the index of import prices in foreign currency) minus the steady rate of change of the sterling exchange-rate. If sterling is steadily depreciating, the rate of domestic inflation is above world inflation rate, while if sterling is appreciating, then domestic inflation is below the world rate.

At the end of the piece on the 1975 model, Ball, Burns and Laury were prepared even to embrace the implications of this identity. With a floating rate:

> our conclusion would be similar to that of the monetarists in that floating the rate provides an extra degree of freedom to pursue a rate of inflation in the long run different from that of our competitors.
>
> (Ball *et al.* 1977: 23)

As a deduction from a very simple abstract model, there is nothing exceptionable here; but, as a statement from the Business School, it is remarkable for three reasons. Firstly, no model results were presented to support its conclusion. Without that, we have no way of knowing either how long (if at all) the economy might take to attain the new equilibrium following a switch to a regime of a steadily changing (appreciating) exchange-rate or what the scale of the consequences would be in the interim. Secondly, as a statement about a macroeconometric model, it makes no sense whatsoever: making endogenous a variable that was previously exogenous (which is what the proper representation of a floating rate entailed) would reduce rather than increase the degrees of freedom.[16] Thirdly, it seeks to shift the question of the control of inflation to the long-run. This is profoundly significant because the whole thrust of the argument hitherto has been to show that, in the long-run, exchange-rate changes have no effect on either output or employment. If an analysis of the control of inflation could be shifted to the long-run, then the inconvenience of having to consider its consequences for output and employment could be avoided.

MODELLING THE EXCHANGE-RATE: INTERNATIONAL MONETARISM

In spite of the fact that the 1975 model represented the effects of exchange-rate changes so clearly. it was not in itself an adequate model of them. This was because the nominal exchange-rate continued to be treated as an exogenous variable. Changes in the parity could be represented and the results that were produced accorded with the theories to which the Business School economists now adhered. But, in handling the matter in that way, the model was operating under conditions that had disappeared as long ago as 1971. The demands of realism required that the model represent the exchange-rate as an endogenous variable; but more than realism, the model needed further development if it was properly to embody the International Monetarist view. The Business School therefore laboured to redesign the model so as to incorporate within it a mechanism that would explain the exchange-rate of an open economy operating under a regime of floating rates. The properties and structure of this model, which I shall refer to as the 1978 version, were reported in 'An Exercise in International Monetarism'.[17]

Looked at superficially, the 1978 model still had much in common with the 1975 one: the income–expenditure framework with its sectoral disaggregation remained; the size was little altered; and, even though monetary variables were then rather unimportant, they were nevertheless present in the 1975 model. Changes in a small number of equations, however, served to alter the character of the model fundamentally. Although the old income–expenditure model remained, it was now placed in a framework whose principal concerns and interconnections related to prices and monetary variables rather than to output and employment. In this new framework, the exchange-rate played the pivotal role.

The first key change entailed the introduction of a three-equation sub-system that determined the effective-exchange rate and that related this variable indirectly to the government's borrowing requirement. Equation one made the UK's share, in international currency units, of the world money stock (the ratio of $E.M_{UK}$ to M_W) a function of the ratio of UK real income to world real income. This equation implied that, taking real incomes and the world money stock as fixed, a rise in the UK's money stock would be associated with an equi-proportional fall in the effective exchange-rate. Equation two then related the change in the UK money stock to domestic credit expansion and the current account of the balance of payments. Equation three in its turn related domestic credit expansion to a number of variables, notably the government borrowing requirement, with which it moved on a one for one basis. Taken together these three relationships created a chain that linked a rise in the government's borrowing requirement ($+\Delta PSBR$), via domestic credit expansion and the UK money stock, to a fall in the effective exchange-rate ($-\Delta E$):

$$+\Delta PSBR \rightarrow +\Delta DCE \rightarrow +\Delta M_{UK} \rightarrow -\Delta E.$$

The second key change concerned the wage–price sub-system. The pair of equations that gave the 1975 model its characteristic properties was replaced by a sub-system that approximated to the Scandinavian inflation model. This was one of the alternatives that had been considered but not used for the 1975 model. The key equation here was that the price of goods in the traded sector (identified here as exports), P_x, was equal to the world price of traded goods divided by the exchange-rate. In terms of their rates of growth, the Scandinavian model expressed wages in the traded goods sector (this identified as average earnings in manufacturing) as equal to the difference between prices and productivity. Further equations then linked wages, prices and productivity in the manufacturing and export sectors to wages, W, and prices, P, in the economy as a whole. This created a second chain that linked a fall in the exchange-rate to rises in export prices, wages and domestic prices:

$$-\Delta E \rightarrow +\Delta P_x \rightarrow +\Delta W \rightarrow +\Delta P.$$

The coefficients on the equations that made up this chain were such as to mean that, in the long-run, a fall in the exchange-rate would cause an equi-proportional rise in both wages and prices.

The third key change concerned the personal sector consumption function. The empirical problem that motivated it was the experience of the middle 1970s when the savings ratio rose at the same time as the rate of inflation rose. A consumption function with this property was introduced to replace the old one, which could not accommodate this empirical result. The theoretical justification for it was rooted in a postulated relationship between the desired level of nominal wealth and the level of nominal income. In exhibiting a positive relationship between the savings ratio and the inflation rate the equation performed in a manner similar to that of the shortly to be published 'DHSY' consumption.[18]

There are, of course, other links between the variables that appear in these chains, one of which is the accounting identity that, given levels for the real variables, takes wage and price inflation, through taxes and current price government expenditure, back to the PSBR. A full-scale macroeconomics model provides this type of link, which can be represented as:

$$(+\Delta P, +\Delta W) \rightarrow (+\Delta G_\pounds - \Delta T_\pounds) \rightarrow +\Delta PSBR.$$

Taking these three chains together, we can see that an initial increase in the PSBR works its way through the system to provide a further increase in PSBR, with the principal variables in this circuit, in order, being the money supply, the exchange-rate and domestic inflation. This loop is not closed – there are effects too on the real variables – and the fact that the mechanism has a positive feedback does not in itself mean that it is unstable. However, the Business School economists did emphasise the point that the model was now rather sensitive to the precise assumptions that were made about such things as tax rates and tax allowances; small variations here could, in an inflationary situation, feed through into large variations in the PSBR.

The effect that these amendments had on the model's performance can be seen from the results that were published for two simulations, one for a tax cut and another for an increase in public expenditure,

Table 7.1 LBS model (1978): effect of tax cut of £400 million per annum
(1970 prices)

	Year 1 (1976)	Year 8 (1983)
PSBR (current prices)	+£870m	+£2,610m
Exchange rate (year end)	−2.2%	−14.1%
Price inflation (annual rate)	+0.9%	+1.7%
Consumer expenditure (1970 prices)	+£122m	−£154m
Trade balance (1970 prices)	−£49m	+£145m
GDP (1970 prices)	+£66m	+£21m

Source: Ball *et al*. (1979), tables 4.1 and 4.2.

each of £100 million per quarter (at 1970 prices). Selected results for
the tax cut simulation, for the first and eighth years (figures were
reported for thirty-two quarters), are set out in table 7.1.[19]

If we look at the first-year effects, the reduction in taxes, which was
financed by a rise in the public sector borrowing requirement (note
that £100 million per quarter at 1970 prices revalues approximately to
£870 million per annum at 1976 prices), causes an almost equal change
in domestic credit expansion and hence an immediate fall in the
exchange-rate (−2.2 per cent in the first year). As a result, the domestic
rate of inflation rises, although there is something of a lag in this
effect. The cut in taxation leads to a rise in consumer expenditure,
although the marginal propensity to consume is only a little more
than one-quarter. This is because the rise in inflation causes a rise in
the savings ratio, immediately damping down the boost to income.
The trade balance deteriorates and thus the increase in GDP is less
than the rise in consumption.

The key to understanding the results for the eighth and final year of
the simulation is to note that the cut in taxation has set up a pretty
steady depreciation in the exchange-rate, at something under 2 per
cent a year on average (causing a cumulative fall of over 14 per cent).
The wage-price sub-system transmits this steady depreciation into a
comparable rate of domestic inflation (peaking at a little over 2 per
cent per annum in the second year and gradually falling away over the
next seven years). This in its turn is of sufficient size to ensure that the
direct boost to consumption administered through the tax cut is more
than offset by the rise in the savings ratio; consumption is therefore
down in real terms. The much improved trade balance all but offsets
this; in total the change in GDP is still positive after eight years,
although well down on the initial effect.

A VERY BRITISH MONETARISM

The interpretation that Ball and his colleagues placed on these results was that they showed both output and consumption to be either close to, or at least moving (albeit slowly) towards, their control levels.[20] If we are willing to accept this interpretation then it would seem as if this model succeeded in giving form to a Monetarist vision of how the economy operated, marking the culmination of the move away from Keynesianism.

The 1975 model had succeeded in demonstrating that, if enough time were allowed to go by, devaluation of the exchange-rate would have no effect on either output or jobs. This served to dispose of Kaldor's proposal for radical reform, which Ball and Burns had once lobbied for as enthusiastically as anyone, for exchange-rate depreciation to be used to secure competitive advantage for the UK so as to sustain higher growth and lower unemployment. The 1978 model completed this process by showing that, under a regime of floating exchange-rates, variations in the PSBR would have no lasting effect on output or jobs. Thus neither the traditional Keynesian instruments of fiscal policy, nor the radical Keynesian instrument of the exchange-rate, could have any lasting effect on the very variables that Keynesianism placed highest in importance, namely aggregate income and total employment.

Conversely, by giving form to Monetarism, this model can be seen as lending credibility to the three major tenets of the economic orthodoxy of the 1980s: firstly, that control of the public sector borrowing requirement is the key to the control of the money supply and hence inflation; secondly, that the exchange-rate is a key element within the mechanism by which inflation is brought under control; and thirdly, that this battle against inflation need have no lastingly harmful effects on output or employment.

This was, however, a particular, and perhaps even peculiar, form of Monetarism. All Monetarists would probably subscribe to the third of the three tenets but, since it just describes the wholly beneficial outcome that follows from the pursuit of Monetarist policies, it is the defining article of faith that is beyond dispute among adherents. The first two tenets, which relate to the means by which this happy outcome is to be achieved, are a different matter because here there is room for considerable dispute among Monetarists.

I could hardly believe my eyes when I read, in the first paragraph of the summary chapter [of the Green Paper on

Monetary Control], 'The principal means of controlling the growth of the money supply must be fiscal policy – both public expenditure and tax policy – and interest rates'. Interpreted literally, this sentence is simply wrong. Only a Rip Van Winkle, who had not read any of the flood of literature during the past decade and more on the money supply process, could possibly have written that sentence.

(Friedman 1980: 57)

This reply, from Milton Friedman, was part of long and detailed response to the inquiry of the House of Commons Treasury and Civil Service Committee into the conduct of monetary policy. Friedman here was attacking the primacy that was accorded to the control of the PSBR (control that necessarily was achieved by fiscal policy) in the fight against inflation. Yet this was the mechanism – PSBR and interest rates determine domestic credit expansion, which in turn determines the money supply – that was at the core of the Business School model.

What about the next link in the Business School chain, from the money supply to prices and wages via the exchange-rate? 'Do you agree', asked the Committee's questionnaire, 'that, for the UK under floating exchange rates, the principal "transmission mechanism" between monetary policy actions and the ultimate targets is via changes in the exchange-rate?'

I strongly disagree. Monetary policy actions affect asset portfolios in the first instance, spending decisions in the second, which translate into effects on output and then on prices. The changes in exchange-rates are in turn mostly a response to these effects of home policy and of similar policy abroad. This question is topsy-turvy. Floating exchange-rates are necessary in order for a monetary policy proper to be possible. They are a facilitating mechanism, not a 'transmission mechanism'.

(Friedman 1980: 61)

There are two conclusions here. The first is that the Monetarism of the Business School model was evidently far removed from – even quite at odds with – the understanding of the man who could reasonably be regarded as the leading Monetarist of all time. Really all that they agreed on – of course – was the fundamental article of faith, namely that the effects of a good dose of Monetarism would be largely painless and immensely beneficial.[21] The second conclusion is this: the Business School economists had to *interpret* economic theories in order to cast them in the form of a macroeconometric model; and they had always had to do so to some extent. The problem is to decide the legitimate bounds to interpretation.

THE CORRUPTING OF A MODELLING TRADITION

In 1979, the incoming Conservative government of Margaret Thatcher began to pursue economic policies to which the Business School's model could be seen to give support. Certainly, the Business School economists gave full support in the *Sunday Times* column: the 'fight against inflation' should remain the 'cornerstone' of strategy; continued monetary restraint, which was 'essential', would 'in due course' bring about a fall in the inflation rate; 'it would be wholly wrong for the government to change its policies now'.[22] This resolution was in spite of a forecast of a 2 per cent fall in GDP in 1980 followed by zero growth in 1981, with unemployment heading towards 2 million. Pessimistic enough in itself, this forecast proved to be far too optimistic in the light of what actually happened.

The recession of 1980 and 1981 showed just how wrong the Business School model was. In particular, the effect of a rise in the exchange-rate was not to bring inflation smartly under control with no harmful, lasting side-effects. Instead, it simply destroyed the international competitiveness of British industry, thereby destroying a large chunk of British industry in the process and pushing unemployment above 3 million. How did a mistake of this seriousness come to be made?

We can begin to see what is wrong simply by looking once more at the simulation results for the model and, in particular, the interpretation that was placed on them. Whenever the identification of a long-run effect rests on the interpretation of output from a computer simulation (as opposed to an algebraic analysis), judgement is inevitably involved. In this case, however, the interpretation of the effect was based on the self same theory that had been used to build the model. Any gap between what the model actually showed and what it was designed to show was closed down in favour of theory.

The weight attached to the theory was even more evident in the case of the second simulation shown in the paper, namely that of an increase in public expenditure. This simulation quite unambiguously produced a long-run increase in output. This increase was caused by the different import propensities underlying public and private expenditure, a shift to the former from the latter lowering imports. This could have been an insight but, such was the strength of their prior belief about the neutral effects on output in the long-run, Ball and the others preferred instead to disavow the result, claiming that it went beyond what could be reasonably inferred from such a model.[23]

When the long-run is tied down by economic theory, it is still possible for the econometric model to contribute insight into the matter of the nature of the path to the long-run and the time taken to approach closely to it. That, however, depends on the criteria used to determine the model's dynamics. In their account of the model, Ball and his colleagues indicated the influence of the new and up-coming 'time-series econometrics', exemplified in the DHSY consumption function, on their equations. In fact, however, their interpretation of what the new econometrics permitted almost beggars belief. It is to this that we now turn, as part of a more deep-seated assessment of what went so wrong with modelling in the late 1970s. What will matter here is less the econometrics – far less, in fact – than the interpretation and misinterpretation of the economic concepts to which the econometrics relates. Chief among these concepts is the long-run.

Part III

EVALUATION AND CRITIQUE

8

THE TURN TO THE LONG-RUN (1)

How soon is the long-run?

The turn to the long-run was the key conceptual shift in the macroeconometric transition from Keynesianism to Monetarism. Looking back over this account of the evolution of the income–expenditure models, it is easy to see the status of this concept, as measured by the frequency with which it appeared, increasing as the model developed. Thus, in chapters 3 and 4, which covered the establishment of the income–expenditure model and its early, and untroubled, growth, the concept of the long-run was not mentioned at all; in chapter 5, on radical reform, it made an appearance, although nothing of substance followed from it there; in chapter 6, under the guise of the 'ultimate effects', it began to appear often; while in chapter 7, the long-run was the recurring theme throughout.

The emergence of the long-run as the central point of reference of a macroeconometric model came about from the intersection of two lines of development. The first was the simple extension of the horizon over which policy simulations could be projected, from the short term, traditionally no more than eighteen months or two years, to a longer time-frame. This extension was made possible by the sheer power of the computer. Although the forecasts that were published still looked no further forward than two years, it was sometimes thought necessary to publish policy simulations over nearly ten years. Figure 4.1, depicting the GDP multiplier for the 1972 Business School model, is just such an example and it shows why this was necessary because, as can be seen (and as was mentioned in chapter 4), the behaviour of that multiplier in the third year and beyond is rather different from the value attained after just two years.

The second line of development was the revival of the equilibrium tradition within economics in general. Of course, the IS–LM was an equilibrium construction but, although it pervaded the textbooks, it was not the basis of the UK macroeconometric models. The income–expenditure approach, in contrast, was part of the alternative tradition within economics of the circular flow. These two traditions have jostled through two centuries: the motif of the circular flow goes back to the *Tableau Economique* of the eighteenth century Physiocrat, François Quesnay, and recurs within the work of both Karl Marx and Keynes himself; the equilibrium motif was given its highest expression by the neoclassical economists of the late nineteenth century, although it can be seen too, much earlier in the century, in the writings of David Ricardo.

The two lines of development converge at the long-run. In its econometric usage, the 'long-run' has a precise meaning within the context of a dynamic economic model expressed in algebraic form: the long-run is the position of rest towards which the dependent variables tend following some change in the independent variables.[1] In the graphs of the 'what if?' policy simulations, in chapters 4, 5 and 7, the long-run is therefore just the value at which the variable graphed there ultimately settles.[2] Where equilibrium economic theory comes in is as the basis for judging, or even specifying, what that value ought to be.

For the moment, I will leave aside the question of whether any of the problems of macroeconometric models can be blamed on the notion of equilibrium itself or the content of the equilibrium economic theories that were employed. Instead, I will concentrate in this chapter on the way in which the long-run concept was handled by the builders and users of macroeconometric models over the period when the old Keynesianism was falling back under the onslaught of New Keynesianism and International Monetarism.

The key issue that we are going to look at here is the time that it takes, in the modellers' judgement, to reach the long-run. Since the long-run is an expression that has two quite different meanings attached to it, it is unavoidable that we begin with a clarification of the concept itself.

KEYNES AND SARGAN ON THE LONG-RUN

In ordinary (non-economic) usage, the 'long run' means a long spell of time or a long time into the future. In econometric usage, in contrast, the 'long-run' is not a quantity of time at all but the value of a variable: the limit of a sequence. As such, the long-run has nothing *intrinsically* to do with time; the question therefore of 'when' the long-run is attained is (except in a few special cases) unavoidably a matter of judgement. For example, on the one hand, a model 'never' actually reaches its long-run value, in the sense that the sequence $\{1/_1, 1/_2, 1/_4, 1/_8, 1/_{16} \ldots\}$ 'never' reaches its limit of zero.[3] On the other hand, we may (arbitrarily) define a model to be very close to its long-run after just a short space of time, in just the same way as we could choose to describe terms in this sequence smaller than, say, $1/_{16}$ as being negligibly different from zero.

The fact that the long-run has nothing intrinsically to do with time means that it is neither synonymous with the 'long term' – a long spell of time[4] – nor even necessarily a phenomenon of it; neither should it be mixed up with the economic notion of the long *period*.[5] Indeed, in certain situations, we could reasonably conclude that the long-run was in effect reached within a space of time conventionally defined as the 'short term'.

With the revival of the equilibrium tradition and its reintroduction into UK macroeconometric modelling by the London Business School, the matter of 'when' the long-run is (in effect) reached became all-important: the quicker that it is deemed to arrive, the more relevant are equilibrium theory and the propositions derived from it. I now want to give three instances where this matter was explicitly discussed.

The first is a comment by Ball and Burns on a comparative study of the multiplier properties of various US macroeconometric models. The authors of the study, Alan Blinder and Robert Solow, had concentrated on the multipliers over three years, during which period one of the largest multipliers was that of the MPS model.[6] The Business School economists' comment was that this study had

> omitted to make the point that with full adjustment the multiplier in the MPS model will go to zero. By implication, one concludes that this fact is not regarded as significant in comparing multiplier performance on the grounds that the time period of full adjustment is too long to be of practical importance.
>
> (Ball and Burns 1979: 316)

The second example is Keynes' famous aphorism: 'in the long-run we are all dead.' The whole point of this sentence is that 'long-run' carries both of its meanings simultaneously. For polemical purposes, it is meant to be understood in its ordinary sense, which makes the sentence a statement of the obvious. As a substantive point, though, it is meant to be understood in its other sense, that is, that the long-run takes a very long time to arrive. This is clear from the context, where Keynes was attacking a simplistic interpretation of the quantity theory of money, that doubling the quantity of cash (n) would have the effect of raising prices (p) to double what they were previously.

> Now 'in the long-run' this is probably true. If, after the American Civil War, the American dollar had been stabilised and defined by law at 10 per cent below its present value, it would be safe to assume that n and p would now be just 10 per cent greater than they actually are ... But this long-run is a misleading guide to current affairs. In the long-run we are all dead. Economists set themselves too easy, too useless a task if in tempestuous seasons they can only tell us that when the storm is long past the ocean is flat again.
>
> (Keynes 1923: 80)

The last example comes from Denis Sargan's 1964 'Colston' paper and it is highly pertinent for a number of reasons. The paper from which it comes was the founding paper of the 'time-series' approach to econometrics, which has dominated British econometrics since the late 1970s, following its breakthrough at that time with the DHSY consumption function. Thanks especially to its 'error-correction' form, this approach helped to promote equilibrium economic theory within econometrics since it allows the 'equilibrium relationship' derived from that theory to appear explicitly within a dynamic equation. The London Business School economists explicitly signalled an allegiance to this approach in their 1978 model. Sargan drew his material from the Oxford model of Klein, Ball, Hazelwood and Vandome. What he did with this model that is relevant here was to re-estimate the wage and price equations and examine both their dynamic and long-run properties. As part of this, he dealt with the question of how long it took the long-run to arrive. This question, moreover, was addressed specifically with respect to a change in the exchange-rate.

Solution of Sargan's long-run equations for wages and prices yielded two relationships, for the indices of wages rates (w) and retail prices (p), each one of which was modelled in terms of an import price index (p_I), consumption taxes (T_i), unemployment (U), industrial productivity (R) and a time trend (t):

$$w = p_I + 5T_i - 0.22U - 0.58R - 0.015t$$
$$p = p_i + 5T_i - 0.18U - 0.58R - 0.010t.$$

For our purposes, what matters in these equations is the unit coefficient on p_1: following a change in import prices, and assuming all else equal, both wages and retail prices would ultimately change in the same proportion.[7] 'This means', said Sargan, 'that in this model devaluation has a purely temporary effect.'[8]

But an examination of the dynamics of adjustment towards the long-run led Sargan to qualify this conclusion. The dynamic behaviour of wage rates was captured by an equation that expressed the proportionate change in the wage rate as a function of an error-correction term (which is all that is important here) and other variables:

$$\Delta w_t = -0.054(w_{t-1} - P_{\mathrm{I},t-3}) + f(U, T_\mathrm{i}, R, t).$$

The interpretation of this equation is, again assuming all else equal, that the wage index changes by 5.4 per cent of the gap between that wage index one quarter ago and the index of import prices three quarters ago.[9] Even assuming, then, that the effect of a devaluation on import prices is immediate and full, it would take a full four years from the time of the devaluation for the wage rate to go 50 per cent of the way towards its long-run value and over eleven years to move 90 per cent. 'In the light of these rather long lags,' concluded Sargan, 'the force of the statement that devaluation has only a temporary impact is weakened.'[10]

THE ENCOMPASSING OF KEYNESIANISM AND MONETARISM

The attention that was devoted in the middle 1970s to the effects of policy beyond the original two-year forecasting horizon can be understood as a rational response by macroeconomists who had been working on policy to the repeated disappointments that they had suffered over the previous decade. These disappointments had stemmed not so much from a failure on the part of government to adopt their proposals as from the ultimately unsatisfactory outcomes of the policies that they had advocated that *had* been adopted by governments.

The Cambridge Economic Policy Group economists were the first of the macroeconometric modellers to make this point. The criticism, however, was an old one dating back to the 1950s and the complaint, made by Keynesian economists, that government mismanagement of the economy had caused the alternate booms and recessions known, derogatively, as 'stop–go'.[11] As we saw in chapter 6, Godley and Cripps now traced the problem to the models themselves. They acknowledged that the models were quite adequate in the way that they represented the initial response of the economy to policy changes; the criticism was directed instead at their failure to represent the very different pattern that would emerge ultimately. Similarly, the Business School's argument against devaluation as the route to steady growth did not involve rejecting their own older (Kaldorian) view of the way in which the economy first responded; instead, the modification of view related to the long-run effect of policy.

The difference between the Business School and the Policy Group was that, whereas Godley and Cripps believed that the ultimate effects came to dominate the immediate impacts really rapidly, perhaps even within a year, Ball and Burns represented the long-run as something that took more like half-a-dozen years to arrive. The great advantage of leaving the long-run that much more time to arrive was that it allowed the Business School to reconcile the old understanding of the effects of devaluation with the new. The 1975 model continued to reproduce the old view, but that view was now seen simply as a special case, limited to the short term. After five or six years, provided fiscal policy was neutral, the initially beneficial effects of devaluation on output and employment wore off almost completely, leaving a lasting effect on the price level only.

This can be seen as a classic example of intellectual advance through 'encompassing': both the new (1975) and the old (1972) models were capable of providing an explanation of the well-attested impacts of devaluation over two or so years but only the new model was able to account *as well* for the ultimate failure of that policy. Without entering into the wider question concerning its status as the hallmark of scientific progress,[12] we can see that the advantage of 'encompassing' was that it allowed Ball and Burns to explain how the initial impacts (which were widely accepted) turned into the ultimate effects (which were far more contentious).

In doing so, we can see them as answering the very *type* of question that Richard Kahn and Michael Posner had posed, without receiving a satisfactory response, to the Policy Group economists (see chapter 6). Kahn and Posner's question was a conventional one and the Business School could have answered it and used their model to support and illustrate that answer. The substance of the answer and whether or not it would have been accepted is immaterial here beside the point that a discussion *could* have been joined in which both sides understood the nature of the question and the nature of the answer that was required.

The 1975 model, and therefore the conclusion drawn from it, was far from being beyond challenge,[13] but it did succeed in accommodating two views, the Keynesian and the International Monetarist, which previously had been thought to be entirely antagonistic. It managed this accommodation by assigning them to two different time-frames: the Keynesian view to the short term, over the first two years, and the Monetarist to the point reached after about six years, and beyond.[14]

In a world of floating exchange-rates, this model was unsatisfactory in so far as it continued to treat the exchange-rate as an exogenous variable. The need to make the exchange-rate endogenous was therefore an entirely reasonable objective for model development; since International Monetarism was a theory that purported to explain the rate, it was certainly a potential source from which to draw inspiration for the design of the equilibrium properties of a new Business School model. The problem was, though, that proponents of International Monetarism saw its propositions as applying not to the medium term but to the short term. Thus the specific statement of the monetary position that Ball, Burns and Laury used to motivate even their 1975 exercise was that 'a country's price level is pegged to the world price level and must move rapidly in line with it'.[15] Rapidly? Even allowing that judgement is always involved, an effect that takes half a decade to appear can hardly be described as rapid.

This created a tension at the very heart of the Business School's move to Monetarism. The disavowal of Keynesianism – the explanation for the failure of the policy of export-led growth through devaluation – located the Monetarist effects in the medium term. The statistical basis for the result was uncertain, but the essence of the conclusion, that the effects of devaluation were temporary, had been proposed more than a decade earlier by Denis Sargan. This arrangement, though, was nowhere near good enough to provide a basis from which to argue the case for the pursuit of Monetarist policies to control inflation, since the model indicated that the cost of such policies would be some five years of lower output and higher unemployment.

With sufficient imagination, it is just about possible to conceive of an honest case being made for Monetarist policies that did indeed take these costs into account. Public and political debate on economic policy in Britain is not marked, however, by the sober assessment of the costs and benefits of alternative courses of action. Policies must be marketed as miracle cures. In order to market Monetarism in this way, the Business School economists had to play up the long-run; and the sooner it could be persuaded to arrive, the better.

A PRICE WORTH PAYING?

When the Business School economists wished to emphasise the benefits that were to be had in the long-run, they played down the invariably adverse short-term effects (on employment and output) of the policies that they were promoting. The best way to do this was to draw back from emphasising the point that the long-run was, at quickest, a medium-term phenomenon and to try instead to give the impression that it was itself of the short term.

When the thrust of Business School advice turned, around the end of 1975, to the control of inflation via the manipulation of the exchange-rate, specific policy proposals seem to have been of two types: on some occasions they were for exchange-rate stability and on others for exchange-rate appreciation. Broadly speaking, it seems as if appreciation was proposed (especially in 1977) when the immediate problem was one of mitigating existing inflationary pressures, whereas stability was proposed in those times (1976 and 1978) when the pressing problem was to prevent the re-emergence of those pressures. But we do not find these proposals being supported by arguments informed by a balanced, encompassing perspective. Instead, what happened was that the disadvantages that would be experienced on the way – the 'Keynesian' short term effects on unemployment and output – just disappeared from view.

This disappearance happened in one of two ways. One was simple neglect. For example, the first time that the case for exchange-rate stability was put in the *Sunday Times* column was in the spring of 1976: fiscal and monetary policy should be directed towards the balance of payments and the objective of maintaining a stable exchange-rate in order that inflation could be 'controlled in the medium term'.[16] This is an accurate interpretation of the properties of the 1975 model but even stability, if the choice lies between that and a depreciation, incurs short-term costs in the areas of lost output and higher unemployment. A strict case for stability would reckon with these and would present a basis for trading off the disadvantages against the long-run benefits.

On occasions, though, neglect turned into outright denial. At the beginning of 1977, authorship of the column in the *Sunday Times*, as well as responsibility for the forecasts, had shifted to Terry Burns and Alan Budd. Budd had been responsible for forecasting at the Treasury until 1974. The two set out their views on the conduct of policy and on the best means to achieve a reflation. Rather than loosen fiscal and monetary policy, a better way, they argued, to reflate an economy with a still high inflation rate would be to allow the exchange-rate to appreciate within fixed targets for domestic credit expansion. This exchange-rate appreciation would lower the inflation rate, interest rates and the savings ratio, and the lowering of the savings ratio would cause the sought-after expansion.

> Many will oppose increases in the exchange-rate on the grounds that the export effort and manufacturing industry will suffer. *We deny that. There is no evidence that attempts to manipulate the exchange-rate have had any long-term success.* If the exchange-rate is not allowed to adjust, domestic prices adjust instead. If the exchange-rate is allowed to rise, the result should be a fall in interest rates and an overall improvement in the basic financial position of companies.
>
> (*Sunday Times*, 2 January 1977; my emphasis)

While it was reasonable to infer from the model that attempts to manipulate the exchange-rate had had no effect in the long term, the outright denial of adverse effects on exports and output flew right in the face of what their own model said. The justification for exchange-rate appreciation that was given here involved denying consequences that could be expected to last for some few years. In emphasising the long-run in this way, the Business School economists gave a highly selective reading of their own model. Far from an argument based on the balanced perspective, encompassing both their old view and their new, this extreme position rested on the long-run alone. The old perspective was obliterated entirely. In so doing, Burns and Budd were consigning to oblivion the legacy of ten years of model-building.

Now, certainly, there were occasions when the adverse consequences of exchange-rate changes were mentioned.[17] However, in that same year (1977), Burns and Budd went on to advocate a 'longer-term financial plan'[18]. They made contact with the Conservative politician, Nigel Lawson, who was calling for something similar.[19] In 1980, as Financial Secretary to the Treasury in the new Conservative government, Lawson was responsible for implementing the fruits of that thinking in the form of the 'Medium-Term Financial Strategy', a strategy that was arguably responsible for the severity of the ensuing recession. Burns himself left the London Business School to take up the post of Chief Economic Adviser to the Treasury at the beginning of that same year. In personal terms, this was a considerable achievement.[20] Although the question of the influence of individual economists over the conduct of government economic policy is outside the scope of this book, it is hard to believe that clever politicians would not have seen the Business School economists' arguments as a convenient academic cover for their own designs.

THE 1978 MODEL: THE REPRESENTATION OF A VIEW

It is against this background that the 1978 version of the Business School model must be seen. It was not simply another stage in the development of the Business School model ('making the exchange-rate endogenous'), but rather one in which, for the first time, the long-run became the focus of policy. In order to support the case for the control of inflation via reductions in the PSBR, the model had both to exhibit the required long-run properties and to ensure that this long-run arrived as quickly as possible.

Perhaps, when they set out, they hoped that these changes could be accomplished as satisfactorily as the changes that had been made in both 1972 and 1975. After all, each of these models represented a view. In practice, though, this was not possible and the evidence for this is to be seen, not only in the model itself, but also in the defence of it that was mounted by its authors, Ball, Burns and Peter Warburton, to the effect that it represented a new approach to model-building.

Traditionally, they suggested, the model builder started with a collection of dependent variables; the programme of work was then directed towards finding the equation for each that was best in statistical terms; these 'building blocks' were then brought together and it was only at this stage that the character of the whole 'building' emerged. This approach was the one that Ball himself had enunciated in his review of the Cambridge Growth Project model in the early 1960s; it was the line that, hitherto, the Business School itself had followed. In contrast, the approach represented by the new model was one that started with a clear idea of the building and proceeded to seek the materials necessary to construct it. Ball and his colleagues admitted that this contrast, between the traditional and the new approaches, was something of a caricature, but even so:

there is a difference in emphasis between those whose models are more deeply rooted in what they expect the data to tell them and those who adopt what might be described as thinking more in systems terms, and therefore choosing specifications that are consistent with one overall view in preference to others that on other grounds might be seen to be preferable ... In practice, model builders will no doubt lie along a spectrum between the two extreme points of view. For the present, at any rate, we fall by and large into the category of those who are concerned to work from the overall view back to the detailed specification of individual relationships rather than the other way round.

(Ball *et al.* 1979: 88)

It is easy to see from the model itself why such a defence was necessary. Although the parameters of the model were estimated by formulae provided by statisticians, the mere use of such formulae in no way imbues the resulting empirical model with statistical validity. For that to happen, it is necessary that various statistical assumptions be shown to hold for the empirical equations in question.

In keeping with the practice of the time, the only evidence that was presented by the Business School to judge this matter was the statistic for the Durbin–Watson (DW) test.[21] Among the six new equations (three in the block linking the PSBR to the exchange-rate and three in the wage–price block), the only one that passed the test was the equation for the nominal wage rate. In two cases, the test itself could not be applied. In the other three cases – the equations for the exchange-rate (as a function, among others things, of the money stock), domestic prices (as a function of export prices and unit labour costs) and the minimum lending rate – test statistics, ranging between 0.47 and 0.54, showed conclusively that the equations had no statistical basis to them.[22]

Looking back over earlier versions of the Business School model, such values for the DW test are not unprecedented, although their sheer concentration in such a crucial area was without precedent. Here, though, the problem is more serious because an implication of a low DW statistic is that the discrepancies between the actual historical values of the dependent variables and the historical values predicted by the model tend to be in the same direction for a long time, even though they average to zero overall. This is quite the opposite of what would be required to substantiate the view that long-run equilibrium was restored rapidly. The transformation of the

Business School model into a vehicle for International Monetarism could be achieved only at the expense of forfeiting all claim to statistical validity.

Even after letting this go, there were still difficulties. Taken one at a time, the crucial individual equations were all designed so as to exhibit the desired long-run property. This was done either through the use of a suitable functional form (notably the error-correction form) or by the imposition of coefficients. Of the six equations, one was of the error-correction form while four of the other five can be interpreted as having had the necessary long-run properties built in to them through the imposition of coefficients reflected in the choice of independent variable. It is also possible to influence the speed with which the long-run arrives in an individual equation; *in extremis*, by the use of static equations (which imply an instantaneous long-run). Two of the equations were unambiguously of this form: the one for the exchange-rate and the one for nominal wages.

Yet, after all this attention, the model still failed to give a very convincing rendition of the Monetarist line. The simulations from the model, which were discussed in chapter 7, were by no means robust, being sensitive to specific assumptions about the details of fiscal policy. In the case of the government spending simulation, the results produced were ones that Ball and his colleagues preferred to discount. The problem that the simulations reveal is the difficulty of specifying equations one at a time. Individual equations – even sub-systems of equations – can be designed to behave as required, but this behaviour is always conditional on 'all else being equal'. In a complete model, however, all else is not equal but is instead determined somewhere in the rest of the model. In this case, the main 'else' was GDP; when this was determined simultaneously, the fragility of the Monetarist propositions became apparent.

THE UNANSWERED QUESTION: WHAT DETERMINES THE LONG-RUN?

Let me summarise the argument. The defeat of old Keynesianism was achieved by restricting the effects that it perceived to the short term only. For that to happen, it was sufficient that the long-run be reached after five or six years. The positive promotion of Monetarism as the 'miracle cure' required that the long-run be attained much more rapidly than that. The construction of a model to represent this new view necessitated abandoning any claim to statistical validity; moreover, the resulting construction was so flimsy and ill behaved that a disinterested observer might regard it as evidence against the view it was representing, rather than for it.

However, in dismissing the 1978 version Business School model in this way, it is important to recognise that what is rejected is the positive case for this particular brand of Monetarism. The earlier critique of Keynesianism, including the radical variant proposed by Kaldor and pursued enthusiastically by the Business School economists themselves for a time, is untouched by the 'failure' of the 1978 model. The thrust of this critique was that, when their long-run effects were examined, Keynesian policies appeared incapable of addressing the secular problem of the British economy's low growth and rising unemployment: fiscal policy was ineffective while the use of the exchange-rate principally affected the price level rather than growth. Even if we judge the Business School's whole critique, starting with the 1975 model, to be unfounded, there is, still, the critique of the anti-Monetarist Cambridge Economic Policy Group economists to contend with. The Policy Group's argument did not quite rely on the long-run in the same way as did the Business School's. It depended not on demonstrating the *complete* absence of any lasting effects but only on the fact that the scale of the problem was now too great, in the middle 1970s, relative to the size of the effect that conventional, or even radical, Keynesian policies could reasonably be expected to have. This raises the question therefore of what it is that determines the course of the underlying position of the economy through time. If neither fiscal policy nor exchange-rate policy can have any appreciable effect on the underlying position, how was this position determined and what, if anything, could be done about it?

9

THE TURN TO THE LONG-RUN (2)
Policies for the long-run

Throughout the last chapter, models' long-run properties were looked at in the context of an exercise in comparison. The question there was always one of how the economy's long-run position would *change* were the values of some economic variables to be altered; usually, these alterations involved changes in either fiscal or exchange-rate policy. Beneath these exercises in comparative statics lies the base, or 'underlying', position that is attained in the long-run. The London Business School addressed this matter directly as far as the price level and the exchange-rate were concerned, but the only models that explicitly examined the underlying positions of the real variables, and their path through time, were those of the Cambridge Economic Policy Group and Liverpool. Although the Policy Group was the first to look at them, Liverpool was the first to give them a name – the 'natural rates'.[1]

The importance of the economy's underlying position began to receive much more emphasis in the middle 1970s. To understand why this was so, we need to consider what the circumstances would be under which exercises in comparative statics conducted with standard macroeconometric models would, or would not, be sufficient for policy purposes. An exercise confined to comparison would be all that was required whenever the long-run effect of a policy was *large* relative to the problem that was being addressed. For example, suppose that unemployment stood at 500,000. If the government wanted to reduce this to 300,000, and if its economists believed that a sustained reduction of the necessary size could be achieved through a fiscal expansion, then neither these advisers nor their critics would trouble themselves with the question of why unemployment was 'still' as high as 300,000. Both sides would concentrate on the validity of the claim that the particular package of fiscal measures would bring about the desired sustained reduction of 200,000; and attention would also be paid to the side-effects of such a policy, for example an increase in the rate of inflation. But if, conversely, the long-run effects of conventional policies were *small* relative to the size of the problem, then the question of what determined the underlying position would be of primary importance. For example, if unemployment stood at 1 million, and if the best that fiscal policy could do was to reduce it by the same 200,000, then the question of what caused it still to be at 800,000 would be crucial.

A transition from the first set of circumstances, when the effects of fiscal policy were large relative to the problem, to the second, when they were small, is something like the process that took place between the middle 1960s and the middle 1970s. Only when the 'conventional' policies ceased to deliver an adequate solution, in the 1970s, did the underlying position become the focus of modellers' attention. This idea that the underlying position of the real variables was deteriorating – that the 'secular' trends within the economy were adverse – was precisely what motivated both Liverpool and Cambridge to switch their attention to the question of what determined this position. Here is Liverpool:

> Surprising though it seems on reflection, very little of macro-economics is devoted to explaining y^* and e^* [the natural rates of output and employment], and the implied natural rate of unemployment. Nevertheless, the new classical analysis has, when confronted by the UK post-war experience, driven the Liverpool Research Group into formulating an explanation of the natural rates and integrating it into the Liverpool Model. The reason is plain – UK unemployment has risen steadily and dramatically since the mid-1960s, apparently (and certainly according to the model) quite independently of the business cycle. A group concerned with policy towards unemployment needs must develop such an explanation.
>
> (Minford *et al.* 1984: 33)

Macroeconomics may have had little to say about it, but the Policy Group economists had been preoccupied with this very matter for over a decade. Here is an example of how they saw the problem, taken from a piece that, it should be noted, drew attention to the fact that the Group had been advancing this kind of analysis since 1972:

While during the past 25 years the changes in the direction of policy, at the time they were made, had come to seem inevitable, there were underlying trends of a most disturbing kind continuously at work which should have been apparent ... Since 1960, exports have risen at 4–8% *per annum*, whereas imports have risen at 8–12% *per annum*. Exports were so much higher at the beginning of the period than imports that for many years the absolute gap between the two was roughly constant. But the continuation of past trends of imports of manufactures relative to exports would more recently have meant that the gap would close and that imports would come to exceed exports by a large margin. The necessary consequence is that growth of GDP has had to be sacrificed to hold down growth of imports and protect the balance of payments ... So far as unemployment goes the picture is a clear one; after remaining nearly stable and very low until about 1965 there has been a marked, indeed sensational, turn for the worse.

(Cambridge Economic Policy Group 1978: 2–3)

The main business for this chapter is to explain how both Liverpool and the Cambridge Economic Policy Group represented the underlying path of output (and other real variables) in their models and to assess whether these models gave any legitimate support to the case that each was trying to make for policies designed to alter that path in the future. In order to do this, a certain amount of detailed analysis of each model is required. Its end result, in each case, is a rather simple expression of all the factors involved. In part, this is why it is worth the trouble to dwell on the detail, but in part also it is why the detail is necessary since it is vital to try to show that such simple expressions fairly represent the essentials of each model on this question.

In the light of the attention devoted by Liverpool and Cambridge, it is initially surprising that the London Business School economists did not focus on this problem too. This is particularly so in view of the fact that a major point of the International Monetarist model was that neither fiscal nor exchange-rate policy had any lasting effect at all on output or employment. Why this question was not of interest, and the implications of this, will be looked at briefly. Finally, I will discuss the factors that each model *left out* of its explanation of the secular decline of the UK economy.

MODELLING THE ECONOMY'S UNDERLYING POSITION

The first step is to look at the way in which models of the 'underlying' position are constructed. This position is an abstraction, from which the actual position of the economy generally differs, and it must therefore be defined by those who are attempting to analyse it. This is accomplished by the use of one (or more) conditions of an equilibrium-like nature that, crucially, are not believed to characterise the economy's actual position. The underlying position, at some point in time, is therefore where the economy would be were these conditions to hold exactly.

The conditions themselves can be either economic (for example, that all expectations are fully realised) or mathematical (the steady-state) or a combination of both. Models of the underlying position can therefore be thought of as models of the economy's actual position onto which these equilibrium conditions are grafted. How did the Policy Group and Liverpool define the underlying position?

The definition employed by the Policy Group was purely economic. The main condition used took the form of a constraint on the balance of payments: at different times, either the current balance or the basic balance.[2] Speaking loosely, the underlying levels of GDP and employment are those that would pertain were the value of exports to equal the value of imports.[3] Except for the Group's devaluation projection, the underlying position was further defined by the condition that the exchange-rate should adjust so as to maintain constant cost competitiveness in export markets. As I showed in chapter 6, these conditions on export cost competitiveness and the balance of payments were two of the four targets that were imposed on the model but were not part of it. If we observe this distinction, then the Policy Group's model represented the actual position of the economy. However, since all published projections observed at least the balance of payments condition, these projections were always of the underlying position.[4]

In contrast, the Liverpool model defined the underlying position, or natural rates, using both economic and mathematical conditions. The key to understanding the way this worked is to visualise the Liverpool model as being made up of two related but distinct sub-models, one of the actual path of the economy (the 'macro' model) and the other of the four natural rate variables (the 'supply side'). The natural rate variables were output (y^*_t), unemployment (U^*_t), the real exchange-rate (RXR^*_t) and real wages (W/P^*_t). The natural rate sub-model was derived as the steady-state (static) solution to four equations in the 'macro' model with two further economic conditions imposed besides: firstly, a zero trade balance and, secondly, equality between the actual price level at time t and the expectation, one period earlier, of that level. The second condition is a natural choice for a 'rational expectations' model; the first is a very strong echo of the condition that was employed by the Policy Group. With natural rate variables present in the model in their own right – quite distinct, it should be noted, from their 'macro' counterparts, y_t, U_t, RXR_t and W/P_t, which describe the actual values of output, unemployment, the real exchange-rate and real wages at time t – it is possible both to obtain projections of the underlying position and to analyse the factors that determine it. As Minford and his colleagues noted, the consequence of this dual treatment was that it made the model able to track 'not merely the business cycle but also the evolution of the "secular trends"'.[5] In its ability to do this, the Liverpool model was unique.

EXPLAINING THE ECONOMY'S UNDERLYING POSITION

Obviously, both Liverpool and the Policy Group were interested in modelling the underlying position and its evolution through time in order to represent measures by which that path could be altered. Fortunately, we can find straightforward expressions for these underlying paths for both these models that display all the factors involved quite clearly.

The starting point for this analysis of the Policy Group model is the balance of payments condition. In itself, all that this says is that 'exports' (X) minus underlying 'imports' (M^*) divided by the terms of trade[6] (TT) must equal some target (B):

$$B = (X - \frac{M}{TT})$$

M^* is, by definition, equal to underlying output (Q^*) multiplied by the average propensity to import (m), so:

$$Q^* = TT \cdot \frac{(x - B)}{m}$$

154

The key question is the way in which X, m and TT are determined, because on this depends the model's ability to explain *how* the future course of Q^* can be improved. In the Policy Group's model, these variables are governed by four sets of factors:[7] firstly, various deterministic time trends (one per behavioural equation); secondly, the volume of world trade (WT); thirdly, three terms reflecting the price of UK goods relative to the price of competing goods (exports of goods and services, imports of semi-finished manufactures, and imports of finished manufactures); and, fourthly, the quantitative import control 'instrument' variable (μ_{CON}). The price terms in their turn depend on: an index of the UK's export cost competitiveness $(E.RFC)$, where E is the effective exchange-rate; the world terms of trade (TT_W);[8] and tax rates on exports (t_x) and imports (t_m).

This collection of structural equations, in the balance of payments section of the Policy Group's model, can be reduced to one single equation, which expresses underlying output in terms of the exogenous variables of the model. This relationship, which is linear in either the variables or their natural logarithms, is composed as follows (note that this assumes that the target (B) equals zero):[9]

$$Q^* = f\{TREND, -(\mu - \mu_{CON}), +WT, -TT_W, +t_m, -t_x, +(E.RFC)\}$$

The signs attached to the variables in this equation express the direction in which Q^* will change as the variable changes: thus, world trade, tax rates on imports and export cost competitiveness are positively related to output, while the world terms of trade and tax rates on exports are negatively related. The term $(\mu - \mu_{CON})$ works as follows: μ is the average import propensity if export cost competitiveness is equal to unity and taxes on imports are zero; μ_{CON} reflects the degree of quantity control on imports with a value of zero corresponding to the absence of such controls. As μ_{CON} increases so Q^* increases.

The final point here on the Policy Group model concerns the export cost competitiveness term $(E.RFC)$. Although relative factor cost in 'own' price terms (RFC) is an endogenous variable, the combined term is in effect exogenous. This comes about from the way in which the model was used: a value for $(E.RFC)$ was one of the four targets (or conditions) imposed on the model and the exchange rate (E) was the instrument used to achieve it.

Turning now to the Liverpool model, I mentioned before that the key to understanding this model was to visualise it as containing two linked, but nevertheless separate, parts. The great thing here is that the nature of the relationship between the two parts is such as to allow us to look at the natural rates without having to deal with the 'macro' part, for, whereas endogenous variables pertaining to the actual economy depend on natural rate variables, natural rate variables (which are all endogenous) depend only on each other and on exogenous variables. As well as the usual deterministic elements (intercept and trend), these explanatory variables are as follows: a measure of real unemployment benefits (B); the average amount lost in taxes and national insurance by a married man with two children (T_L); national insurance contributions paid by employers (T_F); the working population (POP); the trade-unionisation rate (UNR); and the volume of world trade (WT).[10]

In the model, the four equations are written down in such a way as to make each natural rate variable depend on at least one other natural rate variable (that is, the equations appear in structural form). But thanks to the linearity of this system of four equations, we can substitute out to obtain four equations, one for each of the natural rate variables, in which the only right-hand side variables are exogenous variables (that is, the reduced form). I shall just concentrate here on the equation for Q^*, but there are similar equations for RXR^*, U^* and W/P^*. The equation for the natural rate of output, which is linear in the variables or their natural logarithms, is:[11]

$$Q^* = f\{TREND, -(b + T_L), -T_F, +POP, -UNR, +WT\}.$$

Again, the signs attached to the variables indicate the direction in which a change in the variable affects Q^*. Thus, increases in the working population and world trade cause the natural rate of output to rise, while increases in unemployment benefits, employee taxes paid by employers, income taxes, and the level of trade unionization cause the natural rate of output to fall.

Before taking this further, we need to look briefly at the London Business School model. The first point about it is that, unlike the other two, this model explicitly represented only the *actual* position of the economy.[12] However, since the key International Monetarist properties applied to the long-run, it is reasonable to regard the underlying position as being defined, implicitly, by the mathematical condition of the steady-state.

Inspection of the model[13] confirms that deterministic components, along with world trade and various terms-of-trade variables, would all have been involved. These, though, are not within the province of the UK authorities to alter and clearly do not constitute means by which the underlying path of the real variables might be altered. In comparison with the Policy Group model, the Business School model did not contain an import control variable or import tariffs. It appears, in fact, that there were no variables that could perform this role.

Evidence for this interpretation is to be found in a contemporary paper by Ball and Burns on the subject of long-run portfolio equilibrium and balance of payments adjustment. This paper contained an abstract discussion supported by simulations from a small, almost 'toy', twenty-equation computerised model.[14] In the paper, the long-run level of output was modelled in the most rudimentary fashion possible – as a constant. The abstract analysis was one step more advanced in treating it as a constant rate of growth. Both cases, though, were deterministic; neither of them therefore admitted any possibility of changing the value.

The explanation for this failure to examine the underlying position of these variables is, of course, that the very question itself had ceased to be important to the London Business School economists. In effect, when they abandoned the exchange-rate, in 1975, as an instrument by which to achieve a sustained, higher rate of growth, it was not only the instrument that went but the objective too.

POLICIES FOR THE LONG-RUN: IMPORT CONTROLS VS. THE SUPPLY SIDE

What should we make of the explanations of the secular trends contained in the Liverpool and Policy Group models and their implications for policy? To aid this discussion, table 9.1 summarises the explanatory factors as they appear in the two models. The elements shown there are divided into four groups. The first of these is the deterministic component; the others are categorised according to whether they are internal to the UK, external to it, or whether they mediate between the UK and the rest of the world. Within each category, variables are grouped according to whether they are positively or negatively related to underlying output.

The main thing that this table shows is that the fundamental difference between Liverpool and the Policy Group concerned the location of the means for solving the adverse underlying trends in the UK economy. Clearly, neither the deterministic component nor external factors offer any means by which an improvement might be achieved, however much they may contribute both to the explanation of past trends and to the likely course of future events. The only

Table 9.1 Factors explaining the underlying path of UK output (by category and direction of effect)

Variable by category	Model	
	CEPG	LPL
1. *Deterministic factors*	+	+
2. *External factors*		
World trade	+	+
World terms of trade	−	
3. *Internal factors*		
Working population		+
Employee taxes; income taxes; trade unionisation; social security benefits		−
4. *Intermediating factors*		
Import taxes; export cost competitiveness; import controls	+	
Export taxes	−	

variables that could possibly be used to alter that future course are the ones shown here in the third and fourth categories, that is, the internal variables and those intermediary variables that are controlled by the UK. The point is that it is to internal variables that Liverpool looked while the Policy Group relied on the intermediary ones.

This must place a question-mark over the Cambridge Economic Policy Group's analysis of the phenomenon of the UK's secular decline. Without for one moment accepting Liverpool's view of what the relevant factors are, the idea that *some* internal factors might be responsible is one that seems overwhelmingly likely. The external situation facing each one of the western European and northern American economies has certainly been far more hostile in the fourth quarter of this century than it was during most of the third; yet some have coped better than others and internal factors must be pertinent in explaining this difference.

However, the real difficulty with this model concerns the way in which it represented the effects of the strategy of import controls, a strategy with which the Policy Group is inextricably associated. The way in which the effect of import controls was represented in the model was by an intercept adjustment term that served to scale up or down the quantity of imports of finished manufactures to the UK business sector. The limitation with the use of an intercept adjustment to represent a policy variable is that it necessarily restricts the wider effects of that policy to those that are transmitted by the dependent variable in question – in this case, the quantity of imported finished manufactures. In the Policy Group model, this quantity affected neither the terms of trade nor the volume of exports. As a result, thanks to the fact that the model was solved under a balance of payments condition, a reduction of imports via import controls inevitably meant higher output and employment.

But this type of demonstration was unconvincing because the very construction of the model ruled out the question that is at the heart of the dispute about protection, namely whether or not protection has any adverse effects on the efficiency of domestic industry. Were the model to have included channels that represented the paths along which these adverse effects were transmitted, there would still have been an argument about the merits of protection but it would then have been one that was concerned with the *magnitudes* of the effects involved.

Moreover, this is precisely how devaluation was handled by this model. The mechanism internal to the economy by which changes in the exchange-rate were transmitted to nominal wages and then prices not only was well represented but had also been the subject of intensive research by economists within the Group since its inception. As a result, the alternative strategy of devaluation was analysed by the model but ruled out on the grounds that the magnitudes involved were such as to be implausibly large.

For import controls, no quantitative justification was available because the model did not represent the arguments that the opponents of import controls were making. Without some representation of the way in which industry would react, the import control projections in effect presupposed the very things that were at issue in the strategy.

In principle, as table 9.1 shows, the model contained two other variables besides import controls that could make a difference: higher import tariffs and a higher level of export cost competitiveness achieved via the exchange-rate. The latter had, as we saw in chapter 6, been ruled out as being infeasible; projections of both conventional policies and import controls were based on the assumption that the exchange-rate could adjust to whatever level was required to maintain a constant level of export price competitiveness. Although the model could represent the effect of import tariffs (via changes in the price of imports relative to the price of domestically produced goods), no projections based on tariff variation were published by the Policy Group.

The Policy Group's consistent advocacy of the strategy of import controls began in 1975 and was to continue until the research funding for its model ceased in the early 1980s. The majority of professional economists regarded the strategy as a heresy; but what the Group was involved in was far more than just an academic squabble. The strategy was at odds with both GATT and the regulations of the European Community. In the middle 1970s, the United Kingdom's continued membership of the Community was still an open issue. The import control strategy was an element within the 'Alternative Economic Strategy' of the Labour party's left wing. Francis Cripps served as an adviser to the leading politician of the parliamentary left, Tony Benn. That this constituency should be attracted to an approach in which import controls were presented as the means by which to restore and maintain low unemployment is all too understandable.

In every sense, the argument that Minford and his colleagues put forward for the cure of low output growth and rising unemployment was the complete opposite of the Policy Group's. This was nowhere more true than in the colour of their politics, which was unashamedly right wing. The key feature of the Liverpool model's explanation of the phenomena was that the effect of the variables that harmed the natural rates, namely trade unionisation, benefits, employers' labour taxes and income taxes, was strong. This strength is particularly evident as far as their effects on the natural rate of unemployment are concerned: a 10 percent rise in the real level of benefits is sufficient to cause unemployment to rise by almost one-third; an increase in the trade unionisation rate of 2 percentage points increases unemployment by almost a quarter; and 4 percentage points on income tax, or 2 percentage points on employers' labour taxes, would increase unemployment by more than one-tenth.[15] The supposed policy implications of all this, especially as far as trade unions and social security benefits are concerned, are unambiguous.

The Liverpool model is not vulnerable to the same types of criticism as those advanced against the Policy Group; in particular, it did contain a representation of the internal mechanism by which these effects were supposed to come about and it did not employ an intercept shift as its principal policy instrument. Even so, there is no more reason to believe this model's account of what could be done to arrest and reverse the rise in unemployment than there was to believe the Policy Group's remedy.

The principal reason for this is that no evidence was put forward to substantiate the scale of the effects that these exogenous variables were claimed to have on the natural rate variables. Although the coefficients of the 'macro' part of the model were estimated, the coefficients of the natural rate equations were not; we have seen already how they were obtained, as a result of the algebraic process that created those equations. Since the natural rate equations form a closed, linear system, the practicalities of testing whether the system is a statistically adequate representation of the historical data is straightforward; tests undertaken show that it is not.[16] But this result is no surprise since the Liverpool economists never pretended that their model would do well on this score:

> It must be stressed that the model is intended to represent what we believe;[17] it has not been our intention to *test* the model against past data, rather to use this data to help parameterise the model so that it can be tested by us in forecasting the future.
> (Minford *et al.* 1984: 42)

If the model represented a view, then we might at least have expected it to do so consistently; but this was not so according to Steve Nickell, who argued that the very strong effects for unionisation and benefits arose precisely because the Liverpool model did not include a crucial trend-like variable (labour productivity) that nevertheless appeared in the theoretical specification on which the model was based. This in fact was just one of a number of such variables that failed to appear in the computer model, but it was the most important. 'Minford's estimates', concluded Nickell, 'are vastly too large simply because of his use of an estimated model which is mis-specified relative to his own theory.'[18] For a model that purported to represent a view, this seems a particularly damning observation.

REPRESENTING A VIEW: SHOULD WE BELIEVE MACROECONOMETRIC MODELS?

It is difficult to detect any real difference between the defences of Minford – 'the model is intended to represent what we believe; it has not been our intention to test it against past data' – and Ball and Burns – 'we fall by and large into the category of those who are concerned to work from the overall view back to the detailed specifications rather than . . . those whose models are more deeply rooted in what they expect the data to tell them'.[19] In each case, the model was an expression of belief and both teams of economists freely admitted that they had gone ahead and created their computer models even where they were unable to reconcile the beliefs with past data.

Up to a point, it is entirely proper that a macroeconometric model should be constructed so as to 'represent a view' of how the economy works in order to promote the case for some particular policy or strategy. Every model is inevitably partial and highly simplified. Given certain phenomena to be explained, the model builder has to select the factors that he or she believes to be the important ones. Necessarily, the model can capture only a fragment of reality. Macroeconometric models deal with critical issues of great social-importance. The modellers who build them are attempting to influence and persuade politicians, policy makers and the general public. They are bound to use their models to try to support their arguments.

However, the translation of a set of beliefs from the language in which they were originally expressed – verbal, abstract algebraic, graphical – into the language of the computer is a process that should be undertaken with great scrupulousness. The reason for this is simple: although, in principle, the status of a computer model is no different from that of the same model expressed in any other medium, in practice such a model enjoys a higher public status because of the aura that surrounds computers.

There are some good reasons for this public attitude towards the computer: a preference for modernity; an awe of the technology; a sense of wonderment at its fantastic capabilities; and, above all else, the fact that numerical output is superficially easier to comprehend than the outputs from any of the other languages. Numbers have a familiarity, a brevity, a precision and an air of reality. Moreover, they also deal with the very important question of scale: no doubt there is a scrounger somewhere who would go out to work were the dole to be reduced, but when the Liverpool model assures us that just 10 per cent off benefits would reduce the underlying rate of unemployment by one-third, what was previously mere saloon-bar prejudice becomes a serious contender for policy. If the computer did not convey these advantages, it is hard to see why otherwise rational economists would go to all the trouble and expense of using the medium simply to represent what they believed.

What are the criteria, then, by which we should judge whether a model properly added anything to the case that it was being used to support? Firstly, justification has to be given for the quantification that has gone into turning an abstract model, or structure of beliefs, into an empirical model. It has to be a justification, moreover, that does not simply rest on those beliefs alone, even though it will of course conform to them. Formal econometrics (for example, the 'time-series econometrics' hybrid dominant in the UK) provides one basis on which to build such a justification. By virtue of being a systematic approach, it confers the advantage that the necessary justification can be provided in a concise and rather standardised way. However, although its strict application to a multi-equation model is in principle straightforward, its practical limitations are still considerable.[20] Other, less systematic, approaches therefore have to be used as a supplement; what matters is that the evidence for the inferences drawn by these other means is presented and discussed as thoroughly as possible.

Secondly, the model should have included some representation of the counter-view to the policy that was being promoted. Obviously the model would have shown those counter-effects to be small; but that would then simply have shifted the argument to the first matter, of how the model was quantified.

On this view, the proper role of the macroeconometric model is to contribute decisively on the question of the size and timing of effects. Empirical questions are the special province of the computer form of model. Computers are quite capable of handling any additional complexity in the model structure due to the need to represent the opposite view. In order for this to happen, though, both criteria must be satisfied and in none of these three cases was this so. The Policy Group emphasised its affiliation to the idea that the model should conform to a whole range of empirical evidence[21] but, by allowing no possibility of there being adverse effects arising from the policy of import controls, could not examine any counter-views. Both Liverpool and the Business School willingly forfeited their claims to conform to the data. Moreover, the very way in which the Business School modelled the underlying path of output precluded any possibility of Monetarist policies having any harmful effects on it. Given the chief argument against Monetarism, that it would cause a deep recession with lasting harm, this is remarkable.

THE ABANDONMENT OF THE INCOME–EXPENDITURE FRAMEWORK

These three models differed substantially from one another in the factors that were deemed capable of altering the adverse trends in the underlying level, or natural rate, of output. What they shared in common, however, was the belief that none of the variables in the (extended) income–expenditure framework had any role to play. While they might certainly be important in the process of adjustment towards that position, the values that these variables took were ultimately completely determined, or constrained, from outside.

It is important to be clear about the implications of this. What these models were all saying was not just that the variables in the income–expenditure framework were irrelevant as far as the levels of underlying aggregate income and employment were concerned – this is extraordinary enough given that we are talking here among other things about private sector investment, company sector finances, gross trading profits, even the money supply and bank lending – but also that the actual relationships between these variables are completely unproblematic. If we take these models literally – and how else can we take them? – they each endorse a view that says that none of the secular problems of the British economy are to be traced, for example, to the availability of finance for investment, or to the institutional arrangements that seem to require companies to maintain dividend payments (to the personal sector via life assurance and pension funds) irrespective of the profit position. At bottom, it does not matter, according to this view, how the City of London is organised or what its aims are or how it is regulated or what the relationship is between it and industry. Neither does it matter how the public sector spends its money, whether on infrastructure or consumption; it is all the same. The same indifference to how money is spent applies equally to the private sector. Above all else, this view quite excludes the idea that the key variable in a capitalist economy is investment. In sum, the marginalisation of the extended income–expenditure framework in the manner of these models amounts to saying that neither the channels through which finance, expenditure and income flow, nor the uses to which they are put, have anything to do with either the slow but steady relative decline of the British economy, or the seemingly inexorable rise in unemployment over a quarter of a century.

The abandonment of the income–expenditure framework as the focus for analysis was not, however, the same thing as the abandonment of a rich legacy of economic understanding of these matters. We have seen, in earlier chapters, that, while the great increase in computational power that was afforded by the electronic computer made the completion of the income expenditure model possible, nothing existed to guide this development. What was needed was an economic theory whose scope was commensurate with that of the complete framework; yet none was used and seemingly none existed. The result was that the development was piecemeal and ad hoc. Nothing exhibits this weakness better than the treatment of gross trading profits and, by association, the financial surplus of the company sector. Far from being the subject of exhaustive study of both its determinants and its effects, the profit of the company sector was the overwhelming favourite for the choice of the passive 'sink' variable that served to bring the aggregate measures of income and expenditure into equality.

When, in 1973, the New Cambridge economists first reached the edge of this income–expenditure world (that is, the sectoral financial surpluses), the key variable in Robert Neild's analysis was the financial surplus of the company sector and its behaviour over the cycle. Yet when the New Cambridge insights were formalised, by Cripps, Godley and Fetherston, this separate treatment of what might be thought to be a crucial variable was lost, submerged into an undifferentiated private sector. Indeed, if there was one moment when the development of the income–expenditure model took a fatal wrong turning it was then: instead of sinking the company sector into the private, the Cambridge economists should have split the company sector into two by separating the banks from other companies. The fact that *four* sectors is one too few to represent the economy can be seen from table 4.1, which showed the extended income–expenditure framework. Since the relationship in which banks stand to money is, by definition, different from the relationship of other companies, it is necessary to split the company sector in order to show the money supply. A wholly consistent representation would therefore have required five sectors and not four. To have gone in this direction would have taken the avowedly anti-Monetarist Cambridge economists into the heart of the enemy's terrain, with the risks and the challenges that that would have presented.

How should this 'wrong turning' be explained? Part of the reason must lie in the importance that was attached to forecasting by the Policy Group economists, in particular to the forecasting of the balance of payments, which was indisputably a problem of the first rank in 1974 and 1975. A stable relationship for the private sector's surplus provided a firm foundation for the forecasting of the current account deficit, conditional on the government's deficit. A much more important part of the reason for the turn, though, arises from the fact that the source of Britain's economic problems was seen by these Cambridge economists as lying in the relationship between

Britain and the rest of the world; in the external relationships, in other words, rather than the internal.

They were led to this by Nicholas Kaldor. The radical reform, of export-led growth, was motivated by the idea that the relative failure of the old consumption-led approach was caused by the Keynesians' neglect of what was involved in transferring Keynes' closed economy model to the situation of an open economy. The problem, even then, was therefore seen in terms of Britain's external relations. Both devaluation as a tactic and export-led growth as a strategy were judged unworkable by Godley and his colleagues; import controls and managed world trade were proposed instead. This signalled a change of means, but the basic analysis of the problem remained the same, namely that the difficulties lay in the external relationship. With this perspective, there was little point in unpacking the private sector into its company and personal parts and less point still in extracting the banks and other financial institutions from the industrial and commercial companies. This type of disaggregation would greatly have increased the model's size and complexity without adding a jot to the representation of what the Policy Group thought the essentials to be.

I mentioned, at the beginning of the last chapter, that the income–expenditure view was a representative of the paradigm of the circular flow rather than of the paradigm of equilibrium. The recent dominance of the latter, at least within what could be called the Anglo-American tradition of economics, means that these income–expenditure models seem rather alien. They are, however, still very much within the wider tradition of macroeconometric modelling, for, as Mary Morgan has argued, Tinbergen's original conception of a macroeconometric model involved a synthesis of the 'sequence' or 'process' analysis of the Swedish School of macroeconomics with the statistical microeconometric models of supply and demand developed in the 1920s and 1930s.[22] This synthesis did not survive long, as Morgan shows in her account of the dispute in the 1940s between Wold (sequence analysis) and Haavelmo and the Cowles Commission (simultaneous equations models of equilibrium). The former position lost out, to some extent therefore pre-figuring the eclipse of the 'sequential' income–expenditure model. But the dispute between Wold and the Cowles Commission was conducted within the framework of econometrics, whereas what we are concerned with here is the dispute within economics.

Ultimately, the problem with the development of the income–

expenditure model is that it was not supported by the right sort of economic research. What was needed was research that was directed towards articulating the channels through which finance, income and expenditure flowed through the system. This research would have had to have studied the institutions within the economy. It would have had to look at their practices; at the rules, formal and informal, that governed their conduct; at their objectives; at the constraints that they imposed on other institutions. The object of the research would have had to have been to codify all this in such a way that it could be represented as set of quantified, behavioural relationships. The challenge would have been to have assembled these in a manner that nevertheless observed the accounting identities, which in principle actually hold in each period (as opposed to equilibrium, which does not). What was needed, in short, was an analysis directed towards uncovering the real processes by which income, expenditure and finance flowed round the system.

That this research did not happen is partly a result of the very nature of the Keynesianism with which we have been dealing here. The 'management of the economy' was in the first instance an activity unto itself and, as such, macroeconomics did not need to concern itself with what happened within society. In particular, Keynesianism was not an interventionist philosophy but, rather, one that was intended to complement and indeed buttress 'laissez-faire'. It is to the development of this view of Keynesianism, and to the analysis of its consequences, that we now turn.

10

CAN WE RETURN TO KEYNESIANISM?

The 1990s have already been better years for Keynesians than were the 1980s. The prolonged recession that began at the start of the 1990s, when unemployment reached its low point of 1.6 million, has naturally made a doctrine that is committed to the reduction of unemployment an attractive candidate; calls for a 'return to Keynesianism' are frequently to be heard. The principal purpose of this final chapter is to assess the viability of this idea against the background of this account of the transition from Keynesianism to Monetarism.

It may perhaps be thought that a return to Keynesianism has been taking place for some time now. Economic policies and policy instruments that were condemned during the 1980s have since been rehabilitated one by one: the virtues of an expanding public sector deficit in times of recession; the virtue of public expenditure *per se*, especially where this is expenditure directed towards improving the infrastructure, be it physical or human; the wisdom of allowing the exchange-rate to depreciate in order to boost external demand; the need for explicit government guidelines on pay increases; even the merits of sometimes raising taxes.[1] But where these ideas have received official sanction, it has tended to happen only after the event, to provide justification for a reversal of policy that was forced on the authorities. In no way does it signal the beginnings of either a return to the perspectives of the heyday of Keynesianism, in the 1950s and 1960s, or the formulation of a new, coherent strategy. On the contrary, at times it seems much more to be an exercise born of some desperation: in a situation where 'events' appear to be in the control of the authorities, rather than the other way round, it is as well to rule out nothing in principle in case the doing of it suddenly becomes unavoidable. But events also conspire to force further reversals: a revival of inflation, a crisis in public sector funding, or a complete loss

168

of confidence in sterling induce measures of a distinctly non-Keynesian kind.

In this chapter, I am going to develop two arguments. The first, which has a number of stages to it, sets out to account for the demise of Keynesianism. The first stage of the argument offers a characterisation of Keynesianism: not a brand of economics but rather an autonomous system for solving the problems of a market economy that was specific to the circumstances of its time. The second stage looks at the political and social consequences of that system, consequences that stemmed primarily from this autonomy of demand management. The third stage develops the explanation for the demise of Keynesianism: as the circumstances changed, Keynesianism struggled to adapt; the adaptation, though, was both far more fragile and ultimately at odds with the very character of Keynesianism itself. The final stage examines the extent to which Monetarism and its supply-side accretions have nevertheless drawn on central aspects of Keynesianism to provide legitimation for themselves.

The second argument is brief and positive. The transformation from Keynesianism to Monetarism within macroeconometric models was a progression that had a certain logic to it, but it was not inevitable. This is because the course that was actually followed depended on a number of decisions that were made on the way. In some of these cases, the decisions made were seriously wrong. One of these, above all others, entailed the gradual eclipse of the very problem that had been the reason for the Keynesian system in the first place. This was the problem of investment in a capitalist economy. We cannot return to Keynesianism, but we should turn our attention once more to the problem that it identified.

THE AUTONOMY OF MACROECONOMICS

Why was Keynesianism popular? It had the attraction that, contrary to the orthodox view, which held – and holds – that the law of the market is the final arbiter of all things economic, Keynesianism permitted a certain freedom from economics. The key to this freedom was that Keynesianism, through the practice of demand management, would *itself* look after the society-wide economic variables, especially the total level of employment and the overall level of income. One way of putting this is to say that the sphere of macroeconomics, and the practice of demand management, enjoyed a degree of autonomy from the sphere of microeconomics.

The basis for this view lies in the old macroeconometric models themselves. Here, the main economy-wide aggregates – the macro-economic variables – were explained solely in terms of one another. Microeconomic variables, and any notion that macroeconomic variables depended on them, were absent. Demand management would certainly impinge upon society, directly through fiscal policy itself and indirectly through the benefits to be had from a higher level of aggregate income. However, although the actions of individuals and institutions contributed greatly to shaping the situation to which the skills of demand management had to be applied, they did not mediate the actual practice of it or hinder it achieving its objectives.

The view of the economy that the models express is essentially a technocratic one. It relies on the idea that, however free our behaviour may be as individuals, in the aggregate we are somehow constrained to behave in a regular way. This behaviour is, moreover, both comprehensible and quantifiable: the models express those regularities and their interrelationships. Expert economists, working through the government on behalf of society, can exploit those regularities for the good of all.

Yet it is precisely their lack of 'microeconomic foundations' that most economists now regard as the most damning weakness of these macroeconometric models. The hostility towards macroeconometric models to which this criticism gave rise is particularly strong among economists in the United States.[2] In Britain, the re-founding of macroeconometric models on 'firm, microeconomic foundations' was one of the main items on the model builders' research agenda during the 1980s – evidence that the criticism was accepted even by those who were closest to the models.

So is not the idea of an autonomous macroeconomics simply absurd? If we conceive of 'economic theory' as something that is universally true, then the idea that the sphere of macroeconomics exists apart from the sphere of microeconomics cannot but seem ridiculous. If nothing else, extreme situations must exist – for example, if employers were determined to engage in a coordinated campaign of sackings and lock-outs in order to break the power of the trade unions – in which no amount of Keynesian demand management could possibly hope to maintain full employment. The reason why so many economists nowadays see the old, autonomous macroeconomic models as absurd stems precisely from the fact that it is now an article of faith among many economists that economic theory *is* something whose truth is timeless. Rooted in a conception of 'economic man' as a rational, self-seeking individual, the laws of economics are held to be on a par with the laws of physics.[3]

But Keynesianism was never intended to be a construction of this type. It was, instead, specific to its circumstances – in a word, it was 'contingent'. We can see this firstly in its methodology. In an essay on Kaldor, the economist Tony Lawson has described this methodology as the 'realist approach to economic analysis'.[4] It insists upon abstraction, without which there can be no theory, but the abstractions themselves have to be 'appropriate' to the situation under consideration. The key entities within this methodology are 'stylised facts'; these are facts that are held to be important but, since 'importance' is a designation that can be conferred only on the basis of a theory, they are facts that are themselves a product of a theory.

The contingent nature of this Keynesianism is to be seen secondly in its affinity to 'operations research'. Although there is a considerable degree of overlap between economics and operations research, the latter's proud self-designation as an 'applied' science reveals an outlook wholly different from that of many academic economists, for whom 'applied work' is derivative, necessarily inferior to the work of the 'theorist'. Operations research is all about problem solving, particularly where large systems are involved. The old macroeconometric models, based on the circular flow, portrayed the economy as a system. The first detailed description of the London Business School's macroeconometric model appeared in the *Journal of the Operational Research Society*. Operations research dates back to the 1930s. It gained considerable momentum during the 1940s from a host of military applications. One whom it influenced at that time was Kaldor:

> I became aware of this more pragmatic approach during the war when it was used by scientists for the purposes of 'operational research'. It is an approach which in one sense is more modest in scope (in not searching for explanations that derive from a comprehensive model of the system) and also more ambitious in that it directly aims at discovering solutions (or remedies) for real problems.
>
> (Kaldor 1978: xvii)

THE POLITICAL ECONOMY OF KEYNESIANISM

An autonomous macroeconomics is a paternalist notion: expert economists will look after society's big economic problems for it without having to call on individuals or institutions for help in that task. The great advantage of such paternalism is that it opens up a space within which society, through its institutions, can decide on a whole range of matters internal to it without having to concern itself with the overall, economic consequences. This was the political economy that, for a generation, Keynesianism made possible.

An example of the opportunities that this new-found freedom permitted concerns the question of the distribution of income. Demand management would dictate the overall level of tax that was required, and this would necessitate sometimes a reduction and sometimes an increase in the overall, or average, rate of tax. Within that constraint, however, the tax system (the instrument by which the desired distribution of income was to be achieved) could be designed with social objectives in mind; the extent to which these objectives could actually be realised would be limited far more by what was politically acceptable to the majority than by any economic consideration.

By treating macroeconomics as a world apart, Keynesianism set politics free from economics. So long as the constraints, of an essentially accounting nature, laid down from above by the economists were adhered to, other (and non-economic) considerations could be used to guide the reform of almost every aspect of society. This was an enormous change. Its principal political effect was to make the Labour party, committed on the one hand to ending the scourge of unemployment and on the other to extensive social reform, viable as a party of government. In parallel, the position of reform-minded Conservatives, such as R. A. Butler and Harold Macmillan, was greatly strengthened too.

Keynesianism's great achievement was to open up a space for the moral and the social within politics. Political parties could pursue their social agendas – a more egalitarian distribution of income, achieved through a progressive taxation system; a new balance between public and private expenditure; the extension of the social security system to eliminate poverty; a health service free at the point of use; subsidies for essential services; minimum wage legislation; houses built according to need; public ownership of strategic industries – all of these became possible and, with it, government by a political party committed to them. Of course, moves could also be made in the opposite direction, but again, provided the requirements of demand management were adhered to, there need be no harm to the overall level of well-being. There was room for real and deep political disagreement, yet, for society as a whole, the effects of that disagreement were bounded.

THE DEMISE OF KEYNESIANISM

The changing circumstances of the British economy, which first became manifest in the middle of the 1960s, eventually made the autonomy of the macroeconomic sphere unsustainable. In itself, of course, this statement is no more than a truism that follows directly from the characterisation of Keynesianism as 'contingent'. Any living form will be threatened, perhaps mortally, by a change in its environment; in order to account for its disappearance, we must explain why the efforts that it made to adapt were ultimately unsuccessful.

The evidence that the environment in the middle 1960s had become more hostile was that GDP was now growing too slowly, relative to the rate of growth of output per head, to be able to maintain unemployment at the low levels that had been a feature of both the 1950s and early 1960s. The growth of imports seemed always to outstrip expectations and the unfavourably high income elasticity of demand for imports, relative to that of the world's elasticity of demand for exports, seemed to doom the UK to a long-term rate of growth lower than that of other major economies. GDP could be boosted through fiscal expansion, but such attempts invariably had to be thrown into reverse in order to correct a fast-emerging imbalance of foreign trade.

Devaluation was not the only solution that was proposed for this problem,[5] but it was the one that was actually implemented, in 1967 and again in the boom of the early 1970s.[6] The use of the exchange-rate for this purpose was advocated by Kaldor as the means by which to manage the economy in a new manner, through export-led growth. This was to replace the old approach, of consumption-led growth, which was flawed in two ways. Firstly, there was a problem of timing caused by the fact that a fiscal boost increased consumption ahead of production or investment. As a result, imports increased to take up the slack yet this was the very thing that caused a trade gap to emerge, provoking the need for deflationary measures. Secondly, investment that was introduced to meet rising consumer demand tended to be concentrated on services rather than manufacturing; yet it was manufacturing, in Kaldor's view, that held the key to a sustained higher rate of growth of productivity. Export-led growth, in contrast,

173

suffered from neither of these flaws: the export boost would inevitably lead the boost in imports, thereby avoiding the worsening trade gap that invariably brought consumption-led growth to a halt; and, since the manufacturing content of exports was higher than that of consumption, manufacturing performance would be strengthened.

There are two points of note about this analysis. Firstly, although international competition presented an increasing problem, the Keynesian reformers attributed the fact that the British economy was in the wrong shape to meet that competition to a fault within Keynesianism itself. Secondly, the argument for the new approach to demand management, via export-led growth, rested on the superiority of its effects compared with those of the old approach. Although Kaldor set out the mechanism by which the new approach operated, this emphasis on its benefits, 'if only' it would work, tended to divert attention from the character of the mutation to Keynesianism that was proposed.

One aspect of this mutation was that demand management was now to operate at one remove: under consumption-led growth it had operated directly on one of the macroeconomic variables – personal and public sector consumption – through fiscal instruments; under export-led growth, in contrast, it operated indirectly, via the exchange-rate and relative prices. Not only was the new approach more indirect, it was also considerably more fragile. One of the things to be said for taxes as an instrument of policy is that at least the tax rates themselves are under the control of the authorities. Although the question of their effect depends on myriad other factors, at least one component of the mechanism is secure. No such certainty surrounds the exchange-rate. It is questionable whether the government is free to use it. Even if it is, it is subject to many other forces that the authorities may find hard, or even impossible, to cope with. A robust, if deficient, system had therefore been replaced by one that promised far more but that used an instrument over which the government's hold was tenuous at least.

The other aspect of the mutation was that the new system of demand management depended on a shift *within* society itself. Devaluation achieves its end by transferring income from wages and salaries to profits, in order both to lower domestic costs relative to those of overseas competitors and to increase industry's profits and therefore the incentive to invest and produce. In addressing this matter, Kaldor suggested that there was no reason why some measure of redistribution should not be possible. When posed in these abstract terms it is hard to dispute the argument; a great deal will depend on the circumstances, including the magnitude of the redistribution and the benefit (to society as whole) that it will bring, as well as the extent to which those who will suffer, in this case wage and salary earners, can take action to offset the effect. Discussed in this way, the argument against devaluation that was decisive was the kind that was advanced years later by Godley and his colleagues, namely that the *scale* of the reduction in real wages that was required to restore unemployment to its former low level was far beyond that which workers would be willing to tolerate. Practically, this explained why the strategy had not worked when it was tried in the early 1970s and why it would not have worked, in the sense of restoring growth and lowering unemployment sufficiently, were it to have been tried in 1976 or 1977.

The real significance of devaluation was that it undermined the very basis of Keynesianism itself. The success of export-led growth depended on there being a redistribution within society. At the level of the Business School's model, macroeconomics came to depend on a microeconomic response; the sphere of macroeconomics has ceased to be autonomous. However, this retreat at the level of theory was but a pale reflection of the consequences in reality. There, the expert economists had to admit that they were no longer able, alone, to manage the economy on society's behalf; instead, they had now to call for help – and some sacrifice – from society itself.

Once macroeconomic performance came to depend on microeconomic response in this way, the barrier that Keynesianism had constructed between politics and economics began to disintegrate. This set two processes in motion. Firstly, politics was increasingly called upon to support economics because, once the management of the economy came to depend on measures that harmed one part of society at the expense of another, political legitimation was required. Secondly, economics began to recolonise areas of life from which Keynesianism had expelled it. This too was inevitable since, once the macroeconomic performance depended on the microeconomic response, decisions that had previously been taken on purely political grounds had now to take economic considerations into account.

Both of these developments were to the disadvantage of politics and, in particular, to the Labour party. On the one hand, Labour's commitment to low unemployment and a sufficiently high rate of growth meant that it had little choice but to lend support to whatever measures were deemed necessary for their achievement even if this brought the party into conflict with the core of its supporters. Devaluation, and the contemporary attempts to control wages in order to maintain the competitive advantage afforded by it, are cases in point here. On the other hand, Labour's social priorities had at the very least to be circumscribed by the need to take account of the economic implications of the reforming measures that they wanted to introduce.

Since the London Business School had been the most fervent advocates of the devaluation strategy, it is perhaps fitting to use one of their last Keynesian pronouncements to illustrate the extent of the breach that had been made in the dyke that separated economics from politics and how sharp the conflict between the two had become in the second half of the 1970s. In the situation where wage bargainers could resist the reduction in real wages imposed initially by devaluation, the model simulation showed that the balance of payments could nevertheless be improved if those in receipt of transfer incomes from the public sector, such as social security or unemployment benefit, were not compensated for devaluation's inflationary effects. At the expense of one group in society, some aspects of the economy could be improved. Ball and his colleagues most certainly did not approve of this – 'the balance of payments is indeed adjusted in the right direction, but the burden of adjustment is most inequitably distributed . . . being borne by pensioners, recipients of unemployment benefit, etc'[7] – but the implication is unavoidable: certain key aspects of the welfare state were now inimical to the well-being of the economy.

We can summarise this argument in the following terms. The increasingly hostile circumstances (which were partly of Keynesianism's own making) had forced the Keynesians themselves to redesign the system. The redesign that they came up with was both far more fragile and, crucially, undermined the very separation of politics from economics that lay at the root of its popular appeal. Sold on the basis of the superior results that it would deliver were it only allowed a free run, it was in fact far less well adapted than its predecessor and failed to cope with the extremely hostile circumstances of the 1970s.

How, then, can we seriously contemplate a return to Keynesianism? The old but robust form was identified as being responsible for the sclerosis within the economy; the new one was fragile and, in its reliance on transfers of income to achieve macroeconomic aims, basically anti-Keynesian.

DWELLING AMONG THE RUINS

Although this book has been about the transformation from Keynesianism to Monetarism (and, at times, beyond), the two have by no means been treated equally. The reason for this is the perception that, since the fall of Keynesianism, we have been living among its ruins. Those in control have given up any attempt to construct anything on the old scale. Instead, different parts of the Keynesian edifice have been put to use when it suited, although the ends that they now serve are often the opposite of the original ones. One instance of this sort of appropriation, mentioned in the introduction to this chapter, is the recent rehabilitation of certain Keynesian nostrums, for example the virtues of devaluation; the point here, however, is deeper than that.

Initially, I think, Monetarism did attempt a project on the scale of the old Keynesian one. The objective was different – the defeat of inflation rather than the maintenance of growth – but what was proposed echoed Keynesianism in its simplicity, its scope and the key role to be played by expert economists working above society. By the simple device of cutting the public sector borrowing requirement, these economists (or those senior government ministers whom they advised) would initiate a process that rapidly, and with no lasting harm, would bring down the rate of inflation. These experts could not work the trick quite on their own, since firms and trade unions would need to curb price and wage rises. Nevertheless, the appreciation of the exchange-rate, brought about by the reduction in the public sector borrowing requirement, would, it was promised, provide a sufficient inducement to workers and firms to behave in the required way. This was not the original idea of an autonomous macroeconomics but it was akin to the export-led growth mutation, albeit turned upside down. In particular, that most fragile of instruments, the exchange-rate, was once more called upon to play the main role.

This pretence, that Monetarism could achieve grand solutions at only a small and temporary cost, has long since been abandoned. Pain is now the order of the day, to such an extent that senior government ministers are emboldened enough to boast of its virtues. The pain from recession is all of a piece with the pain inflicted by the measures recommended by supply-side economics. On the surface, these look to have nothing whatsoever to do with Keynesianism. Indeed in one sense they are quite its opposite: the very things that had previously been precisely the kind of matter that society could decide upon without consideration for the macroeconomic consequences – trade union membership, social security benefits, income and labour taxes – are now held to be directly responsible for the high and rising level of unemployment and the poorer than desired level of aggregate income. The Liverpool model first introduced these; as we saw, the model was extreme in the magnitudes of the effects that it attributed to these variables and could be discounted. But, as we saw in the previous chapter, some of Liverpool's sharpest critics have themselves adopted not only the natural rate framework but also the principal policy conclusions, notably the adverse effects of benefits and the extent of unionisation on the natural rate. Although the influence of the Liverpool model on the 'labour market' policies of the 1980s was probably distant at best, the basic affinity between the ideas represented there and the policies that have been pursued, is unmistakable: the emasculation of the trade unions through a series of legislative measures; the cuts in benefits and the removal of entitlement to benefit, especially for young adults; the abolition of wages councils and minimum wage legislation; the British government's refusal to sign up to even the very limited provisions of the social chapter of the Maastricht agreement; the talk of a limit on the duration for which benefits are paid to the unemployed.

The connection between these policies and Keynesianism itself is that they draw their legitimacy from the Keynesian focus on macro-economics and the whole system of values to which it gave rise. Chief among these is the notion of 'the economy' itself and the idea that its health and progress are inextricably linked with the general welfare of society. 'The economy' is seen through the macroeconomic variables, chief among which are aggregate income and unemployment on the real side, and the rate of inflation on the money side. Although the cases of both unemployment and inflation are slightly more complicated, we have been long accustomed to thinking that a higher level of aggregate income is to be preferred to a lower level. 'In the traditional credenda of the economist', wrote E. J. Mishan, 'more is better.'[8] This identification of national income with national well-being was one of the cornerstones of the Keynesian system, yet it was taken over by those dedicated to that system's overthrow. Thus the party that ruled in the 1980s did not hesitate to boast about how well 'the economy' was doing during the boom times of the late 1980s, even though it was careful to exclude from view the disastrous performance at the beginning of the decade.[9]

In a society that was economically homogeneous, with low unemployment and a relatively narrow distribution of incomes among those in work, the association between movements in the aggregate income and each individual's well-being would be quite close. Certainly, British society was very much more homogeneous in these two respects even in the 1970s than it is now.[10] But it is not homogeneity itself that matters here but rather that society is free to reallocate the fruits of a higher aggregate income among its members. Of course there must be limits on this but, when we look, for example, at the Liverpool model, the whole thrust of supply-side economics, directed not only at those in receipt of benefit but also at those in work, seems to be directed towards reducing the scope for redistribution almost to zero. Attempts to alleviate poverty, through increases in unemployment benefit or indeed any other kind of benefit if it requires an increase in taxation, are harmful to GDP, real wages and unemployment. Any attempt to increase the degree of control that employees have over their workplace and their liveli- hood would, if it caused trade union membership to rise, likewise harm aggregate income and worsen unemployment.

Mishan's argument against the almost automatic association that economists make between growth and welfare was thorough and impassioned, yet the economistic perspective that *he* was attacking was one that still admitted that the distribution of output was a legitimate economic concern:

> But if we are genuinely interested in the welfare, and the character, of society, we should be unwilling to reconcile ourselves to this restriction on our judgement – to accept that the smooth operation of competitive markets, and the level and distribution of outputs, are the only criteria to be respected.
>
> (Mishan 1977: 35)

If redistribution too is now inimical to the growth of GDP, it is hard indeed to see what grounds remain for the association between the well-being of the economy and society's welfare.

As long as the independence of macroeconomics from the rest of society remains tenable then the concept of 'the economy' as some- thing that can be 'managed' by expert economists is perhaps a benign one. But, once this condition ceases to hold, the notion of 'the economy' becomes something malign. On the one hand, it serves as a spectre with which to terrorise large parts of the population; in its name, sacrifices on a large scale are called for – and unavoidable. On the other, it serves to define the 'national interest', thereby giving legitimacy to actions that favour Britain at the expense of other countries, even though it is far from clear that the real interests are national at all. For example, a long-lasting solution to British unemployment is unlikely to be found that does not deal too with the same problem in other European countries.

This takes the argument against the idea of returning to Keynesianism a stage further. Following its demise, central elements of Keynesianism were appropriated by the new order that replaced it. The problem that this poses is that to call for a return to Keynesianism in such circumstances serves as much to reinforce the current regime as it does to undermine it.

THE PROBLEM OF INVESTMENT

What is the positive contribution that an historical study can make to the search for a way forward? Although this book has been an attempt to construct a logical account of the demise of Keynesianism, it would be wrong to assume that this could only possibly result in a negative conclusion that served simply to reinforce the status quo. On the contrary: the transformation from Keynesianism to Monetarism was a progression that had an order and a sense to it, but it was also one that depended on choices that were made along the way. 'Logical' in this context is therefore by no means synonymous with 'inevitable', and this in itself gives rise to the first positive point: our present position is one that has been reached through our own volition and not because of the working out of ineluctable 'forces' or 'laws'. There *was* nothing inevitable about it and there *is* nothing inevitable about its continuation. A number of the wrong decisions have been mentioned in the last chapters but there is just one that I want to mention here: above all else what was lost in the progression to Monetarism was the significance that Keynesianism had attached to the problem of investment.

Now, of course, all economists agree that investment is crucial; what made Keynesianism special was its belief that there was nothing in the mechanism of a market economy to guarantee that sufficient investment would be forthcoming so as to ensure full employment. The system of demand management was designed to overcome this weakness. Its rationale was that the chief inducement to investment was the prospect of an effective demand large enough to ensure that the goods that would flow from that investment would be sold. It was not, according to Kaldor, through deficit financing[11] *per se* that Keynesianism had sought to achieve the goals of steady growth and full employment, but rather through the encouragement that the maintenance of a certain rate of growth of demand would afford to investment.

That Keynesianism was preoccupied with this problem above all others is highlighted in the arguments put forward to justify the switch from consumption-led to export-led growth. The case against the old approach turned on the (relatively) adverse effects that it had had on investment; firstly, it had induced the wrong mix of investment, thereby creating an industrial structure that was ever less capable of competing; secondly, it was obliged, because of balance of payments problems, to choke off the growth in demand just at the point when investment, inevitably belatedly, had begun to respond.

The Keynesian idea that a market economy is incapable of bringing forth a sufficient quantity of investment is one that has long been quite lost from sight. Supply-side economics locates the roots of any problem elsewhere, in the labour market: what capitalists do is always rational and for the best; all that prevents a return to low unemployment is labour market imperfections, which are primarily the responsibility of well-meaning but misguided governments. The Monetarism of the Business School ignored the problem: the control of inflation would do no lasting harm to the real economy and the question of where that real economy might be heading in the medium term was one that polite economists preferred to leave discretely to one side. Even the impolite economists of the Cambridge Economic Policy Group contributed to the marginalisation of investment through their concentration on private expenditure; investment was no longer special but just one category of this whole.

But if investment *is* the central problem, why did Keynesianism fail to solve it? Since the argument thus far has located the reason for Keynesianism's demise in the fragility of the adaptation of export-led growth secured through exchange-rate manipulation, the answer required here involves explaining why it was that the older system was replaced with something so fragile. The explanation is that the Keynesian solution for the management of demand, directed towards investment, was always one that operated at a distance. The problem of investment was *not* to be solved by more direct methods: for example, nationalisation of the leading industrial and financial concerns. The shift to export-led growth increased the distance but remained faithful to that principle of non-interference.

In his essay 'The End of Laissez-Faire', Keynes set out a vision of how the state might in future support the activities of individuals without actually supplanting them in any way:

> The most important *Agenda* of the State relate not to those
> activities which private individuals are already fulfilling, but to
> those functions which fall outside the sphere of the individual,
> to those decisions which are made by *no one* if the state does not
> make them. The important thing for government is not to do
> things which individuals are already doing, and to do them a
> little better or a little worse; but to do those things which at
> present are not done at all.
>
> (Keynes 1926: 291)

Citing uncertainty and ignorance as the source of many of the great
evils of the day – inequalities of wealth, the unemployment of labour,
the impairment of efficiency and production – Keynes went on to
outline the nature of the remedy that he had in mind:

> I believe that the cure for these things is partly to be sought in
> the control of the currency and of credit by a central institution,
> and partly in the collection and dissemination on a great scale of
> data relating to the business situation, including the full
> publicity, by law if necessary, of all business facts which it is
> useful to know. The measures would involve society in exer-
> cising directive intelligence through some appropriate organ of
> action over many of the inner intricacies of private business, yet
> it would leave private initiative and enterprise unhindered.
>
> (Keynes 1926: 292)[12]

Some have taken this passage, with its idea that the state should obtain
and broadcast 'all useful business facts', as being consonant with the
type of indicative planning system operated in France (but not, except
for a brief period in the early 1960s, in Britain).[13] The crucial point,
though, concerns the character of Keynes' proposal rather than its
detail: action by some 'directive intelligence' that would nevertheless
'leave private initiative and enterprise unhindered'. Although there
are many differences between Keynes and Keynesianism, not least in
the area of econometrics and macroeconometric models,[14] Keynes'
notion here of 'action from above' seems to accord with the character
of practical Keynesianism.

Previously, we saw how Keynesianism had afforded a space that
made possible the pursuit of social reforms; here we see it representing a guarantee to business that firms could carry on behaving as they
had behaved before and making decisions according to the same

criteria. They would make different decisions under a Keynesian regime, of course, but that was only because they would be induced so to do by an alteration in circumstances. Keynesianism may have created a space within which the pursuit of social reform became possible, but that same space also guaranteed the continued independence of capital to pursue its interests free from the interference of the state. Through its promise to banish depression and slump while leaving the private ownership of the means of production intact, Keynesianism was an attempt to repair capitalism and not replace it.

Had the attempt to reform Keynesianism moved away from consumption-led growth towards the more direct control of investment and output, then it would have undermined this independence. Since the preferred reform, towards the use of the exchange-rate, was itself one that undermined the independence of macroeconomics, it might be argued that the decision to follow a road that relied on a shift from wages to profits showed the true 'class nature' of Keynesianism, with labour, rather than capital, being asked to make the sacrifice. However, although the road that was *not* taken could have led to a form of state socialism, it also led towards more socialised and coordinated approaches to investment and output that were still unequivocally capitalist, such as the forms of industrial and financial ownership and control favoured in Germany and Japan.

The Keynesian reforms of the late 1960s eschewed the route towards more direct control. In 'The End of Laissez-Faire', Keynes showed that he was ready at least to contemplate 'coordination' in the area of investment:

> I believe that some coordinated act of intelligent judgement is required as to the scale on which it is desirable that the community as a whole should save, the scale on which these savings should go abroad in the form of foreign investments, and whether the present organisation of the investment market distributes savings along the nationally most productive channels. I do not think that these matters should be left entirely to the chances of private judgement and private profits, as they are at present.
>
> (Keynes 1926: 292)

The question is how far the poor economic performance of the last twenty years can be attributed to a shortage of well directed investment. Certainly, the one really impressive spell of growth over that period, between 1986 and 1989, was an example of both the power of consumption-led growth to generate investment and the consequences of trying to achieve it in that way, a strong expansion being brought to a shuddering halt by the need to stem the enormous current account deficit that had opened up as a result. There is little in the record since the late 1970s to suggest that the principal problem with which Keynesianism grappled – how to secure both a sufficient level and a correct mix of investment – has now been satisfactorily solved by other means. It is surely time once more to restore that problem to centre stage.

NOTES

1 WHY STUDY MACROECONOMETRIC MODELS?

1 See, for example, the evidence to the Treasury and Civil Service Committee, especially the memorandum submitted by the Treasury itself (HM Treasury 1991) and Wallis and Whitley (1991).

2 The most frequent explanation for the models' forecast failure over this period traced the error to the part of the model that forecast expenditure by consumers. Studies by the Macroeconomic Modelling Bureau, at Warwick University, suggest that other factors are at work. The Bureau was set up by the Economic and Social Research Council in 1983 to promote the understanding of models and to conduct comparative research. Since its inception, it has published a considerable number of thorough and detailed studies on the models' properties.

3 Peter Warburton, of the brokers, Robert Fleming. Warburton appeared fifth in a league table, published by the *Financial Times* newspaper (20 October 1992), which ranked forty-one economic forecasters according to how well they had forecast the growth of the UK economy in each of the three years, 1990, 1991 and 1992. Although any ranking based on such a simplistic criterion is of doubtful value, the table revealed the quite staggering fact that, out of the 123 individual forecasts reported there, no fewer than 120 were wrong through having been too *optimistic*, in many cases wildly so. Warburton was one of only two people (Tim Congdon was the other) to have erred, once, on the pessimistic side.

4 However, as Pesaran and Smith (1985) argue, the question of how far to go in the direction of improving a macroeconometric model's forecasting capability can be decided only in the light of the model builder's objectives and the costs and benefits involved. It is quite wrong to suppose that we should be aiming for one single model that outperforms all other models and methods: this flies in the face of what Adam Smith taught about the benefits to be had from division of labour and specialisation. To condemn a macroeconometric model because it does not forecast as well as a model designed specifically for that purpose may be no more sensible than criticising a bread knife for the poor job it makes of peeling potatoes.

5 The resulting concoction – 'time-series econometrics' – has been the

dominant strand of UK econometrics for over a decade now. What gave this amalgam such a boost was the fact that it seemed to have overcome the forecasting failures of the early and middle 1970s, which culminated in the general failure to forecast the depth of the 1975 recession.

6 Kaldor (1971: 1).
7 This is a matter of dispute within Monetarism. The 'international' variety, favoured in Britain, allotted it a role but, as we shall see in chapter 7, this was an anathema to mainstream proponents such as Milton Friedman.

2 MACROECONOMETRIC MODELS: A PANORAMIC VIEW OF THEIR HISTORY

1 They have also been subject to an enormous amount of scrutiny, especially by the ESRC Macroeconomic Modelling Bureau, led by Ken Wallis, which has led to a wealth of published information and discussion.
2 Although published separately, the tabular survey (Nerlove 1966) did not stand alone but was accompanied by a number of lengthy discussions ('fragments of a critical survey') of various models contained therein. For example, Nerlove (1962) dealt with Klein's Oxford model while Nerlove (1965) dealt with that model, and Tinbergen's UK model.
3 Radice (1939).
4 Although not published until 1951, Tinbergen had carried out the work a decade earlier.
5 The final equation was $z = 1.27z_{-1} - 0.60z_{-2}$ (Tinbergen 1951: 116) where z was non-labour income and where the unit of time was between eight and nine months. The choice of which variable to use for this 'final equation' is irrelevant to the dynamic properties so revealed.
6 See Morgan (1990) for a discussion.
7 Cairncross (1952).
8 The model was also discussed at length in various papers by Nerlove (1962, 1965).
9 Bodkin et al. (1991).
10 Nerlove (1962: 154).
11 The task of estimation, or at least some of it, was carried out on a computer and a whole chapter of the book was devoted to discussing aspects of this matter, including the merits of different machines.
12 The original forecast appeared in the paper by Ball et al. (1959) which was later the subject of a post-mortem by Hazelwood and Vandome (1961). The forecast for 1961 appeared in Klein et al. (1961b).
13 In a review of the Institute's forecasting record since 1959, Neild and Shirley (1961) contended that the Oxford model's forecasts were inferior to those obtained from informal methods, pointing out in particular that, whereas the model had forecast a substantial fall in industrial production in the first half of 1959, the outcome had in fact been an increase. They also noted that reworking the forecasts on an *ex post* basis by including the true values of exogenous variables improved some elements of the forecast but worsened others.

14 'A Programme for Growth' eventually produced a series of a dozen papers in as many years. I have drawn here particularly on numbers 1 (Stone and Brown 1962), 5 (Stone 1964), 6 (Stone 1965) and 9 Stone *et al.* 1970).

15 Stone (1965).

16 The problem was eventually overtaken by the change of the original model to a dynamic form.

17 Brown (1964: 171).

18 Pearce (1970) gave the first general description of the Southampton model. Heathfield and Pearce (1975) contained the best detailed description of the model equations, although it should be noted that even at this stage (that is, 1972) the equations were still in abstract form only. Pearce *et al.* (1976) reported some simulation results on a version of the model.

19 It should be understood that these figures, and their detailed breakdown by block shown in table 2.1, give only a broad indication of the composition of the model. This is because the information for this model has been gleaned from what was still only an abstract listing of the behavioural equations along with the variables in the model. The basis of the classification is that a variable appearing as the dependent variable of one of the reported relationships has been used to classify a (behavioural) equation, while all other endogenous variables have been assumed to be determined by identity. It was also necessary to decide whether the variable involved applied to a sector or to the economy as a whole; usually this was clear (although it was not always so). This has, however, led to an over-counting since many sectoral variables do not, in fact, exist for all fourteen sectors. Finally, excluded altogether from the count are the 196 relationships for each of the input–output coefficients (keeping consistency here with the CGP model).

20 Pearce (1970: 30).

21 Stone (1954).

22 *Sunday Times*, 27 November 1966.

23 Byron (1970: 7).

24 Ball *et al.* (1975a: 3).

25 These began as the annual 'Economic Survey'. See Cairncross and Watts (1989).

26 This information, as well as a general discussion of the forecasting and modelling at the National Institute is discussed by Worswick (1975).

27 The 1972 version of this model was described in Bispham (1975a).

28 Bispham (1975a).

29 Barker (1978) and Barker *et al.* (1980) provide accounts of the developments to the Cambridge Growth Project.

30 The Department of Economic Affairs was created by the new Labour government, which came to office in 1964, as a counterweight to the Treasury. Anne Sowerbutts (1970) explained that one difference was that, while the Treasury was concerned with a horizon of no more than two years, the new department wanted to look at the consequences of government policy decisions over a longer time span. The model was annual, estimated by ordinary least squares and contained about 260 relationships, of which just under half were identities. A key feature of it was that it determined the real level of output along the lines argued by

Godley and Shepherd (1964) in 'Long-Term Growth and Short-Term Policy' and Shepherd (1968) in 'Productive Potential and the Demand for Labour'.
31 Godley and Cripps (1974a: 58).
32 Kahn and Posner (1974).
33 See, for example, Ball (1978: para. 315).
34 Davidson *et al.* (1978).
35 Cripps and Fetherston (1979: 45).
36 Wall *et al.* (1975).
37 The Committee's report (Ball 1978) contained a considerable amount of general information on macroeconometric models and the processes of forecasting and policy analysis, which they supported.
38 Details of model III are taken from a National Institute (1977) discussion paper.
39 Minford *et al.* (1984: 42).

3 KEYNESIAN DEMAND MANAGEMENT: THE EMERGENCE OF THE MODEL AS THE FORMALISATION OF A VIEW

1 In a later publication of the Growth Project, Stone (1964) referred approvingly to this section of Ball's review. It is evident therefore that in this respect, if no other, the models of the Growth Project and the Business School were informed by the same philosophy.
2 Note that, in this respect, perhaps the critical difference between the Oxford and Business School models was that, whereas the former calculated GDP from the output side, the latter forecast it from the expenditure side.
3 The reasons why the Cambridge Growth Project model has remained on the margins of UK modelling would constitute a substantial study in its own right. Its survival over many years attests both to the fact that it 'works' and to the fact that there is a market for its output.
4 Cairncross (1952).
5 Notwithstanding its substantive points, Cairncross's review was very prejudiced. For example, Tinbergen's approach, we are told,

> [is] uncompromisingly econometric. The statistical series are hurriedly introduced – over a hundred of them – and reduced to nine-year moving averages, with a mumbled footnote or two to tell us where they come from. The machine is then set in motion and presto! regression equations and correlation coefficients come pouring out.
> (Cairncross 1952: 872)

This quite misrepresents not only the quantity of work involved in computing regressions by hand but also (and much more importantly) the very nature of applied econometrics practised by Tinbergen and his successors.
6 Cairncross (1965).
7 Ibid.: 123.

8 Cairncross gave a concrete example of this in a later paper (Cairncross 1969) when he noted that, between the first quarters of 1966 and 1967, the expenditure measure of GDP rose by 2 per cent, the income measure fell by 0.5 per cent while the output measure remained unchanged.

9 In his Presidential address to the Royal Economic Society in 1969, he reiterated the need for synthesis while at the same time insisting that the 'information system' was more important than the 'model', because, while it was 'quite possible to make forecasts of short-term prospects without a model', it was 'impossible to make quantitative forecasts without quantitative data' (Cairncross 1969: 799).

10 At its simplest, this is an exogenous variable (one for each behavioural equation) that appears on the right-hand side of the equation and changes the value of endogenous variable on the left-hand side by a constant amount.

11 Worswick (1975: 72).

12 Shepherd *et al.* (1975: 48).

13 Ibid.

14 Wallis (1989).

15 For an account of the US experience see Epstein (1987).

16 Surrey (1971).

17 Worswick (1975: 72).

18 Ibid.: 67.

19 Treasury forecasts, prepared three times a year, were intended to inform decision making with regard to the overall level of domestic activity as well as the balance of payments. The GDP forecast was constructed as the sum of forecasts of the individual components of aggregate expenditure: exports, fixed investment, public authorities' consumption, investment in stocks and personal consumption. Forecasts were also made of imports, of invisible trade and of the interest, profit and dividend flows necessary to complete the current balance. Further details are contained in HM Treasury (1964).

20 Forecasts of the prospects for the UK economy over the short term (that is, twelve to eighteen months) had been published by the National Institute and the London and Cambridge Economic Service since the 1950s. Forecasting at the Treasury dated back much further, to the Second World War, and, although these forecasts had for the most part remained secret, there was a period from 1947 when official forecasts to the end of the year were published.

21 House of Commons (1966: 469–70).

22 In this case 'men' included a number of women who had Treasury experience, for example, Kit Jones.

23 House of Commons (1966: 471).

24 Godley and Shepherd (1965).

25 Surrey (1971: 87–8).

26 See relationship 3.5 (Surrey 1971: 32).

27 Ball and Burns (1968: 231–2). As well as using Board of Trade data, the National Institute conducted its own 'Industrial Enquiry'.

28 This does not seem to have been an issue that model builders felt obliged to address, much as they felt under no obligation to address econometric

matters such as identification.

29 Albeit with a coefficient that was conventionally insignificant (*t*-ratio of about 0.7) in both the early listings of this model: Ball (1967) and Ball and Burns (1968).

30 It should be noted that this is a major difference between the UK and US macroeconometric models. See, for example, the interview with Lawrence Klein in Mariano (1987).

31 Ball and Burns (1968: 232).

32 Chick (1973: 58).

4 KEYNESIAN 'NORMAL SCIENCE': THE ELABORATION OF THE INCOME–EXPENDITURE MODEL

1 Kuhn (1970: 23).

2 Ibid.: 58.

3 This diagram is based on the 'Sector Summary' to be found in the UK Central Statistical Office's *Blue Book* (for example, table 11.1 of the 1992 edition).

4 These constraints apply in principle to both the output from a model and the historical data series; in practice, however, the data series are such that GDPY and GDPE are not equal and neither do total financial transactions by sector equal the financial surplus or deficit. These discrepancies, which are due to measurement problems and which have at times been very substantial, appear as balancing items within the accounts. What usually happens is that a number of the variables within the model (that is, within the table) are adjusted to take up the discrepancies.

5 It should be noted that the income variables in the Business School model were calculated in current prices while the expenditure variables were calculated in constant prices. This hints at the point that, in fact, a complete income–expenditure model has to complete not one such for each period but two: one at current prices and one at constant prices. The two are not directly related to one another since different price deflators are used for different variables.

6 Ball *et al.* (1975a).

7 The size of the 1978 model, given in table 2.1, suggests that, notwith-standing this sentiment, the model was still in fact to grow much further.

8 The case for disaggregation must rest in the first place on the view that different components of an aggregate variable behave in very different ways. This would be the rationale for treating consumption and invest-ment separately, since it is believed in the traditional Keynesian view that the factors on which each depends are quite different from each other.

9 We can recognise this as a variation on Walras' Law: equilibrium in any two of three markets for goods, bonds or money implies equilibrium in the third. In this case we are dealing not with 'equilibrium' but with 'accounting balance', but the principle applies just as well.

10 For example, House of Commons (1966: 470).

11 Figure 4.1 is the same as the first panel of figure 7.1 given in Ball *et al.*

NOTES

(1975b) and has been drawn from the data presented in table 7.2 of that paper.

12 For example, suppose the model is just $Y = X^2$. If X rises by 1 from 5 to 6, then Y will rise by 11, whereas if X rises by 1 from 9 to 10, Y will rise by 19. This problem does not arise with a linear model (such as the one in the appendix to chapter 1) but, in practice, non-linearity is a characteristic of all macroeconometric models, the most usual reason being that behavioural equations are usually linear in the logarithms of the variables while identities are linear in the variables themselves.

13 Undercutting both these positions, it would also have been possible in principle to have dismissed such a projection altogether; the model was a short-term model and its mechanical application beyond eighteen months neither represented some new finding nor did it constitute something by which the model's validity over the short term could be judged. The modellers themselves of course did not take this view, although there are some formal explanations of why the model should be valid for the short term only – the absence of a supply side is one and a belief that the confidence intervals associated with the prediction are too wide beyond only a few quarters is another – and the first of these was part of the explicit motivation for at least one later attempt to build a new type of UK model (see Beenstock et al. 1986).

14 Ball et al. (1975b: 183).

15 Ibid.: 183–96.

16 See, for example, the discussions of the Treasury and National Institute models, presented to the same 1972 Conference (Renton 1975).

5 KEYNESIAN REFORM: KALDOR'S RADICAL CRITIQUE AND THE EXCHANGE-RATE

1 See, for example, Ball and Burns' discussion, just weeks after the devaluation, of the problems that they and other forecasters had to confront in forecasting the effects of devaluation (*Sunday Times*, 31 December 1967).

2 Stone et al. (1970).

3 It was only much later that the modellers would come to consider the reverse problem, that is, the effect that the behaviour of the domestic economy might have on the exchange-rate.

4 Ball et al. (1975b: 210).

5 Ibid.

6 *Sunday Times*, 2 January 1972.

7 *Sunday Times*, 2 April 1972.

8 Kaldor (1971).

9 See Thirlwall (1987).

10 Kaldor (1971: 11).

11 Tinbergen (1952).

12 Kaldor (1971: 11).

13 Ball et al. (1977: 4).

14 Of course, the need to champion a cause becomes pressing only when that

cause is under threat. To an extent, the very fact that it was not, even until the late 1960s, necessary to argue for the goals is evidence of their still widespread and largely unquestioned acceptance. When articulate people find it necessary to promote that which until recently had been taken for granted, it is probably to be seen as a premonition of imminent demise.

15 *Sunday Times*, 28 December 1969.
16 *Sunday Times*, 23 August 1970.
17 Ibid.
18 *Sunday Times*, 29 August 1971.
19 *Sunday Times*, 2 January 1972.
20 *Sunday Times*, 15 April 1973.
21 GDP in fact grew in 1973 by over 7.5 per cent. On records going back to 1855 (Feinstein 1972), this is the highest rate for any calendar year apart from 1940.
22 The forecast (made in September 1973) for 1974 illustrates this sensitivity. The base assumption for import prices in 1974 was that they would rise by 6 per cent; but it would take a rise of no more than 11 per cent for the balance of payments deficit to be double the figure in the base case.

6 KEYNESIAN CRISIS: NEW CAMBRIDGE AND THE ATTACK ON SHORT-TERM DEMAND MANAGEMENT

1 The 'headline' rate of inflation, as measured by the retail price index, remained above 20 per cent for thirteen months, from March 1975 to March 1976. At over £3 billion, the 1974 current account deficit represented nearly 11 per cent of current account credits. This represented a deterioration, in only three years, from a balance of payments surplus of over £1 billion in 1971, equivalent to 7.5 per cent of credits at that time. (Note that these figures are of a recent vintage – 1991 CSO *Pink Book*.)
2 C. ıbridge Economic Policy Group (1976: 1n).
3 The association between the *Bulletin* and *The Times* newspaper began in 1952, when the *Bulletin* began to appear as part of the newspaper's quarterly 'Review of Industry'.
4 Neild (1973).
5 *Sunday Times*, 31 December 1972.
6 Godley and Cripps (1973).
7 Neild (1973).
8 This constancy – at around 3 per cent of GDP – dated only from 1961. The eight or so years shown before that date reveal a steady rise, from a deficit at the beginning of about 2 per cent. Neild put this rise down to the spread of occupational pension schemes at that time.
9 It is certainly of note here that Cripps, Godley and Martin Fetherston, in their evidence to the House of Commons Public Expenditure Committee (for more on which, see below), described the 'treatment of company behaviour' as 'a major weakness in conventional short term forecasting systems' (Cripps, Godley and Fetherston 1974).

10 For example, the 'deplorably large errors' in the budget of March 1974, which meant that, instead of being highly contractionary, the fiscal stance actually turned out to be highly expansionary (Cambridge Economic Policy Group 1975: 4).
11 Cambridge Economic Policy Group (1975: 8, emphasis in original).
12 Note that it is not that s, the marginal propensity to save of the *personal* sector, is zero; persons can save but the saving is then passed on and spent elsewhere.
13 Kahn and Posner (1974).
14 Corden, Little and Scott (1975).
15 Bispham (1975b).
16 Cripps, Fetherston and Godley (1976).
17 Much better known is the very similar property, this time for the *personal* sector (that is, excluding companies), reported by Davidson *et al.* (1978).
18 Kahn and Posner (1974).
19 Such model multipliers did appear though, in the form of a 'CEPG ready reckoner', in the third and subsequent editions of the technical manual that described the model (Fetherston and Coutts 1978).
20 Godley and Shepherd (1964).
21 Coutts (1977: 93).
22 Fetherston (1976).
23 Cambridge Economic Policy Group (1976: 1n).
24 Atkinson (1976).
25 Cambridge Economic Policy Group (1976: 66).
26 Fetherston (1978: A16).
27 But caution is in order. For example, in 1990 itself, when unemployment stood at around 1.5 million, the Policy Group's 1978 forecast would have looked absurd if taken literally. A proper assessment of the accuracy of the Policy Group's forecasts therefore requires an estimation of the underlying, or trend, level of unemployment, and not the headline figure, which may be above or below that trend owing to cyclical effects. Moreover, account has to be taken of whether the policies that have actually been pursued since those forecasts were made bear any relation to the policies on which the projection was based. Indeed, an accurate forecast might be rather worrying because it would suggest either that the actual policies of the 1980s made no real difference or that those policies would have been inevitable whoever had been in government.
28 Cambridge Economic Policy Group (1976: 16).

7 KEYNESIAN DEMISE: THE RISE OF MONETARISM

1 Ball *et al.* (1977).
2 The paper on model properties did not give a listing of the model used. However, the 1972 model (Ball *et al.* 1975a), which was the one discussed in chapter 5, was referred to as 'an early version'. A more up-to-date version (Ball 1976) was mentioned as being closer to that used for the

simulation. It was not, however, identical and this is a point to which I shall return below.

3 Ball *et al.* (1977: 4).

4 Ibid.: 5.

5 It should, however, be noted, that the property required by the Business School economists of their model was consistent with a zero coefficient on the unemployment term in the real wage equation. Moreover, Ball and his colleagues emphasised that, 'thus far', it had been 'difficult to estimate significant and stable effects of the impact of unemployment upon wage changes' (Ball *et al.* 1977: 8).

6 Graphs are drawn directly from data given in the appendix tables of Ball *et al.* (1977) for the variables *GDP*, *PC* (the index of consumer prices) and *FO* (the negative of the overseas sector's net acquisition of financial assets, that is, the current account balance) for simulations I and III in that paper.

7 Ball *et al.* (1975a: 210).

8 Ball *et al.* (1977: 20).

9 Although corporate profits played the role of the buffer in the listing of the model given by Ball (1976: 333), another listing of the model, 'as at 25th April 1975', reported in a London Business School discussion paper (1975), shows the buffer role being taken by the sum of corporate profits, the public sector trading surplus and income from self-employment. Each of these was modelled separately, and then the discrepancy between their sum achieved that way and the sum that they were required to have in order to balance income and expenditure was allocated to the three variables proportionately.

10 Coutts, Tarling and Wilkinson (1976).

11 For a discussion of this, see *Ball et al* (1977: 10–12). The published model listing (Ball 1976) does not include such a relationship; but the almost identical internal listing (London Business School 1975: 18), referred to in note 9 above, does.

12 Nordhaus and Godley (1972).

13 In chapter 8, I shall explain in similar terms what it was about the Cambridge model that *disabled* Godley and company from making the same shift.

14 *Sunday Times* 21 April 1974.

15 Ball and Burns (1976).

16 Note that 'degrees of freedom' is not meant here in its statistical sense.

17 Ball *et al.* (1979).

18 Davidson *et al.* (1978).

19 Ball *et al.* (1979).

20 Ibid.: 101.

21 Thus, from the same response to the Committee, Friedman opined that the reduction of inflation to single figures by 1982 would have as a side-effect 'only a modest reduction in output and employment' while 'the effect on investment and the potential for future growth will be highly favourable' (Friedman 1980: 61).

22 *Sunday Times*, 2 March 1980.

23 Ball *et al.* (1979: 103).

8 THE TURN TO THE LONG-RUN (1): HOW SOON IS THE LONG-RUN?

1 For example, suppose that the relationship governing some variable, Y, at time t depends, firstly, on the contemporaneous value of another variable X and, secondly, on the values of Y and X at time $t-1$:

$$Y_t = 1.1X_t + 0.5Y_{t-1} - 0.8X_{t-1}.$$

The 'long-run' is defined as the situation when the X variable takes the same value in every time period, say X^*. The long-run value of Y, Y^*, can then be worked out by solving:

$$Y^* = 1.1X^* + 0.5Y^* - 0.8X^*,$$

which yields:

$$Y = 0.6X^*.$$

2 From a mathematical point of view the questions of interest are the existence of a long-run equilibrium (the model may not be stable) and the nature of the path towards it. In the very first macroeconometric models – Radice's for example – it was the questions of existence and stability that were the ones of primary interest.

3 Assuming that we proceed through the terms in the series at a constant rate. This is exactly the manner in which these discrete time econometric models approach their long-runs.

4 The word 'term' denotes a spell of time; the short term, medium term and long term are just arbitrary divisions of time and the usage of these expressions is governed by nothing more than convention. The strongest convention as far as macroeconometric models are concerned is the use of 'short term' to designate a spell of time of about two years. 'Terms' though can be fuzzy; they can overlap; and they can be comparative (in the sense of the 'longer term'). Notice the difference from 'run' here: the 'short-run' is the complement of the long-run; they don't overlap; and, although definition is free, it is hard to see that expressions such as 'shorter-run' or 'medium run' can sensibly have any meaning.

5 There is, among economists, a third possible sense to the distinction between the 'short' and the 'long', which relates to the status of the capital stock. The distinction in question goes back to the Marshallian separation between the short period, when the capital stock was fixed, and the long period, when it was allowed to vary. Almost all UK macroeconometric models have been short-period models in the sense that they treat the capital stock as fixed, the major exception being the model built in the 1980s (but not for long maintained) by Michael Beenstock and his colleagues at the City University Business School. It is very reasonable to question, as the City University economists did, whether a short period model would be suitable for medium-term analysis and forecasting. However, although this suggests a symmetry between the short period and the short term on the one hand, and the long period and the long term on the other, the actual concepts are still quite distinct.

6 The MPS (MIT–PENN–SSRC) model of the US economy was begun in

the late 1960s, originally as a project of the Federal Reserve Board.

7 The wage and price variables in these equations are the logarithms of the indices in question.

8 Sargan (1964: 48).

9 The time indices in this error-correction term are rather unusual.

10 Sargan (1964: 48).

11 See, for example, J. C. R. Dow's study of the British economy between 1945 and 1960 in which he concluded that 'the fluctuations in the growth of demand in the years 1952–60 were due in large part to fluctuations in policy' (Dow 1964: 391). Dow, though, believed that the problems had been caused by an insufficient degree of gradualism in the policies of that period. Thus, unlike the Policy Group, Dow's was a criticism of the *practice* of demand management rather than the principle.

12 This view, which originated from the philosopher of science Imre Lakatos in the 1960s as a reaction to the more revolutionary, or at least 'discontinuous', model of scientific progress advanced by Thomas Kuhn, has held enormous sway within UK time-series econometrics over the last fifteen years.

13 In particular, the coefficients of the crucial wage equation seem to have been imposed without the benefit of any statistical support.

14 Since the Monetarist view was the long-run view, we could sum this up by saying that, in the 1975 model, the long-run was a medium-term phenomenon.

15 Ball *et al.* (1977: 5).

16 *Sunday Times*, 25 April 1976.

17 For example, the *Sunday Times* column of March 1978.

18 *Sunday Times*, 16 October 1977.

19 Keegan (1989: 47 *et seq.*).

20 Burns, the son of a colliery worker from County Durham and a product not of Oxford or Cambridge but of Manchester University, was appointed to this post at the very young age of 35. Keegan suggests that he and Lawson 'together ... supervised the drawing up of the "Medium-Term Financial Strategy"' (Keegan 1989: 90). Now, as Sir Terence Burns, he is the Permanent Secretary to the Treasury.

21 The estimate of a coefficient is just a guess at its 'true' value; the guess is obtained by putting numbers into a formula, a task that computers make trivial. If various assumptions hold, then the formula has certain desirable properties that allow us to regard the estimate as being a good guess at the truth. But, as econometricians nowadays emphasise, the empirical equation must be tested to see if the assumptions hold. The Durbin–Watson test is a test of this sort. If the assumptions are found not to hold, then there is no statistical basis for claiming that the estimates are a good guess at the truth.

22 The critical value against which to compare these statistics is about 1.5. Values of the statistic above that (and below 2.5) indicate an equation with statistical validity, while values below indicate that the validity is lacking. The values obtained here were therefore way below what was necessary. It is true that the concept of co-integration (developed in the 1980s) could now possibly be used to restore legitimacy to these

equations. What this could not restore, however, is the idea that the effects represented operate rapidly.

9 THE TURN TO THE LONG-RUN (2): POLICIES FOR THE LONG-RUN

1 I will nevertheless restrict the use of the expression 'natural rate' to the Liverpool model only, firstly because it is an expression that is rather laden with associations and secondly because it would be anachronistic to use it for models of the 1970s.

2 The current account balance is defined as exports less imports plus the net flows of interest, profits, dividends and other transfers to the overseas sector. The basic balance is the current account balance plus net direct and portfolio investment flows.

3 The 'underlying' position should not be confused with the 'par' position, which was another abstraction employed for some years by the Cambridge Economic Policy Group. The 'par' economy was defined by the condition of full employment.

4 The Policy Group's model proper was not a steady-state model and no steady-state conditions were attached to it for projections. With one important exception, however, I think that its properties would have been little different had it been a steady-state model. This is because the most common form of dynamic equation employed was a first-order, finite distributed lag. This – the 'least dynamic' of the dynamic forms – has the feature that the steady-state is achieved, precisely, after just one period. The exception – and the reason why the Policy Group's model cannot, in general, be reduced to a steady-state as it is usually understood – is that the relationship between employment and output makes the rate of growth of labour productivity depend positively on the rate of growth of output. Inflation is steady in the model only if productivity is growing at the same rate as workers' target real wages. Since there is nothing to guarantee this latter condition, a steady rate of inflation is the exception, rather than the rule, for this model.

5 Minford *et al.* (1984: 38).

6 The index of export prices divided by the index of import prices.

7 This analysis is based on the listing given by Fetherston (1976), especially section two of that document, which describes the balance of payments sector.

8 The index of world raw material prices divided by the index of world 'competitive' products.

9 It should be emphasised here that, in contrast to the similar expression for the Liverpool model given below, the actual structural-form equations in the Policy Group model (described in Fetherston 1976) could not be reduced to a single analytical expression. This is because some of the variables in the relevant equations, in the balance of payments part of the model, appeared sometimes as levels and sometimes as logarithms. However, equation 'T8' in the formal analysis of the model (Cripps and Godley 1976) is similar to the expression given here, the only difference

being that this one shows the deterministic component and the import control variable explicitly, as per the listing of the proper model.

10 It should be emphasised that, in the subsequent discussion, the Liverpool variables are taken as given. In practice, however, variables such as B, the measure of unemployment benefits, have themselves been criticised on the grounds that the reduction of the complexities of a changing social security system to a single, unchanging variable is far too simple a treatment. See, for example, Atkinson and Micklewright (1985).

11 For the derivation of the reduced-form equations for the natural rate equations of the model see Kenway (1991).

12 Although it contained a number of static (that is, instantaneous) equilibrium-like conditions, for example the relationship connecting the money stock to the exchange-rate, these were intended to hold exactly in every period. These conditions, therefore, characterised the actual rather than the underlying position of the economy.

13 London Business School (1978).

14 Ball and Burns (1979). Variants of this almost 'toy' model, which, unlike the real thing, could be guaranteed to behave as required, were employed by Business School economists on a number of occasions to support theoretical discussions. It is rather tempting to believe that this model, which originated with Michael Beenstock, was in fact the one that represented the way in which the Business School economists believed the economy to work.

15 Minford et al. (1984: table 1).

16 Kenway (1991).

17 In its entirety, the Liverpool model is a non-linear rational expectations model that is capable of solution only by advanced numerical techniques using considerable computer power. It is far from obvious that such a thing will always do as its proprietors wish. But inside this creation sits a four-equation linear, static sub-model whose reduced form can therefore be obtained analytically. As a result, the sub-model's behaviour is entirely predictable under all circumstances. The existence of this self contained sub-model helps explain why the Liverpool economists could be so sure that the model would indeed represent what they believed.

18 Nickell (1984: 951). The consequence of omitting the productivity variable was that the coefficient on the lagged dependent variable was increased above what it would otherwise have been. This in turn increased the size of the long-run effects of the other regressors.

19 Ball et al. (1979: 88). I have distorted the order here; the original quote, in proper order, appears in chapter 8.

20 Aris Spanos (1990) shows how the approach can be extended from its traditional, single-equation setting to a simultaneous model. The practical limitations are firstly, that there must be as many observations on each variable as the total number of predetermined variables in the model as a whole and, secondly, that the model be 'linear' (in the sense that the model cannot contain both a variable and the logarithm of that variable).

21 Cripps and Fetherston (1979).

22 See Morgan (1987).

10 CAN WE RETURN TO KEYNESIANISM?

1 To say that taxes might sometimes be raised is by no means the same thing as saying that they should be raised during a recession.

2 See, for example, Gregory Mankiw's 'Quick Refresher Course in Macroeconomics' in which he attempts to explain the disparity between academic macroeconomics and the applied macroeconomics embodied in the macroeconometric model. Mankiw speaks of a 'chasm between microeconomic principles and macroeconomic practice'; 'large-scale macroeconometric models', he reports, 'are mentioned only occasionally at academic conferences, often with derision' (Mankiw 1990: 1647 and 1645). The criticism would not be true of the current generation of UK models, but (with the exception of Liverpool) it most certainly is true of the vintage of model that we have been considering here.

3 Mankiw's attempt to explain the previously mentioned gulf between academic and applied macroeconomics relies on an analogy with, respectively, the Copernican system and the Ptolemaic system that it replaced.

4 Lawson (1989).

5 Another option proposed was import controls. Ball was one who had argued for the selective control of imports, describing them as the 'least unsatisfactory' of the alternatives. This argument, in the *Sunday Times* newspaper, came only weeks before the sterling devaluation (*Sunday Times*, 17 September 1967).

6 On coming to office in October 1964, the new Labour government imposed a 15 per cent surcharge on imports of manufactured goods. This, though, was intended as a short-term measure, to deal with the specific problem of the £800 million balance of payments deficit inherited from the previous administration, rather than something designed to address more fundamental problems. It was, in any case, in contravention of both the General Agreement on Tariffs and Trade and Britain's obligations under the European Free Trade Area.

7 Ball *et al.* (1977: 18).

8 Mishan (1977: 29).

9 For example, in its manifesto for the 1987 general election, the Conservative party claimed that 'Britain today is in the seventh successive year of steady economic growth. We have moved from the bottom to the top of the growth league of major European countries' (Craig 1990: 418). The claim is quite accurate but it conveniently leaves out of account the recession that immediately preceded those seven years.

10 See, for example, (Stark 1989).

11 Matthews (1968).

12 It is this passage, with its emphasis on the need for information, that Estrin and Holmes cite in favour of indicative planning.

13 Estrin and Holmes (1983).

14 See, for example, Morgan's account of Keynes' criticisms of Tinbergen's model (Morgan 1990).

REFERENCES

Atkinson, A.B. and J. Micklewright (1985) *Unemployment Benefits and Unemployment Duration*, London: Suntory-Toyota International Centre for Economics and Related Disciplines.

Atkinson, P. (1976) 'The External Financial Position', *Economic Policy Review* 2: 42–5.

Ball, R.J. (1963) 'The Cambridge Model of Economic Growth', *Economica* 30: 180–90.

Ball, R.J. (1967) 'Economic Model Building for Control', *The Advancement of Science*, April: 625–42.

Ball, R.J. (1976) 'Quarterly Model of the United Kingdom Economy' in J.A. Waelbroek, (ed.), *The Models of Project Link*, Amsterdam: North-Holland, 301–47.

Ball, R.J. (1978) *Report of the Committee on Policy Optimisation*, London: HMSO.

Ball, R.J. and T. Burns (1968) 'An Econometric Approach to Short-run Analysis of the UK Economy 1955–66', *Operational Research Quarterly* 19: 225–56.

Ball, R.J. and T. Burns (1976) 'The Inflationary Mechanism in the U.K. Economy', *American Economic Review* 66: 467–84.

Ball, R.J. and T. Burns (1979) 'Long-run Portfolio Equilibrium and Balance-of-Payments Adjustment in Econometric Models' in J.A. Sawyer, (ed.), *Modelling the International Transmission Mechanism*, Amersterdam: North-Holland, 311–45.

Ball, R.J., A. Hazelwood and L.R. Klein (1959) 'Econometric Forecasts for 1959', *Bulletin of the Oxford University Institute of Statistics* 21: 1–16.

Ball, R.J., B.D. Boatwright, T. Burns, P.W.M. Lobban and G.W. Miller (1975a) 'The London Business School Quarterly Econometric Model of the UK Economy' in G. A. Renton, (ed.), *Modelling the Economy*, London: Heinemann, 3–37.

Ball, R.J., T. Burns and G.W. Miller (1975b) 'Preliminary Simulations with the London Business School Macro-economic Model' in G.A. Renton, (ed.), *Modelling the Economy*, London: Heinemann, 182–212.

Ball, R.J., T. Burns and J.S.E. Laury. (1977) 'The Role of Exchange Rate Changes in Balance of Payments Adjustment – the United Kingdom Case', *Economic Journal* 87: 1–31.

Ball, R.J., T. Burns and P.J. Warburton (1979) 'The London Business School Model of the UK Economy: An Exercise in International Monetarism' in P. Ormerod, (ed.), *Economic Modelling*, London: Heinemann 86–114.

Barker, T.S. (1978) 'Towards Strategic Paths in Economic Planning' in J.R.N. Stone, and A.W.A. Peterson, *Econometric Contributions to Public Policy*, London: Macmillan, 84–105.

Barker, T.S., V. Borooah, R. van der Ploeg and A. Winters (1980) 'The Cambridge Multisectoral Dynamic Model: An Instrument For National Economic Policy Advice', *Journal of Policy Modeling* 2: 319–44.

Beenstock, M., P. Warburton, P. Lewington and A. Dalziel (1986) 'A Macroeconomic Model of Aggregate Supply and Demand for the UK', *Economic Modelling* 3: 242–68.

Bispham, J.A. (1975a) 'The NIESR Model and Its Behaviour' in G.A. Renton, (ed.), *Modelling the Economy*, London: Heinemann, 75–82.

Bispham, J.A. (1975b) 'The New Cambridge and "Monetarist" Criticisms of "Conventional" Economic Policy Making', *National Institute Economic Review*, November: 39–55.

Bodkin, R., L.R. Klein and K. Marwah (eds) (1991) *A History of Macro-econometric Model-Building*, Aldershot: Edward Elgar.

Brown, J.A.C. (1964) 'Discussion on the Paper by L.R. Klein', in P. E. Hart, G. Mills and J. K. Whitaker (eds), *Econometric Analysis for National Economic Planning*, London: Butterworth, 169–71.

Byron, R.P. (1970) 'Initial Attempts in Econometric Model Building at N.I.E.S.R.' in K. Hilton and D.F. Heathfield, (eds), *The Econometric Study of the United Kingdom*, London: Macmillan, 3–28.

Cairncross, A. (1952) 'Business Cycles in the United Kingdom, 1870–1914. By J. Tinbergen', *Economic Journal* 62: 872–5.

Cairncross, A. (1965) 'Short-term Economic Forecasting at the Treasury', in C. M. Berners-Lee (ed.), *Models for Decision*, London: English Universities Press, 118–24.

Caincross, A. (1969) 'Economic Forecasting', *Economic Journal* 79: 797–812.

Cairncross, A. and N.G.M. Watts (1989) *The Economic Section 1939–61: A Study in Economic Advising*, London: Routledge.

Cambridge Economic Policy Group (1975) 'Review of Britain's Economic Prospects 1975–1978', *Economic Policy Review* 1: 3–14.

Cambridge Economic Policy Group (1976) 'The Strategic Problems of Economic Policy', *Economic Policy Review* 2: 1–18.

Cambridge Economic Policy Group (1978) 'Policy Review', *Economic Policy Review* 4: 1–4.

Chick, V. (1973) *The Theory of Monetary Policy*, London: Gray Mills.

Corden, W.M., I.M.D. Little and M.F.G. Scott (1975) 'Import Controls versus Devaluation and Britain's Economic Prospects', Guest Paper 2, London: Trade Policy Research Centre.

Coutts, K.J. (1977) 'Post Mortem on Five Years of CEPG Forecasting', *Economic Policy Review* 3: 88–97.

Coutts, K.J., R. Tarling and F. Wilkinson (1976) 'Wage Bargaining and the Inflation Process', *Economic Policy Review* 2: 20–7.

Craig, F.W.S. (ed.) (1990) *British General Election Manifestos 1959–87*, Aldershot: Parliamentary Research Services.

Cripps, T.F. and W.A.H. Godley (1976) 'A Formal Analysis of the Cambridge Economic Policy Group Model', *Economica* 43: 335–48.

Cripps, T.F. and M.J. Fetherston (1979) 'Cambridge Economic Policy Group Methodology' in P. Ormerod, (ed.), *Economic Modelling*, London: Heinemann, 40–52.

Cripps, T.F., W.A.H. Godley and M. Fetherston (1974) 'Memorandum on Public Expenditure and the Management of the Economy', *Ninth Report from the Expenditure Committee*, London: HMSO.

Cripps, T.F., M. Fetherston and W.A.H. Godley (1976) 'What Is Left of "New Cambridge"?' *Economic Policy Review* 2: 46–9.

Davidson, J.E.H., D.F. Hendry, F. Srba and S. Yeo (1978) 'Econometric Modelling of the Aggregate Time-series Relationship between Consumers' Expenditure and Income in the United Kingdom', *Economic Journal* 88: 661–92.

Dow, J.C.R. (1964) *The Management of the British Economy 1945–60*, Cambridge: Cambridge University Press.

Epstein, R.J. (1987) *A History of Econometrics*, Amsterdam: North-Holland.

Estrin, S. and P. Holmes (1983) *French Planning in Theory and Practice*, London: Allen & Unwin.

Feinstein, C.H. (1972) *Statistical Tables of National Income, Expenditure and Output of the UK 1855–1965*, Cambridge: Cambridge University Press.

Fetherston, M.J. (1975) 'Statistical Appendix', *Economic Policy Review* 1: 62–91

Fetherston, M.J. (1976) *Technical Manual on the CEPG Model*, Cambridge: Department of Applied Economics.

Fetherston, M.J. (1978) 'Statistical Appendix', *Economic Policy Review* 4: A1–30.

Fetherston, M.J. and K.J. Coutts (1978) *Technical Manual on the CEPG Model*, 3rd edition, Cambridge: Department of Applied Economics.

Friedman, M. (1980) 'Memorandum on Monetary Policy', Treasury and Civil Service Committee, London: HMSO.

Godley, W.A.H. and T.F. Cripps (1973) 'Balance of Payments and Demand Management 1972–1976', *London and Cambridge Economic Bulletin* 82.

Godley, W.A.H. and T.F. Cripps (1974a) 'The Par Model' in G.D.N. Worswick, and F.T. Blackaby, (eds), *The Medium Term*, London: Heinemann, 58–123.

Godley, W.A.H. and T.F. Cripps (1974b) 'Demand, Inflation and Economic Policy', *London and Cambridge Economic Bulletin* 84.

Godley, W.A.H. and J.R. Shepherd (1964) 'Long-term Growth and Short-term Policy', *National Institute Economic Review* August: 26–33.

Godley, W.A.H. and J.R. Shepherd (1965) 'Forecasting Imports', *National Institute Economic Review*, August: 35–42.

Hazelwood, A. and P. Vandome (1961) 'A Post-Mortem on Econometric Forecasts for 1959', *Bulletin of the Oxford University Institute of Statistics* 23: 67–81.

Heathfield, D.F. and I.F. Pearce (1975) 'A View of the Southampton Econometric Model of the UK and its Trading Partners' in G.A. Renton, (ed.), *Modelling the Economy*, London: Heinemann, 83–123.

REFERENCES

HM Treasury (1964) 'Short-term Economic Forecasting in the UK', *Economic Trends*, August: ii-xi.

HM Treasury (1991) 'Memorandum on Official Economic Forecasting', House of Commons Treasury and Civil Service Committee, London: HMSO.

House of Commons (1966) *Fourth Report from the Estimates Committee: Government Statistical Services*, London: HMSO.

Kahn, R. and M. Posner (1974) 'Challenging the "Elegant and Striking" Paradoxes of the New School', *London and Cambridge Economic Bulletin* 85: 19–23.

Kaldor, N. (1971) 'Conflicts in National Economic Objectives', *Economic Journal* 81: 1–16.

Kaldor, N. (1978) *Further Essays in Economic Theory*, London: Duckworth.

Keegan, W. (1989) *Mr Lawson's Gamble*, London: Hodder & Stoughton.

Kenway, P.M. (1991) 'The Long-run and the Natural Rates: An Econometric Examination of the Supply-side of the Liverpool Model', University of Reading Discussion Paper in Macroeconomics, Forecasting and Econometrics, 10.

Keynes, J.M. (1923) *A Tract on Monetary Reform*, London: Macmillan.

Keynes, J.M. (1926) 'The End of Laissez-Faire', *The Collected Writings of John Maynard Keynes*, IX, London: Macmillan.

Klein, L.R., R.J. Ball, A. Hazelwood and P. Vandome (1961a) *An Econometric Model of the United Kingdom*, Oxford: Blackwell.

Klein, L.R., R.J. Ball, A. Hazelwood and P. Vandome (1961b) 'Re-estimation of the Econometric Model of the United Kingdom and Forecasts for 1961', *Bulletin of the Oxford University Institute of Statistics* 23: 46–66.

Kuhn, T.S. (1970) *The Structure of Scientific Revolutions*, 2nd edition, London: Chicago University Press.

Lawson, T. (1989) 'Abstraction, Tendencies and Stylised Facts: A Realist Approach to Economic Analysis', *Cambridge Journal of Economics* 13: 59–78.

London Business School (1975) 'The London Business School Quarterly Econometric Model of the United Kingdom Economy: Relationships in the Basic Model as at 25th April 1975', London Business School Discussion Paper.

London Business School (1978) 'The London Business School Quarterly Econometric Model of the United Kingdom Economy: Relationships in the Basic Model as at October 1978', Econometric Forecasting Unit Discussion Paper.

McKinnon, R.I. (1969) 'Portfolio Balance and International Payments Adjustment' in R.A. Mundell and A.K. Svoboda, (eds), *Monetary Problems of the International Economy*, Chicago: University of Chicago Press, 199–243.

Mankiw, N.G. (1990) 'A Quick Refresher Course in Macroeconomics', *Journal of Economic Literature* 28: 1645–60.

Mariano, R.S. (1987) 'The ET Interview: Professor L.R. Klein', *Econometric Theory* 3: 409–60.

Matthews, R.C.O. (1968) 'Why Has Britain Had Full Employment since the War?', *Economic Journal*, September: 555–69.

Minford, A.P.L., S. Marwaha, K. Matthews and A. Sprague (1984) 'The Liverpool Macroeconomic Model of the United Kingdom', *Economic Modelling* 1: 24–62.

Mishan, E.J. (1977) *The Economic Growth Debate*, London: Allen & Unwin.

Morgan, M.S. (1987) 'The Stamping out of Process Analysis from Econometrics', paper presented to a Symposium on the History and Philosophy of Econometrics, Duke University.

Morgan, M.S. (1990) *The History of Econometric Ideas*, Cambridge: Cambridge University Press.

National Institute of Economic and Social Research (1977) 'A Listing of National Institute Model III', Discussion Paper 7.

Neild, R.R. (1973) 'The Case for a Change in Fiscal Policy: mid 1973', *London and Cambridge Economic Bulletin* 83.

Neild, R.R. and E.A. Shirley (1961) 'Economic Review: An Assessment of Forecasts, 1959–1960', *National Institute Economic Review* May: 12–29.

Nerlove, M. (1962) 'A Quarterly Econometric Model of the United Kingdom: A Review Article', *American Economic Review* 52: 154–76.

Nerlove, M. (1965) 'Two Models of the British Economy: A Fragment of a Critical Survey', *International Economic Review* 6: 127–81.

Nerlove, M. (1966) 'A Tabular Survey of Macroeconometric Models', *International Economic Review* 7: 127–75.

Nickell, S.J. (1984) 'A Review of "Unemployment: Cause and Cure" by Patrick Minford with David Davies, Michael Peel and Alison Sprague', *Economic Journal* 94: 946–53.

Nordhaus, W.D. and W.A.H. Godley (1972) 'Pricing in the Trade Cycle', *Economic Journal* 82: 853–82.

Pearce, I.F. (1970) 'The Southampton Econometric Model of the U.K. and Trading Partners' in K. Hilton, and D.F. Heathfield, (eds), *The Econometric Study of the United Kingdom*, London: Macmillan, 29–52.

Pearce, I.F., P.K. Trivedi, C.T. Stromback and G.J. Anderson (1976) *A Model of Output, Employment, Wages and Prices in the U.K.*, Cambridge: Cambridge University Press.

Pesaran, M.H. and R.P. Smith (1985) 'Evaluation of Macroeconometric Models', *Economic Modelling* 2: 125–34.

Radice, E.A. (1939) 'A Dynamic Scheme for the British Trade Cycle, 1929–1937', *Econometrica* 7: 47–56.

Renton, G.A. (ed.) (1975) *Modelling the Economy*, London: Heinemann.

Sargan, J.D. (1964) 'Wages and prices in the United Kingdom: A Study in Econometric Methodology' in P. E. Hart, G. Mills and J.K. Whitaker (eds), *Econometric Analysis for National Economic planning*, London: Butterworth, 25–54.

Shepherd, J.R. (1968) 'Productive Potential and the Demand for Labour', *Economic Trends* 178, London: HMSO.

Shepherd, J.R., H.P. Evans and C.J. Riley (1975) 'The Treasury Short-term Forecasting Model' in G.A. Renton, (ed.), *Modelling the Economy*, London: Heinemann, 38–65.

Sowerbutts, A. (1970) 'The DEA Medium-Term Macro-Economic Model' in K. Hilton, and D.F. Heathfield (eds), *The Econometric Study of the United Kingdom*, London: Macmillan, 489–94.

Spanos, A. (1990) 'The Simultaneous-Equations Model Revisited', *Journal of Econometrics* 44: 87–105.

Stark, T. (1989) 'The Changing Distribution of Income under Mrs Thatcher' in F. Green, (ed.), *The Restructuring of the UK Ecomony*, London: Harvester Wheatsheaf 177–96.

Stone, J.R.N. (1954) 'Linear Expenditure Systems and Demand Analysis: An Application to the Pattern of British Demand', *Economic Journal* 64: 511–27.

Stone, J.R.N. (1964) *The Model in its Environment*, Number 5 in 'A Programme for Growth', London: Chapman & Hall.

Stone, J.R.N. (1965) *Exploring 1970*, Number 6 in 'A Programme for Growth', London: Chapman & Hall.

Stone, J.R.N. and J.A.C. Brown (1962) *A Computable Model of Economic Growth*, Number 1 in 'A Programme for Growth', London: Chapman & Hall.

Stone, J.R.N., T.S. Barker and R. Lecomber (1970) *Exploring 1972*, Number 9 in 'A Programme for Growth', London: Chapman & Hall.

Surrey, M.J.C. (1971) *The Analysis and Forecasting of the British Economy*, NIESR Occasional Paper XXV, Cambridge: Cambridge University Press.

Tew, J.H.B. (1979) 'Policies Aimed at Improving the Balance of Payments' in F. T. Blackaby, (ed.), *British Economic Policy 1960–74: Demand Management*, Cambridge: Cambridge University Press, 304–59.

Thirlwall, A.P. (1987) *Nicholas Kaldor*, Brighton: Wheatsheaf Books.

Tinbergen, J. (1951) *Business Cycles in the United Kingdom, 1870–1914*, Amsterdam: North-Holland.

Tinbergen, J. (1952) *On the Theory of Economic Policy*, Amsterdam: North-Holland.

Wall, K. D., A. J. Preston, J. W. Bray and M. M. Preston, 'Estimates of a Simple Control Model of the United Kingdom Economy', in G.A. Renton (ed.), *Modelling the Economy*, London: Heinemann.

Wallis, K.F. (1989) 'Macroeconomic Forecasting: A Survey', *Economic Journal* 99: 28–61.

Wallis, K.F. and J.D. Whitley (1991) 'Memorandum on Official Economic Forecasting', House of Commons Treasury and Civil Service Committee, London: HMSO.

Worswick, G.D.N. (1975) 'National Institute Experience with Econometric Models', in G.A. Renton (ed.), *Modelling the Economy*, London: Heinemann, 66–82.

INDEX

as quantitative economic history 19; computerisation of a manual forecasting framework 43, 46–7; criteria for model evaluation 72–4; defined 4, 6; device for consistent incorporation of judgement into forecast 47–8; lack of microeconomic foundations 170; representing a view of how economy works 10, 39, 83–4, 92, 146–8, 161–3; role as extension of single equation applied econometric studies 73–4, 78; *see also* forecasting; structural model (form) 4–6, 156; uses 4, 13–14, 26–7, 75–6

Macroeconomic Modelling Bureau 185–6

Mankiw, N.G. 199

Marx, K. 138

medium term models and analysis *see also* term 34, 40, 94–5, 106

Medium Term Financial Strategy 145–6

Minford, A.P.L. 12, 38–9, 92, 154, 160–1

Mishan, E.J. 178–9

models of the UK economy: Bank of England 33; Byron (A Simultaneous Model of Income, Expenditure and Output) 20–1, 30; Cambridge Economic Policy Group 22–3, 34–5, 40, 85, 91, 107–13, 115, 153–5, 163, 197; Cambridge Growth Project (A Computable Model of Economic Growth) 20–1, 26–9, 34, 40, 44, 54, 74–5, 146, 188; City University Business School (A Macroeconomic model of aggregate supply and demand) 191, 195; Liverpool (A macroeconometric model of the UK) 22–3, 38–9, 92, 151, 153–6, 162–3, 178–9; London Business School 1967 (LBS1a; An Economic Model for Control) 20–1, 29–30, 44, 52–5, 64, 91, 171, 188; London Business

School 1972 (LBS1b) 22–3, 31–3, 64–9, 70–2, 76–8, 112, 115, 142, 193–4; London Business School 1975 (LBS1c) 35–6, 114–21, 127, 131, 142–3, 149, 194; London Business School 1978 (LBS2) 22–3, 35, 37, 91, 127–30, 146–9, 156–7, 190; medium-term model of the Department of Economic Affairs 34; National Institute model I (Surrey/Byron) 22–3, 30, 33, 37, 48–52, 54, 91; National Institute model II 37–8; National Institute model III 22–3, 37–8; Oxford (An Econometric Model of the UK) 20–1, 24–6, 29, 46, 140, 186, 188; Par (Cambridge Economic Policy Group) 34, 85, 108; Queen Mary/Imperial (A Control Model of the United Kingdom Economy) 22–3, 36; Radice (A Dynamic Scheme of the British Trade Cycle 1929–37) 19–21; Southampton (An Econometric Model of the UK and Trading Partners) 20–1, 27–30, 37, 39–40, 44, 187; Tinbergen (Business Cycles in the UK 1870–1914) 19–21, 24, 186, 188; Treasury 22–3, 31–2, 66–7, 112

Monetarism: as heir to the tradition of macroeconomic autonomy 177–8; defined in terms of government's macroeconomic policy objectives 8–9; disputes within 131–3; International 11, 35, 91, 127, 138, 143, 148; monetary approach to the balance of payments 116; *see also* Keynesianism; variants 7

Morgan, M.S. 166

MPS model of the US economy 139, 195–6

National Institute Economic Review 93

National Institute of Economic